G000082211

Cisco® IOS IP Field Guide

Cisco® IOS IP

Gil Held
Kent Hundley

McGraw-Hill
New York   San Francisco   Washington, D.C.   Auckland   Bogotá
Caracas   Lisbon   London   Madrid   Mexico City   Milan
Montreal   New Delhi   San Juan   Singapore
Sydney   Tokyo   Toronto

McGraw-Hill

A Division of The **McGraw·Hill** *Companies*

Copyright © 2000 by The McGraw-Hill Companies, Inc. All rights reserved. Printed in the United States of America. Except as permitted under the United States Copyright Act of 1976, no part of this publication may be reproduced or distributed in any form or by any means, or stored in a data base or retrieval system, without the prior written permission of the publisher.

1 2 3 4 5 6 7 8 9 0   AGM/AGM   0 5 4 3 2 1 0

0-07-212422-9

The executive editor for this book was Steven Elliot, the editing supervisor was Ruth W. Mannino, and the production manager was Claire Stanley. It was set in Stone Serif by Priscilla Beer of McGraw-Hill's desktop composition unit, in cooperation with Spring Point Publishing Services.

Printed and bound by Quebecor/Martinsburg

Contents

Preface   xi
Acknowledgments   xii

Chapter 1   Introduction   1

The Cisco Professional Reference Guide   2
The Role of Routers   2
Basic Configuration Methods   2
EXEC Command Levels   3
   Command Syntax   4
   Obtaining Online Assistance   5
   Error Indications   6
   Entering the Configuration Mode   6
Book Preview   8
   Router Hardware and Software   9
   Working with IP   9
   Interface Configuration   9
   IP Access Lists   10
   IP Routing Protocols   10
   Custom Services   10
   Statistics and IP Traffic Monitoring   10

Chapter 2   Router Hardware and Software Overview   13

Basic Hardware Components   13
   Central Processing Unit (CPU)   14
   Flash Memory   14
   Read-Only Memory (ROM)   15
   Random Access Memory (RAM)   15
   Nonvolatile RAM (NVRAM)   15
   Input/Output (I/O) Ports and Media-Specific Converters   15
   The Router Initialization Process   19
Basic Software Components   23
   Operating System Image   23
   Configuration File   23
   Data Flow   24
The Router Configuration Process   25
   Cabling Considerations   26

Console Access   26
Setup Considerations   28
The Command Interpreter   31
Configuration Command Categories   33
Abbreviating Commands   39
General Console Operations   40
Security Management Considerations   49

Chapter 3   Working with the Internet Protocol   51

The IP Header   52
  Vers Field   52
  Hlen and Total Length Fields   52
  Service Type Field   52
  Identification and Fragment Offset Fields   53
  Time to Live Field   53
  Flags Field   53
  Protocol Field   54
  Source and Destination Address Fields   59
IP Addressing   59
  Overview   59
  IPv4   60
  IPv6   78
Address Resolution   82
  Operation   83
  Cisco ARP Operations   85
Broadcasts   88
  Directed Broadcasts   89
  Use of Nonstandard Broadcast Address   90
Internet Control Message Protocol (ICMP)   90
  The ICMP Type Field   90
  The ICMP Code Field   92
TCP and UDP   95
  The TCP Header   95
  The UDP Header   102
  Router Access-List Considerations   103

Chapter 4   Interface Configuration   105

Working with the `interface` Command   105
  The `interface` Command Options   105
LAN Interface Configuration   106
  Ethernet and Fast Ethernet   107
  Token Ring   115

WAN Interface Configuration   121
  Standard Serial Port Configuration   121
  Serial `interface configuration` Commands   122
High-Speed Serial Interfaces (HSSI)   129
  HSSI Interface Specification   130
  HSSI Interface Configuration Commands   131

Chapter 5   Configuring and Applying Access Lists   133

Overview   133
  Purpose   133
  Application   134
Types of Access Lists   135
  Standard IP Access Lists   135
  Keywords   135
  Source Address   137
  Other Keywords   137
  Extended IP Access Lists   139
  Field Overview   139
  Options   141
  Keywords   142
  Commented IP Access-List Entries   143
Creating and Applying an Access List   143
  Specifying an Interface   143
  Using the `ip access-group` Command   144
  Named Access Lists   145
  Editing   147
  Facilitating the Editing Process   150
  Rules to Consider   151
  Router-Generated Packets   152
Enhanced Access Lists   152
  Dynamic Access Lists   152
  Reflexive Access Lists   157
  Time-Based Access Lists   159
TCP Intercept   160

Chapter 6   IP Routing Protocols   163

Overview   163
IP Path Determination   165
  Entering Static Routes   168
  Determining the Best Match   169
  The Longest Match Rule   171
  Using the Default Route   172

Classless Routing Table Lookups   174
Classless Routing Protocols   176
Load-Sharing Packets   178
Fast Switching   178
Floating Static Routes   179
Types of Routing Protocols   180
Distance Vector (DV) Routing Protocols   181
Link State (LS) Routing Protocols   186
RIP Version 1 and 2   189
RIPv1   190
RIPv2   193
Interior Gateway Routing Protocol (IGRP) and Enhanced
 Interior Gateway Routing Protocol (EIGRP)   195
IGRP   195
EIGRP   200
OSPF   206
Enabling OSPF   207
Neighbor Relationships   208
Areas   208
Summary Routes   209
Types of Areas   210

Chapter 7   Additional IP Services   **213**

IP Functions   213
Hot Standby Routing Protocol (HSRP)   213
IP Maximum Transmission Unit (MTU)   216
Ping   217
ICMP Functions   221
IP Unreachables   221
IP Redirects   223
IP-Directed Broadcast   223
Upper-Layer Services   224
TCP Header Compression   224
Telnet Source Address   224
IP Helper Address   225
IP Forward Protocol   225

Chapter 8   Monitoring IP Network Traffic   **227**

Displaying Interface Statistics   228
Using the show interfaces Command   228
Examining Serial Port Metrics   228
Examining Ethernet Metrics   233

Examining Fast Ethernet Metrics   237
Examining Token Ring Metrics   237
Displaying IP Protocol Statistics   237
Using the `show ip accounting` Command   238
Turning on IP Accounting   239
Viewing IP Accounting Data   239
Viewing the IP Cache   241
Displaying the Routing Table   244
Viewing IP Traffic   246

Index   251

Preface

This field guide focuses on Cisco Internetwork Operating System's (IOS) IP-related commands. This guide reviews the operation and utilization of IOS IP-related commands and provides numerous examples of the use of such commands. Examples show how to configure Cisco routers, including individual interfaces and routing protocols; testing and troubleshooting of network hardware and transmission facilities; and use of different types of data storage to facilitate the storage, retrieval, and updating of router configurations. Numerous examples are presented that can be easily tailored for an organization's specific operational requirements.

Since IOS commands govern the operation of a router, effective use of such commands is a mechanism to control the flow of information through a router. The use of IOS IP-related commands allows you to tailor the operation of both individual routers and groups of routers to form an IP network in addition to controlling the flow of data. This, in turn, permits you to develop a paper concept and turn that concept into a physical reality.

This book is the second in a series of Cisco-related field guides. This guide, as well as subsequent ones being developed by the authors, is oriented toward facilitating knowledge and real-life examples of how to do things for readers. This book first reviews the basics methods for configuring a Cisco router by reviewing the use of the EXEC command interpreter, including key concepts to facilitate the use of IOS in an IP environment. Then, each chapter focuses on a particular IP command–related area. In addition, each chapter provides numerous examples of the use of IOS commands to provide an overview of a network application or requirement that will be implemented via one or more IOS IP-related commands. The intention is to provide real-life examples that can be easily tailored for a specific networking requirement.

As professional authors we highly value reader feedback. Please consider sharing your thoughts with us concerning the scope and depth of topics covered in this book. We would also like your ideas on subjects you would like to see covered in a future edition, or a different Cisco-related topic you would like the authors to cover in a new Professional Reference Guide. You can contact us either through our publisher or directly via email.

Gilbert Held   Kent Hundley

Macon, Georgia   Stanford, Kentucky

gil_held@yahoo.com   khundley@prodigy.net

Acknowledgments

Although you might not realize it, a book is very similar to many sports, representing a team effort. Without the effort of an acquisitions editor with the knowledge and foresight to back a proposal, it would be difficult, if not impossible, to have a manuscript published. It is always a pleasure to work with a knowledgeable acquisitions editor, and Steve Elliot is no exception. Thus, we would be remiss if we did not thank Steve for backing this new writing project.

As an old-fashioned author who spends a significant amount of time traveling to various international locations, Gil Held long ago recognized that the variety of electrical receptacles made pen and paper far more reliable than the use of a notebook that was difficult to recharge. Converting his writings and drawings into a professional manuscript is a difficult assignment, especially when balancing the effort with family obligations. Once again, Gil is indebted to Mrs. Linda Hayes for her fine effort in preparing the manuscript that resulted in the book you are now reading.

Writing is a time-consuming effort, requiring many weekends and evenings that would normally be spent with family. Thus, last but not least, we truly appreciate the support and understanding of our families and friends as we wrote this book, checked page proofs, and verified the techniques presented in this book. Gil would like to thank his wife Beverly for her patience and understanding while he hibernated in his office many evenings and weekends working on this book. Kent would like to extend thanks to his family, friends, and coworkers who have provided assistance and encouragement over the months leading to the completion of this work. He would especially like to thank his mother and father for their guidance and love and his wife Lori for her understanding and support.

CHAPTER 1

Introduction

In the Preface we noted that *Internetwork Operating System* (IOS) commands literally govern the operation of a router, and effective, efficient use of such commands provides a mechanism to control the flow of information through a router. The use of the IOS *Internet protocol* (IP)-related commands allows you to tailor the operation of both individual routers and groups of routers to form an IP network in addition to controlling the flow of data. This, in turn, lets you develop a paper concept and turn that concept into a physical reality.

Although Cisco's IOS supports numerous protocols, this book focuses on the Internet protocol (IP) so we can provide specific information concerning the configuration of routers in an IP environment as well as the use of IP routing protocols, Internet Control Message Protocol (ICMP) operations, and such custom services as *transmission control protocol* (TCP) header compression. We can now do this without diluting specific coverage by digressions into Apple Talk, DECnet, Banyan, Novell and other protocols that, while important to many persons, are of little or no interest in discussing the Internet and corporate intranets. While this book focuses on IOS IP commands, occasionally we will digress to layer 2 since it's important to understand how Ethernet, token-ring, and other *local area network* (LAN) and *wide area network* (WAN) interfaces are configured to work in an IP environment.

This chapter will acquaint you with the contents of the book. First we introduce the concept of the Cisco Professional Reference Guide Series, followed by a brief review of the role of routers and some basic information concerning the Cisco EXEC router command, which allows you to perform different IP-related commands. Once this is accomplished, we provide a preview of this book, briefly focusing on material presented in succeeding chapters. This book preview, in conjunction with the index, will allow you to find the topic of interest to you.

The Cisco Professional Reference Guide

The goal of the Cisco Field Guide Series is to provide information and a series of practical examples on the operation of Cisco equipment that you can easily tailor to specific organizational requirements. This book focuses on router IOS IP-related commands, and provides detailed information on the use of different types of router IP-related commands, how they are used to configure interfaces and protect the flow of data between interfaces, initiate routing between routers, and perform other operations. A series of examples illustrate the use of IOS to perform specific operations. Those operations range in scope from simply obtaining a list of commands supported by your organization's router to configuring a router to support different routing protocols. These are real-life examples you can use as a base for configuring your router to satisfy specific organizational requirements.

The Role of Routers

From an operational perspective the major function of a router is to transfer packets from one network to another. Routers operate at the third layer of the OSI Reference Model. By examining the network address of packets, routers are programmed to make decisions concerning the flow of packets. Another function that goes hand in hand with routing packets between networks is the creation and maintenance of routing tables. Such protocols as the *routing information protocol* (RIP), *open shortest path first* (OSPF), and the *border gateway protocol* (BGP) represent only three of more than 50 routing protocols developed over the past 20 years. With respect to security, the router represents the first line of protection for a network. That protection is in the form of access lists, created to enable or deny the flow of information through one or more router interfaces. Each of the previously described router functions is implemented through appropriate IOS commands. Thus, the setup and operation of an IP network when using Cisco routers is highly dependent upon the appropriate use of IOS IP-related commands.

Basic Configuration Methods

Cisco System routers are configured by using a command interpreter referred to as the EXEC. For those familiar with PCs prior to the arrival of

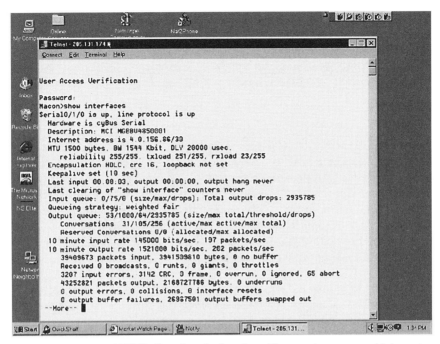

Figure 1-1 Using a GUI Windows-based telnet for a Cisco router command interpreter referred to as the EXEC.

the *graphic user interface* (GUI), better known as Windows, the EXEC represents a DOS-type application since it is command driven. Although you can access a router via a GUI telnet application, as illustrated in Figure 1-1, in reality you enter commands that are interpreted by the EXEC. Several methods are available to configure a Cisco router. This chapter primarily focuses on examples based on the use of telnet, with coverage of other access methods provided in subsequent chapters.

EXEC **Command Levels**

In Figure 1-1 note that the prompt User Access Verification is followed by the prompt Password: which prompts you to enter a password to access what is referred to as the *user level* of access. The EXEC has two levels of access: user and privileged. The IOS commands available at the user level are a subset of the commands available at the privileged level, and are typically restricted to displaying information. In comparison, at the privileged level both display information and change configuration information can be displayed and acted upon.

Again focus on Figure 1-1 and note the line Macon>show interfaces located on the third line in the display. Here Macon represents the system's hostname, which was assigned in this example by one author in honor of his hometown. If you do not set a hostname, a default of Router will be displayed. The right bracket (>) indicates we are in the EXEC's user level of access. When we change to the EXEC's privileged level of access, the right bracket will be replaced by the pound sign (#).

Command Syntax

Again turning attention to Figure 1-1, note the term show interfaces following the right bracket. Here show represents an EXEC command, while interfaces represents a supported parameter, or, in Cisco terminology, a subcommand of the show command. EXEC does not distinguish between upper and lowercase characters, thus you could enter show, SHOW or even ShOw although its probably best to use all lowercase characters for consistency as well as visual verification of each command line. In addition, EXEC also supports abbreviations, so you could enter sh instead of show.

If you make a mistake when typing, you can erase characters one at a time using the BACKSPACE or DELETE key. Pressing either key erases the last character typed. Table 1-1 lists EXEC editing commands, with <ctrl> and <esc> used to indicate the CONTROL and ESCAPE keys, respectively. The plus (+) sign indicates you should press the prefix and suffix keys at the same time to effect the operation.

Table 1-1   EXEC Editing Commands

Command	Purpose
<ctrl>+<p> or up arrow key	Recall the previous command
<ctrl>+<a>	Move to the beginning of the line
<ctrl>+<e>	Move to the end of the line
<esc>+<b>	Move back one word
<ctrl>+<f>	Move forward one character
<ctrl>+<b>	Move back one character
<ctrl>+<u>	Erase the current line
<esc>+<f>	Move forward one word
show history	Show recently used commands

Certain commands, such as show interfaces, can result in the display of more data than you can view through your telnet window. To ensure data does not rapidly scroll off your screen the EXEC will pause at the bottom of your screen and display the prompt –More– (see the bottom of Figure 1-1). To display the following line on a line-by-line basis type a space. To terminate the display operation and return to the user or privilege prompt level type any other character on your keyboard.

Obtaining Online Assistance

By typing the question mark (?) you can obtain a display of user or privilege level EXEC commands supported by the router you are using. By adding a specific parameter after a command and terminating the line with a question mark, you can, in effect, drill down further for additional online assistance.

The value of using online assistance, as well as the primitive manner by which EXEC informs you of errors in command line entries, can be seen by examining a few examples. Figure 1-2 illustrates the use of the ? subcommand at the user access level to obtain information about the use of the show command's interfaces parameter. In examining Figure 1-2 note that the command line entry CISCO7500> indicates that during the setup process the name CISCO7500 was assigned to the router.

Figure 1-2   Obtaining online assistance at the user access level.

```
Cisco7500>show interfaces ?
  Ethernet       IEEE 802.3
  FastEthernet   FastEthernet IEEE 802.3
  Null           Null interface
  Serial         Serial
  TokenRing      IEEE 802.5
  accounting     Show interface accounting
  crb            Show interface routing/bridging info
  fair-queue     Show interface Weighted Fair Queueing (WFQ) info
  irb            Show interface routing/bridging info
  mac-accounting Show interface MAC accounting info
  precedence     Show interface precedence accounting info
  random-detect  Show interface Weighted Random Early Detection (WRED)
                 info
  rate-limit     Show interface rate-limit info
  type           Show vlan types
  |              Output modifiers
```

Figure 1-3 The EXEC's error-handling capability is limited to attempting to indicate where on a command line a possible error occurred.

```
Cisco7500>show interfaces ethernet
% Incomplete command.
Cisco7500>show ethernet interfaces
                ^
% Invalid input detected at '^' marker.
Cisco7500>show Ethernet
           ^
% Invalid input detected at '^' marker.
```

Error Indications

Perhaps one of the mysteries of life for many readers new to the wonderful world of Cisco's IOS is the effect of incorrect entries when working with the EXEC. While the EXEC provides a general indication of where problems reside and a brief statement concerning the problem, unfortunately that is about all it does. An example is illustrated in Figure 1-3 where the authors purposely first entered the command show interfaces ethernet incorrectly. In this example the Ethernet interface number was omitted, resulting in the display of the error message Incomplete command which hints that you failed to include something in your command line entry but does not tell you why the command is incomplete. In the second example in Figure 1-3 we reversed the order of parameters entered with the show command as well as continued our improper use of the ethernet subcommand parameter. Because the command show does not include the parameter ethernet the error message invalid input was displayed. In the third example in Figure 1-3 we continued our errors, again receiving an invalid input message. Note that the response to an invalid input includes the display of a caret (^) character as an identifier that attempts to indicate where the invalid input occurred. Although show is a valid command, the use of the caret implies that the command is invalid when, in effect, command parameters (subcommand) were used incorrectly. Thus, the best thing that can be said about error messages is they alert you to problems.

Entering the Configuration Mode

When you first access a router, you are automatically in its user access level. In this level, which is indicated by the > prompt, you can display certain types of information; however, you cannot change the router's configuration. In order to configure a Cisco router you must enter the privilege mode. To do so you would enter the enable command at the EXEC user level (>) prompt and the applicable privileged level password as shown here:

```
Cisco7500>enable
Password:
Cisco7500#
```

To facilitate security, such as in an over-the-shoulder observation, the password you enter will not be displayed. Assuming you enter the correct password, EXEC displays the privileged-mode system prompt (#), as indicated in the third line of the previous example.

To configure your router you would enter the configure command at the privileged-mode prompt. Since IOS supports the configuration of a router from several data sources, you are then prompted for the source of your configuration subcommands, as indicated here:

```
Configuring from terminal, memory, or network [terminal]?
```

The placement of terminal in brackets indicates it is the default for entering configuration commands and is selected by simply entering a RETURN. A directly cabled terminal or a telnet session can be used as a terminal console. For either connection method, pressing the RETURN key to accept the default enables you to enter configuration commands. Figure 1-4 illustrates the previously described process through the establishment of a telnet session. In this example after we entered the privileged access level through the use of the enable command, we used the configure command at the privileged-mode prompt and selected the default source for configuration commands by pressing the RETURN key. This allowed us to then enter the ? subcommand to determine the configuration commands supported by the version of IOS operating on the router. In examining Figure 1-4, if you have an eagle eye, you might wonder why —More— does not appear at the bottom of the display. In actuality, it did, however, the authors scrolled upward to allow you to view the beginning of the telnet session since the majority of the listing resulting from the use of the question mark was to obtain assistance.

In terms of online assistance, you can obtain help at any point in a command by entering a ?. If nothing matches, the help list will be empty and you must back up until you reach the point where entering a question mark shows available options. Under IOS there are two styles of help available: full and partial. Full help is available when you enter a command followed by a question mark, such as show ? which describes each supported argument supported by a command. Partial help is displayed when you enter an abbreviated argument and want to know what argument or arguments match the input. For example, entering show his would result in the display of history.

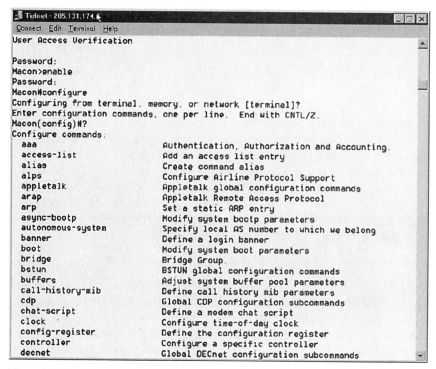

Figure 1-4 Using a telnet session to configure a router.

Now that we have a general understanding of the EXEC and its user and privilege level modes, we will look at the general structure of the remainder of this guide. Since readers have different levels of experience, this preview will allow you to determine if you should read the chapters in the sequence in which they are presented or turn to a chapter that may contain information of an immediate interest.

Book Preview

This section provides an overview of the focus of succeeding chapters in this book. The information in this section is useful by itself or in conjunction with the index as a mechanism to directly locate specific areas of interest. The authors recommend that persons not familiar with the basics of IOS and the use of EXEC commands to configure a router read the chapters in the order of presentation. However, the last four chapters were developed as modular units focused on specific areas of IOS IP commands such as configuring an interface, address assignments, access lists, routing protocols, and tailoring custom services. If you wish, you can read each of those chapters, based upon your need for information and examples on a particular IP topic once you become familiar with the initial three chapters.

Router Hardware and Software

Correct use of IP commands requires an understanding of Cisco router hardware and software. As noted earlier, failure to understand the nomenclature of an interface can prevent configuration of the interface. Thus, knowledge of hardware provides an understanding of how a router operates as well as methods that can be employed to facilitate configuration. Chapter 2 reviews this topic. This begins by examining the basic hardware components of a Cisco router and its software components. The latter topic includes a brief review of how to configure a router through its EXEC mode of operation and an examination of configuration operations, including the use of write, show, console, and reload commands. This chapter concludes with a discussion of global router operations that occur regardless of the specific argument or set of arguments being used. We examine how to assign and change the hostname, set a banner, and boot the host from different sources. In addition, since security is of key importance to all organizations, we also review establishing passwords and different methods of access control. In conclusion we show how to set screen parameters for console operations and the use of the logging facility to direct messages to an appropriate location.

Working with IP

Since this book is a guide to the use of IOS IP-related commands, we devote a chapter to this topic. Chapter 3 discusses IP address assignments, which for many readers are conventional IP addressing methods as well as some techniques that may not be so well known. Examples of the latter include the use of secondary addressing, the use of subnet zero, and the ability to define a broadcast address different from the well-known hex series of *F*'s. Additionally, we cover the *address resolution protocol* (ARP) and, because IP transports ICMP, we also examine the configuration of ICMP.

Interface Configuration

Since all traffic flows occur via router interfaces, Chapter 4 focuses on the manner by which different types of interfaces are configured and examines settings for configuring serial interfaces, Ethernet and token-ring interfaces, as well as HSSI and other types of router interfaces.

IP Access Lists

A router represents the initial point of entry of packets into a network, and its filtering capability can be used to control packet flow. Chapter 5 examines this topic. The chapter begins with a definition of an access list, followed by an examination of the use of different types of access lists, their formats, the use of keywords within each access list format, and, through a series of examples, IOS statements that are required to perform predefined functions through the use of standard and extended access lists.

IP Routing Protocols

The ability of packets to flow between networks depends upon routers knowing where to direct each packet. If we operated in a world where our network was limited to two locations connected by a common transmission facility, we could simply create static routes and never worry about the need to dynamically update routing tables. Because most interconnected networks use a mesh-structured topology, it is important for routers to be able to dynamically update the paths between networks as transmission facilities become temporarily overloaded or if they fail. In an IP environment two key routing protocols are RIP and OSPF, both of which are the focus of Chapter 6. We first review how each routing protocol operates, and then examine how each is configured using IP-related commands.

Custom Services

The TCP/IP protocol suite is a well-thought-out set of applications that operate above transport and network layer services. To enhance the performance of the protocol suite or add support for certain applications you must customize router services. Chapter 7 examines how to configure the Hot Standby Routing Protocol and how to use some advanced features of ping. In addition, we also examine how the *maximum transmission unit* (MTU) is configured and the manner by which TCP header compression is effected. This chapter provides the tools to implement specialized services as well as to enhance the level of performance of the flow of traffic through a network.

Statistics and IP Traffic Monitoring

The book concludes with an examination of the various methods available on a Cisco router to gather statistics and to monitor the flow of packets and frames. Chapter 8 illustrates how the router allows you to determine potential problems, including network error conditions and performance bottlenecks. Included in this chapter are a series of displays so you can determine the ability of the router and the transmission facilities connected to the router to support your network traffic. So, sit back, grab a cup of coffee or a can of soda, get out your magic marker, and relax, as we introduce you to the use of IOS IP-related commands.

CHAPTER 2

Router Hardware
and
Software Overview

This chapter provides an overview of Cisco router hardware and software. We first review the basic hardware components of a Cisco router, followed by an examination of basic router software modules. Once these tasks are accomplished, we examine router operational modes and describe, discuss, and illustrate the use of different router functions.

The overall purpose is to acquaint you with the general operation of Cisco routers and the manner by which they are configured. This chapter includes a number of examples of the use of EXEC commands; these are included as a review for readers who are familiar with Cisco products and provide the necessary information on the general configuration of the vendor's routers for persons who may lack prior Cisco experience. In addition, when appropriate, certain guidelines and hints are included, based on the years of experience from the authors' involvement in configuring and operating Cisco routers. Hopefully, these hints and guidelines may save you hours of puzzlement and make your router experience more pleasurable by being able to take advantage of lessons learned by the authors.

Basic Hardware Components

Cisco Systems manufactures a wide range of router products. Although those products differ considerably with respect to their processing power and the number of interfaces they support, they use a core set of hardware components. Figure 2-1 indicates the key components of a Cisco System's

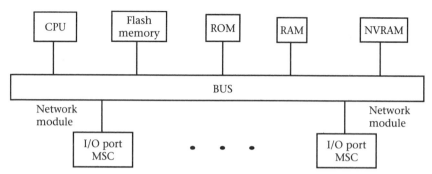

Figure 2-1　Basic router hardware components.

router. While the CPU or microprocessor, amount of ROM and RAM, and the number and manner by which I/O ports and media converters are used can differ from one product to another, each router has the components indicated in Figure 2-1. Examination of the function of each hardware component provides an overview of how the sum of the parts of a router come together to provide its functionality.

Central Processing Unit (CPU)

The CPU, or microprocessor, executes instructions that make up the router's operating system as well as user commands entered via the console or via a telnet connection. Thus, the processing power of the CPU is directly related to the processing capability of the router.

Flash Memory

Flash memory is an erasable, reprogrammable type of ROM memory. On many routers flash memory is an option that can be used to retain an image of the operating system and the router's microcode. Since flash memory can be updated without removing and replacing chips, the cost of this option can easily pay for itself by saving on chip upgrades over a period of time. It is possible to retain more than one operating system image in flash memory, provided enough space is available. This is useful for testing new images. The flash memory of a router can also be used for *trivial file transfer protocol* (tftp) of an *operating system's* (OS) image to another router. In addition, flash memory can be used to store copies of the router's configuration file, which can be useful in situations where a tftp server is unavailable or in emergency recovery procedures.

Read-Only Memory (ROM)

ROM contains code that performs power-on diagnostics similar to the *power-on self-test* (POST) many PCs perform. In addition, a bootstrap program in ROM is used to load operating system software. Although many routers require software upgrades to be performed by removing and replacing ROM chips on the router's system board, other routers may use different types of storage to hold the operating system.

Random Access Memory (RAM)

RAM holds routing tables, performs packet buffering, furnishes an area for the queuing of packets when they cannot be directly output due to too much traffic routed to a common interface, and provides memory for the router's configuration file when the device is operational. In addition, RAM provides space for caching *address resolution protocol* (ARP) information that reduces ARP traffic and enhances the transmission capability of LANs connected to the router. When the router is powered off, the contents of RAM are cleared.

Nonvolatile RAM (NVRAM)

Nonvolatile RAM retains its contents when a router is powered off. By storing a copy of its configuration file in NVRAM, the router can quickly recover from a power failure. The use of NVRAM eliminates the need for the router to maintain a hard disk or floppy for its configuration file. Therefore, there are no moving parts on a Cisco router, which means components last much longer. Most hardware failures in computer systems are due to the wear and tear on moving components such as hard drives.

Since Cisco routers do not have hard or floppy disks, configuration files are usually stored on a PC where they can be easily modified through the use of a text editor. You can then load a configuration directly into NVRAM via the network using tftp.

When using the network for entering a router configuration, the router functions as a client and the PC where the file resides functions as the server. This means you must obtain tftp server software for your PC to support the movement of files to and from your computer. Later in this chapter when we discuss software, we also discuss tftp server software.

Input/Output (I/O) Ports and Media-Specific Converters

The I/O port is the connection through which packets enter and exit a router. Each I/O port is connected to a *media-specific converter* (MSC) which provides the physical interface to a specific type of media such as an Ethernet or token-ring LAN or an RS-232 or V.35 WAN interface.

Under Cisco terminology, various router functions, such as routing protocol updates and access lists, are applied to, or associated with, an interface. However, an interface in effect represents an I/O port configured through an interfaces subcommand, such as `show interfaces`, which would display information about all interfaces in the router. Since the fabrication of I/O ports can vary within a router as well as between routers, it is important to understand how the ports are referenced.

PORT FABRICATION AND COMMAND REFERENCE

If a port is built into a router, it is referenced directly by its number. For example, serial port 0 is referenced in an interface command as follows:

```
interface serial0
```

If a group of ports are fabricated on a common adapter card for insertion into a slot within a router, the reference to a port requires both the slot and port number. Thus, on modular Cisco routers such as the 7500, 7200, 3600, and 2600, the following format is used to specify a particular serial port:

```
interface serial slot#/port#
```

In addition to serial ports, other ports, including Ethernet, Fast Ethernet, and token ring, are specified in a similar manner. Figure 2-2 illustrates the use of the `show interfaces` command with the parameter `FastEthernet1/0` to display information concerning the operation of the Fast Ethernet interface on port 0 on an adapter card installed in slot 1 on the router. At first, we purposely entered the slot/port relationship in error to indicate the importance of knowing and entering the correct parameters for an interface. By using the `show interfaces` command by itself, it is possible to record the configuration of interface modules used in the router, including those presently not operating, as information about nonactive interfaces will also be displayed.

One variation of this format occurs on Cisco 7×00 series equipment where multiple ports can be fabricated on a port-adapter card and multiple port adapters can reside in a slot. In this situation the following command format would be used to reference a specific serial port:

```
interface serial slot#/port-adapter/port#
```

This command format is similar to previous notations and is applicable to different types of interfaces. See Figure 2-3 for an example of this equipment configuration. In this example it was assumed that our router has multiple serial ports fabricated on a port adapter and multiple port adapters can be installed into a common slot. In Figure 2-3 we used the `show interface serial` command to display specific information about serial port 3 fabricated on port adapter 1 installed in slot 0 in the router.

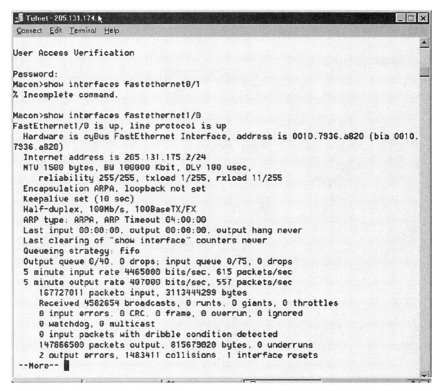

Figure 2-2 Using the show interfaces command to display information about Fast Ethernet port 0 on the adapter card in slot 1 in the router.

In terms of the flow of data within a router, as packets are received from a LAN, the layer 2 headers are removed as the packet is moved into RAM, where the router examines the layer 3 header information. When this occurs, the CPU examines its routing table and performs a lookup on the layer 3 address to determine the port where the packet should be output and the manner by which the packet should be encapsulated.

The process just described is called *process switching mode* because each packet must be processed by the CPU to consult the routing table and determine where to send the packet. Cisco routers also have a switching mode called *fast switching* where the router maintains a memory cache containing information about destination IP addresses and next hop interfaces.

The router builds this cache by saving information previously obtained from the routing table. The first packet to a particular destination causes the CPU to consult the routing table. However, once the information is obtained about the next hop interface for that particular destination, this information is inserted into the router's fast switching cache and the routing table is not consulted for new packets sent to this destination. The

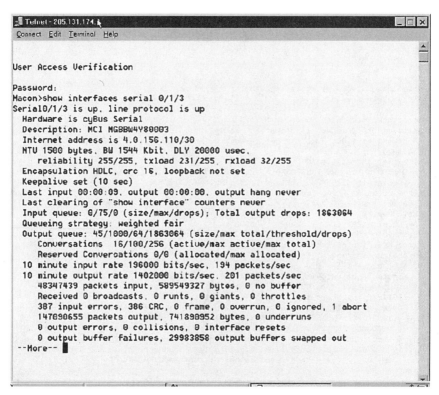

Figure 2-3 Using the show command to display information about the operation of serial port 3 fabricated on port-adapter 1 in slot 0 in the router.

result is that the router can switch packets at a much faster rate and a substantial reduction in the load on the router's CPU.

Some variations on fast switching makes use of special hardware architectures included in some higher-end models like the 7200 and 7500 series. However, the principle is essentially the same for all switching modes: a cache that contains destination address to interface mappings. The one exception to this is a switching mode called *netflow switching* which caches not only the destination IP address but also the source IP address and the upper-layer TCP or UDP (User Datagram Protocol) ports. This switching mode was traditionally available only on higher-end router platforms such as the 7500. However, in the latest version of Cisco IOS, version 12.0, it is supported on lower-end platforms such as the 2600 and 3600 series routers.

A few specific points should be noted about fast switching. First, any change to the routing table or the ARP cache forces a purge of the fast switching cache so that during a topology change, the fast switching cache will be rebuilt. Additionally, the entries in the fast switching cache will vary depending on the contents of the routing table. The entry in the fast switching cache will match the corresponding entry in the routing table. For example, if the router has a route to the 10.1.1.0/24 network, it will cache the destination 10.1.1.0/24. If the router only has a route to the 10.1.0.0/16 network, it will cache the destination 10.1.0.0/16. If there is no entry in the routing table for the network or subnet, the router uses the default route and uses the default major network mask, so it would cache the destination 10.0.0.0/8.

This pattern (*is*) holds true if there is only one route to a particular destination. If there are multiple, equal-cost, nondefault paths, the router will cache the entire 32-bit destination. For example, if the destination IP address were 10.1.1.1 and the router had two routes to the 10.1.1.0/24 network, the router would cache the value 10.1.1.1/32 and match it to the first hop. The next destination on the 10.1.1.0/24 network, say 10.1.1.2/32, would be cached and matched with the second next hop. If there were a third, equal-cost path, the next destination on the 10.1.1.0/24 network would be cached with the third next hop and so on. Notice the caveat that this is true *only* for nondefault routes. If the router must use the default route to send a packet, it only caches the major network number and not the full 32-bit address as described previously.

Essentially, the router uses a round-robin method to cache individual destinations to each successive hop. This means that the router will load share on a per-destination basis. That is, since the fast cache contains a mapping between an end destination and an interface, once the cache has been populated with an entry, all future packets for that destination will use the interface in the cache. The router will not place multiple interfaces in the fast switching cache for the same destination.

In process switching mode, the router load shares on a per-packet basis. Since there is no fast switching cache, each packet is sent in a round-robin fashion to each successive interface. While this leads to a more evenly distributed network load if there are multiple paths, it also increases the load on the router CPU and slows down the rate at which the router can move packets. In most cases, it is better to leave fast switching turned on and live with the unequal distribution across multiple network paths.

The Router Initialization Process

When you power on a router, it performs a sequence of predefined operations. Additional operations performed by the router depend on whether or not it was previously configured. For an understanding of the router initialization process, let's examine the major events that occur when you power on the device.

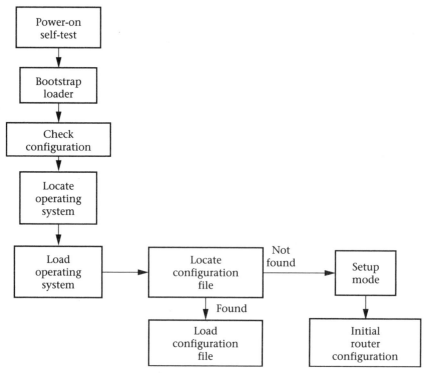

Figure 2-4 Router initialization process.

Figure 2-4 is a flowchart of the major functions performed during the router initialization process. When you apply power to the router, it initially performs a series of diagnostic tests which verify the operation of its processor, memory, and interface circuitry. Since this test is performed upon power up, it is commonly referred to as a *power-on self-test* (POST).

Once POST is completed, the bootstrap loader executes. The primary function of the loader is to initialize or place a copy of the operating system image into main memory. However, to do so it must first determine where the image of the operating system is located since the image could be located on flash memory, ROM, or even on the network.

To determine the location of the image of the operating system the bootstrap loader checks the router's configuration register. The register's values can be set either by hardware jumpers or via software, depending upon the router model. The settings of the register indicate the location of the operating system and define other device functions such as how the router reacts to the entry of a break key on the console keyboard and whether diagnostic messages are displayed on the console terminal.

The configuration register in most current model routers is a 16-bit value stored in NVRAM. It is not a physical entity. In older model routers, such as the MGS and AGS+, the configuration register was a physical jumper with 16 pins. This is the origin of the term register. On both the software and the hardware configuration registers, the last 4 bits (pins in the case of the hardware register) indicate the boot field. The boot field tells the router where to locate its configuration file. The software register is displayed as a four-digit hexadecimal number like this: 0×2102. You can display the configuration register with the command show version. Each hexadecimal number represents 4 bits, so the first number reading from right to left is the boot field. The boot field can range in value from 0 to 15. In the preceding example, the boot field is 2. Table 2-1 indicates how the router interprets the number in the boot field.

In most cases, the boot register will be set to 2, meaning the router will look in the configuration file for boot commands. If none is found, the router will load the first image found in flash memory. If there is no valid IOS image in flash memory or flash memory cannot be found, the router attempts to load an image from a tftp server by sending a tftp request to the broadcast address requesting an IOS image.

Once the configuration register is checked, the bootstrap loader knows the location from which to load the operating system image into the router's RAM and proceeds to do so. After the operating system is loaded, it looks for a previously created and saved configuration file in NVRAM. If the file is found, it will be loaded into memory and executed on a line-by-line basis, resulting in the router becoming operational and working according to a predefined networking environment. If a previously created NVRAM file does not exist, the operating system executes a predefined sequence of question-driven configuration displays referred to as a *Setup dialog*. Once the operator completes the Setup dialog, the configuration information will be stored in NVRAM and will be loaded as the default at the next initialization process. The router can be instructed to ignore the contents of NVRAM by setting the configuration register. If the second hexadecimal value from the right is set to 4, 0×2142, the router will ignore the contents of NVRAM. This feature is used during password recovery on the router so that an administrator can bypass the contents of the configuration file.

Table 2-1 The Meaning of the Boot Field Settings

Boot field value	Router interpretation
0	RXBOOT mode. The router must be manually booted using the b command.
1	Automatically boots from ROM.
2-F	Examines the contents of the configuration file in NVRAM for boot system commands.

Figure 2-5 Initial display generated by a Cisco 4500 router as power is applied.

```
System Bootstrap, Version 5.2(7b) [mkamson 7b], RELEASE SOFTWARE
(fc1)
Copyright (c) 1995 by cisco Systems, Inc.
C4500 processor with 8192 Kbytes of main memory


program load complete, entrypt: 0x80008000, size: 0x231afc
Self decompressing the image :
#################################################
######################################################################
########
############################################################# [OK]

                    Restricted Rights Legend

Use, duplication, or disclosure by the Government is
subject to restrictions as set forth in subparagraph
(c) of the Commercial Computer Software - Restricted
Rights clause at FAR sec. 52.227-19 and subparagraph
(c) (1) (ii) of the Rights in Technical Data and Computer
Software clause at DFARS sec. 252.227-7013.

              cisco Systems, Inc.
              170 West Tasman Drive
              San Jose, California 95134-1706

Cisco Internetwork Operating System Software
IOS (tm) 4500 Software (C4500-INR-M), Version 10.3(8), RELEASE
SOFTWARE (fc2)
Copyright (c) 1986-1995 by cisco Systems, Inc.
Compiled Thu 14-Dec-95 22:10 by mkamson
Image text-base: 0x600087E0, data-base: 0x6043C000


cisco 4500 (R4K) processor (revision B) with 8192K/4096K bytes of
memory.
Processor board serial number 73160394
R4600 processor, Implementation 32, Revision 2.0
G.703/E1 software, Version 1.0.
Bridging software.
X.25 software, Version 2.0, NET2, BFE and GOSIP compliant.
2 Ethernet/IEEE 802.3 interfaces.
1 Token Ring/IEEE 802.5 interface.
2 Serial network interfaces.
128K bytes of non-volatile configuration memory.
4096K bytes of processor board System flash (Read/Write)
4096K bytes of processor board Boot flash (Read/Write)

Press RETURN to get started!
```

Figure 2-5 illustrates the initial display generated by a Cisco 4500 router as power is applied, the bootstrap is invoked, and a previously defined configuration is loaded into memory. Note the prompt at the end of the display which can easily scroll off a screen and which occasionally results in a novice waiting a considerable period of time for something to happen without realizing they need to press the RETURN key to begin to access the system.

Now that we understand the basic hardware components of a router and its initialization process, let's look at router software to learn about the two key software components of a router and the relationship of router commands to the software components.

Basic Software Components

There are two key router software components: the operating system image and the configuration file. This section looks at both; however, because the configuration file allows customization of the operation of a router, most of our attention is devoted to the configuration file.

Operating System Image

The operating system image is located by the bootstrap loader based on the setting of the configuration register. Once the image is located, it is loaded into the low-addressed portion of memory. The operating system image consists of a series of routines that support the transfer of data through the device, manage buffer space, support different network functions, update routing tables, and execute user commands.

Configuration File

The second major router software component is the configuration file. This file is created by the router administrator and contains statements interpreted by the operating system which tell it how to perform different functions built into the OS. For example, included in the configuration file can be statements that define one or more access lists and tell the operating system to apply different access lists to different interfaces to provide a degree of control concerning the flow of packets through the router. Although the configuration file defines how to perform functions that affect the operation of the router, it is the operating system that actually does the work since it interprets and acts upon the statements in the configuration file.

The configuration file contains statements stored in ASCII. As such, its contents can be displayed on the router console terminal or on a remote terminal. It is important to note and remember this if you create or modify a configuration file on a PC attached to a network and use tftp to load the file into your router because the use of a text editor or word processor will normally result in embedded control characters in a saved file that the router will not be able to read. Thus, when using a text editor or word processor to create or manipulate a configuration file, be sure to save the file as an ASCII text (.txt) file. Once the configuration file is saved, it is stored in the NVRAM and loaded into upper-addressed memory each time

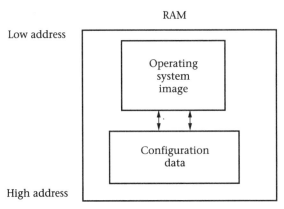

Figure 2-6 Router software components.

the router is initialized. Figure 2-6 illustrates the relationship of the two key router software components with respect to router RAM.

Data Flow

We can learn about configuration information by examining the flow of data within a router. (See Figure 2-7 which illustrates the general flow of data within a router.)

At the media interface, previously entered configuration commands inform the operating system of the type of frames to be processed. For example, the interface could be Ethernet, token ring, *fiber-distributed data interface* (FDDI), or even a (*serial*) wide area network port such as an X.25

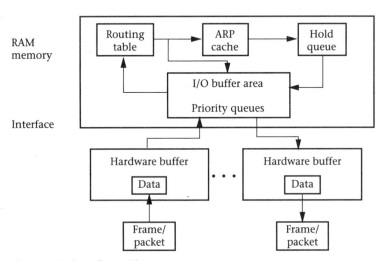

Figure 2-7 Data flow within a router.

or frame-relay interface. In defining the interface you may be required to provide one or more operating rates and other parameters to fully define the interface.

Once the router knows the type of interface it must support, it can verify the frame format of arriving data and correctly form frames for output via that interface or a different interface. In addition, the router can check data integrity on received frames since once it knows the interface, it is able to use an appropriate *cyclic redundancy check* (CRC). Similarly, the router can compute and append an appropriate CRC to frames placed onto the media.

Configuration commands are used within main memory to control the method by which routing table entries occur. If you configure static routing entries, the router will not exchange routing table entries with other routers. The ARP cache is an area within memory which stores associations between IP addresses and their corresponding MAC layer 2 addresses. As data are received or prepared for transmission, the data may flow into one or more priority queues where low-priority traffic is temporarily delayed so the router can process higher-priority traffic. If your router supports traffic prioritization, certain configuration statements are used to inform the router's operating system how to perform its prioritization tasks.

As data flow into the router, the location and status are tracked by a hold queue. Entries in the routing table denote the destination interface through which the packet will be routed. If the destination is a LAN and address resolution is required, the router will attempt to use the ARP cache to determine the MAC delivery address as well as the manner by which the outgoing frame should be formed. If an appropriate address is not in cache, the router will form and issue an ARP packet to determine the necessary layer 2 address. Once the destination address and method of encapsulation is determined, the packet is ready for delivery to an outgoing interface port. Once again, it may be placed into a priority queue prior to being delivered into the transmit buffer of the interface for delivery onto the connected media.

Now that we understand the two key router software components, let's examine how to develop the router configuration file.

The Router Configuration Process

The first time you take your router out of the box and power it on or after you add one or more hardware components, you must use the setup command. This command is automatically invoked in either of the previously defined situations or it can be invoked later at the router's command interpreter prompt level. As mentioned in Chapter 1, the interpreter is referred to as the EXEC. However, prior to running setup or issuing EXEC commands, it is important to note the cabling needed to connect a terminal device to the router's system console port.

Cabling Considerations

The system console port on a router is configured as a *data terminal equipment* (DTE) port. Because the RS-232 port on PCs and ASCII terminal devices are also configured as DTEs, you cannot directly cable the two together using a common straight-through cable because both the router's port and the terminal device transmit on pin 2 of the interface and receive data on pin 3. To correctly work with each other you must obtain a *crossover* or *rollover cable* where pin 2 at one end is crossed to pin 3 at the other end and vice versa. The crossover table also ties certain control signals together so it is actually a bit more than the reversal of pins 2 and 3. However, the cable is easy to obtain by specifying the term crossover or rollover. Once you install the correct cable, you should configure your terminal device to operate at 9600 baud, 8 data bits, no parity, 1 stop bit.

Console Access

A variety of communications programs are available to access the router via its console port. Since Windows 95 and Windows 98 include the hyperterminal communications program, we will briefly explore its use as a mechanism to configure a router. The hyperterminal program that is shipped with Windows NT, however, contains a bug that causes it to oper-

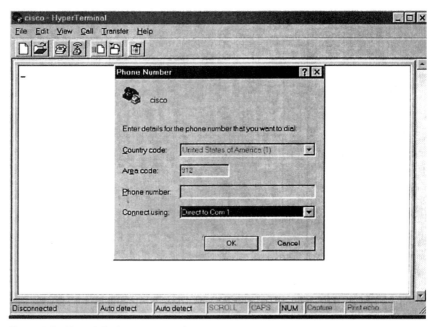

Figure 2-8 Use of the hyperterminal program to create a new connection.

ate incorrectly. If you are using NT to connect to the router, your connection will not work unless you upgrade the hyperterminal program.

Figure 2-8 illustrates the use of the hyperterminal program to create a new connection, appropriately labeled Cisco by the authors. Since you will directly cable your computer to the Cisco console port, you need to configure the phone number entry so it is a direct com port. In the example shown in Figure 2-8, com port 1 is shown as selected. The connection type must be set to direct when cabling a PC directly to the router console port.

Once you select the appropriate direct connect com port and click on the OK button, the hyperterminal program will display a dialog box labeled Port Settings. Figure 2-9 illustrates the Port Settings dialog box for

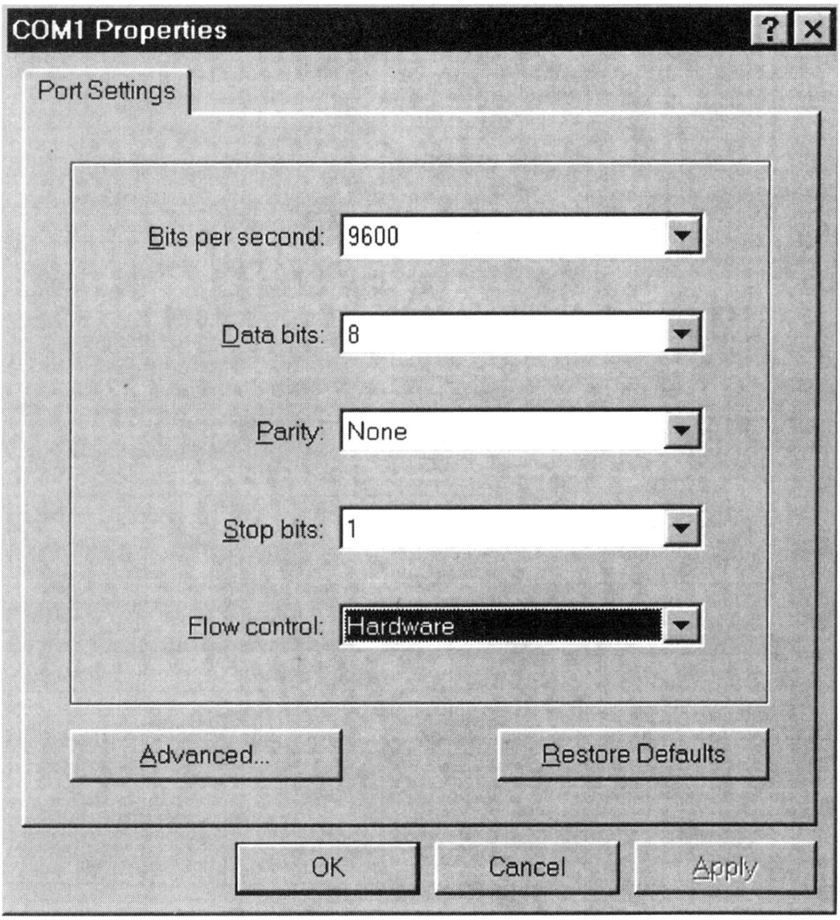

Figure 2-9 The Port Settings dialog box.

the COM1 port previously configured for the connection to be established to the router. The Port Settings dialog box lets you configure the communications parameters used by your computer to match those used by the router console.

In examining Figure 2-9 note the Port Settings dialog box allows you to define the communications settings to be used between your PC and the router port. Since the router console port's default is 9600 bps, 8 data bits, no parity, and 1 stop bit, the configuration in Figure 2-9 is set accordingly.

Setup Considerations

This book is a guide to the use of IOS IP–related commands so we will cover everything you need to know to run setup correctly in an IP environment. However, instead of focusing our attention on setup, which is only run when the router is first removed from the box and perhaps infrequently thereafter, we provide you with information to assist both the setup process as well as the much more prevalent configuration process. However, to facilitate the use of the setup facility you need to prepare for the use of the router. For example, make a list of the protocols you plan to route, determine the types of interfaces installed, and determine if you plan to use bridging. In addition, because setup will prompt you to enter a variety of specific parameters for each protocol and interface, it is highly recommended that you consult the appropriate Cisco Systems router manuals to determine these parameters correctly.

The setup facility allows you to assign a name to the router as well as assign both a direct connect and virtual terminal password. Once you complete the setup, you will be prompted to accept the configuration. After the initial setup process is completed, you are ready to use the router's command interpreters.

Figure 2-10 shows how to use the router setup command and, if desired, to modify one or more previously established configuration entries. In this example the name of the router assigned during a previous setup process was CISCO4000, so that name is displayed prior to a prompt character. The prompt character is a pound sign (#) that indicates we are in the router's privileged mode of operation. Note the enabled password is shown as abadabado. That password must be specified after a person gains access to the router console port and enters the command enable to use privileged EXEC commands that alter a router's operating environment. In addition to the enable password, an administrator may also configure an enable secret password. The enable secret serves the same purpose as the standard enable password, except that the enable secret password is encrypted in the configuration file using MD5. When the configuration is displayed, only the encrypted version of the enable secret password will be seen. This is important for preventing anyone from determining

Figure 2-10 Using the setup command to view an existing router configuration.

```
CISCO4000#setup

        -- System Configuration Dialog --

At any point you may enter a question mark '?' for help.
Refer to the 'Getting Started' Guide for additional help.
Use ctrl-c to abort configuration dialog at any prompt.
Default settings are in square brackets '[]'.

Continue with configuration dialog? [yes]:

First, would you like to see the current interface summary?
[yes]:

Interface       IP-Address      OK? Method   Status
     Protocol
Ethernet0       192.72.46.3     YES NVRAM    up
     down
Serial0         4.0.136.74      YES NVRAM    down
     down
Serial1         4.0.136.90      YES NVRAM    down
     down
TokenRing0      192.131.174.2   YES NVRAM    initializing
     down

Configuring global parameters:

  Enter host name [CISCO4000]:

The enable secret is a one-way cryptographic secret used
instead of the enable password when it exists.

  Enter enable secret [<Use current secret>]:

The enable password is used when there is no enable secret
and when using older software and some boot images.

  Enter enable password [abadabado]:
  Enter virtual terminal password [gobirds]:
  Configure SNMP Network Management? [yes]:
    Community string [public]:
  Configure IPX? [yes]:
  Configure bridging? [no]:
  Configure IP? [yes]:
    Configure IGRP routing? [no]:
    Configure RIP routing? [yes]:

Configuring interface parameters:
Configuring interface Ethernet0:
  Is this interface in use? [yes]:
  Configure IP on this interface? [yes]:
    IP address for this interface [192.72.46.3]:
    Number of bits in subnet field [0]:
```

(Continued)

Figure 2-10 *(Continued)*

```
      Class C network is 192.72.46.0, 0 subnet bits; mask is
255.255.255.0
   Configure IPX on this interface? [yes]:
    IPX network number [110]:

Configuring interface Serial0:
  Is this interface in use? [yes]:
  Configure IP on this interface? [yes]:
  Configure IP unnumbered on this interface? [no]:
    IP address for this interface [4.0.136.74]:
    Number of bits in subnet field [22]:
    Class A network is 4.0.0.0, 22 subnet bits; mask is
255.255.255.252
  Configure IPX on this interface? [no]:

. . . .   . . .
. . . .   . . .

The following configuration command script was created:

hostname CISCO4000
enable secret 5 $1$soiv$pyh65G.wUNxX9LK90w7yc.
enable password abadabado
line vty 0 4
password gobirds
snmp-server community public
!
ipx routing
no bridge 1
ip routing
!
! Turn off IPX to prevent network conflicts.
interface Ethernet0
no ipx network
interface Serial0
no ipx network
interface Serial1
no ipx network
interface TokenRing0
no ipx network
!
interface Ethernet0
ip address 192.78.46.1 255.255.255.0
ipx network 110

. . . .  .
. . . .  .
router rip
network 192.78.46.0
network 200.1.2.0
network 4.0.0.0
network 192.131.174.0
!
end

Use this configuration? [yes/no]:
```

what the enable secret password is by obtaining a copy of the router configuration. The regular enable password may also be encrypted by using the command service password-encryption. This command will also encrypt the passwords used for the vty, auxiliary, and console ports. However, the encryption used is much weaker than that used for the enable secret and many free programs are available on the Internet to crack passwords encrypted in this manner in a few seconds. The authors recommend always using the enable secret password. If both the enable secret and the standard enable password are set, the enable secret password takes precedence.

To save on listing space, a portion of the router's setup configuration was eliminated from Figure 2-10 where the double rows of dots are shown. Note that you can use the question mark at each line entry level to obtain online assistance. Also note that once the configuration is completed, a command script is created by the router. This command script represents the latest configuration changes. You are then prompted to accept or reject the entire configuration.

Since the command interpreter is the key to entering router commands that control how the operating system changes router functionality, including applying access lists to interfaces, let's examine this facility.

The Command Interpreter

The command interpreter, as its name implies, interprets the router commands entered. Referred to as the EXEC, the command interpreter checks each command and, assuming they are correctly entered, performs the operation requested.

Assuming an administrator entered a password during the setup process, you must log into the router using the correct password before you can enter an EXEC command. In actuality, two passwords can be required to use EXEC commands as there are two EXEC command levels: user and privileged. By logging into the router, you gain access to user EXEC commands that let you connect to another host. You can also provide a name to a logical connection, change the parameters of a terminal, display open connections, and perform similar operations that are not considered by Cisco Systems to represent critical operations.

If you use the EXEC enable command to gain access to the use of privileged commands, you can enter configuration information, turn privileged commands on or off, lock the terminal, and perform other critical functions. To use the EXEC enable command you may have to enter another password if one was previously set with the enable-password or enable-secret configuration commands.

The following brief series of router operations will show why the EXEC level should have its own password and why different routers should have different passwords. In this example once we accessed the local router's privilege mode, we initiated a telnet operation to a second router. If you assign the same password to a series of routers, that weak point can make it simple for a hacker to enjoy restructuring your entire network.

```
Cisco7500#
Cisco7500#telnet
Host: 205.136.175.1
Trying 205.136.175.1 ... Open

User Access Verification

Password:
```

USER-MODE OPERATIONS

Once you log into the router, you are in the user command mode. In this mode the system prompt appears as an angle bracket (>). If you previously entered a name for the router, that name will prefix the angle bracket. Otherwise the default term router will appear before the angle bracket.

PRIVILEGED-MODE OPERATION

Since you can only configure a router through its privileged EXEC mode of operation, you can assign a password to this mode of operation. As previously noted, you would use the enable-password configuration command, which means you first enter the privileged mode without password protection to set password protection.

To enter the privileged EXEC mode, enter the command enable at the > prompt. You are then prompted to enter a password, after which the prompt would change to a pound sign #, which indicates that you are in the privileged EXEC mode of operation. If you use the ? command in both user and privilege access modes, the privileged-mode command set includes all user EXEC commands. In addition, the privilege user mode includes the configure command which permits you to apply configuration parameters that affect the router on a global basis.

In Chapter 1 we examined the router response to the entry of the configure command and noted that you can configure the device from a terminal, memory, or via the network. Since a router does not contain a hard disk or a floppy disk, administrators often store configuration files, including access lists, on a network by creating a configuration file using a word processor or text editor and saving the file in ASCII text (.txt) mode. Then you use tftp to transfer the file to the router. To accomplish this you must install a tftp server program on your computer and indicate the location where the tftp server root directory resides. Figure 2-11 illustrates a screen display of Cisco's tftp server software running on one of the authors' PC. If your organization has an appropriate account with Cisco Systems, you can download the software from the Cisco Web site.

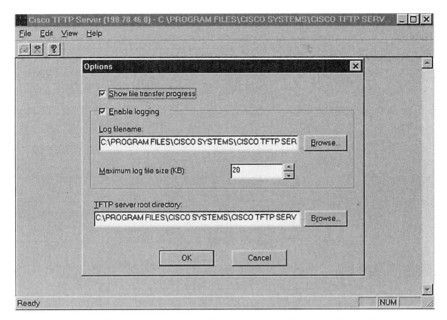

Figure 2-11   Cisco tftp server software allows you to enable or disable logging and specify a server root directory.

Table 2-2 summarizes configuration command entry methods and their operational results, that is, the relationship between the use of different command entry methods and the use of different types of storage for both accessing and storing configuration commands. Cisco changed the format of these commands beginning in version 10.3 of the router operating system. Both forms of the commands are still accepted by the router in the most current releases, although at some point the older version of the commands will probably be phased out. The newer version of the commands are shown in italics.

Configuration Command Categories

Configuration commands can be categorized into four general categories: (1) global, which defines systemwide parameters; (2) interface, which defines WAN or LAN interfaces; (3) line, which defines the characteristics of a serial terminal line; and (4) router subcommands used to configure a routing protocol.

GLOBAL CONFIGURATION COMMANDS

Global configuration commands define systemwide parameters, including router interfaces and access lists applied to those interfaces. Some global

Table 2-2 Configuration Command Entry Methods

Command	Operational result
Configure terminal	Configures the router manually from the console.
Configure memory	Loads a previously created configuration from NVRAM.
Copy startup-config	
Running-config	
Configure network	Loads a previously created configuration from a network server via tftp.
Copy tftp running-config	
Write terminal	Displays the current configuration in RAM.
Show running-config	
Write network	Shares the current configuration in RAM onto a network server via tftp.
Copy running-config tftp	
Show configuration	Displays the previously saved configuration in NVRAM.
Show startup-config	
Write erase	Erases the contents of NVRAM.
Erase startup-config	
Reload	Loads the contents of NVRAM into RAM. Occurs automatically during power-on.

configuration commands are mandatory if you want the router to operate. For example, you must configure your LAN and serial ports to connect to the Internet. Other configuration commands, such as creating and applying an access list, are optional. A list of global configuration commands supported by the router you are using is available by entering the ? command after entering the router's configuration mode. To do so you must use the enable command to enter the privilege access mode as configure is a privilege command. Once this is accomplished, enter the command configure and the router's prompt changes to router(config)#, where router is the hostname assigned to your router and config indicates your location in the configuration command mode. Once in the configuration command mode, enter the ? subcommand, as illustrated in Figure 2-12, for a list of global configuration commands applicable to the router used by the authors.

Figure 2-12 Using the ? command to obtain a list of global configuration commands applicable to a particular router.

```
User Access Verification

Password:
Cisco7500>enable
Password:

Cisco7500#configure
Configuring from terminal, memory, or network [terminal]?
Enter configuration commands, one per line.  End with CNTL/Z.
Cisco7500(config)#?
Configure commands:
  aaa                          Authentication, Authorization and
                               Accounting.
  access-list                  Add an access list entry
  alias                        Create command alias
  alps                         Configure Airline Protocol Support
  appletalk                    Appletalk global configuration commands
  arap                         Appletalk Remote Access Protocol
  arp                          Set a static ARP entry
  async-bootp                  Modify system bootp parameters
  autonomous-system            Specify local AS number to which we belong
  banner                       Define a login banner
  boot                         Modify system boot parameters
  bridge                       Bridge Group.
  bstun                        BSTUN global configuration commands
  buffers                      Adjust system buffer pool parameters
  call-history-mib             Define call history mib parameters
  cdp                          Global CDP configuration subcommands
  chat-script                  Define a modem chat script
  clock                        Configure time-of-day clock
  config-register              Define the configuration register
  controller                   Configure a specific controller
  decnet                       Global DECnet configuration subcommands
  default                      Set a command to its defaults
  default-value                Default character-bits values
  dialer                       Dialer watch commands
  dialer-list                  Create a dialer list entry
  dlsw                         Data Link Switching global configuration
                               commands
  dnsix-dmdp                   Provide DMDP service for DNSIX
  dnsix-nat                    Provide DNSIX service for audit trails
  downward-compatible-config   Generate a configuration compatible with
                               older software
```

(Continued)

Figure 2-12 *(Continued)*

```
dspu                    DownStream Physical Unit Command
dss                     Configure dss parameters
enable                  Modify enable password parameters
end                     Exit from configure mode
endnode                 SNA APPN endnode command
exception               Exception handling
exit                    Exit from configure mode
file                    Adjust file system parameters
frame-relay             global frame relay configuration commands
help                    Description of the interactive help system
hostname                Set system's network name
interface               Select an interface to configure
ip                      Global IP configuration subcommands
ipc                     Configure IPC system
```

The built-in help facility, while cryptic in some ways, provides some information, possibly eliminating the need to consult a reference book. For example, many times during the daily grind of configuring LAN and WAN devices, it is easy to forget blocks of numbers assigned by Cisco to different types of access lists, ICMP type codes, and similar information. By drilling down and using the ? command you may be able to obtain the needed information. Figure 2-13 shows the use of the ? command parameter to obtain information about the access list command. Figure 2-13 shows a list of the numeric range associated with different types of access lists.

In examining Figure 2-13 note that the online help for access lists provides a general review of the number range for different access lists supported by the router. Chapter 6 examines access lists in considerable

Figure 2-13 Obtaining online help on router access lists.

```
CISCO7500(config)# access-list ?
  <1-99>       IP standard access list
  <100-199>    IP extended access list
  <1000-1099>  IPX SAP access list
  <1100-1199>  Extended 48-bit MAC address access list
  <200-299>    Protocol type-code access list
  <700-799>    48-bit MAC address access list
  <800-899>    IPX standard access list
  <900-999>    IPX extended access list
```

Figure 2-14 Using the `interface serial` command followed by the ? command to
display a list of interface configuration commands.

```
User Access Verification

Password:
Macon>show interfaces serial0/1/0 ?
  accounting       Show interface accounting
  crb              Show interface routing/bridging info
  fair-queue       Show interface Weighted Fair Queueing (WFQ) info
  irb              Show interface routing/bridging info
  mac-accounting   Show interface MAC accounting info
  precedence       Show interface precedence accounting info
  random-detect    Show interface Weighted Random Early Detection (WRED)
                   info
  rate-limit       Show interface rate-limit info
  type             Show vlan types
  |                Output modifiers
  <cr>
```

detail, so at this time we will simply note they are numbered and used to
enable or disable the flow of packets across a router's interface.

INTERFACE COMMANDS

Interface commands define the characteristics of a LAN or WAN interface
and are proceeded by an interface command. Figure 2-14 illustrates the use
of the `show interfaces serial0/1/0` command followed by the ? command to display a partial list of interface configuration commands that
can be applied to a serial interface.

The `interface` command allows you to assign a network to a particular port as well as configure one or more specific parameters required for
the interface. For example, `interface ethernet0` informs the router that
port 0 is connected to an Ethernet network.

The most common format of the `interface` command is

```
interface type number
```

Here `type` defines the type of interface to be configured. Table 2-3 lists 10
keywords used to define different types of router interfaces.

LINE COMMANDS

Line commands modify the operation of a serial terminal line. Figure 2-15
illustrates the use of the `line` command followed by the ? command to
display a list of lines that can be configured.

Table 2-3 Keywords That Define the Type of Router Interface

Keyword	Interface Type
async	Port line used as an asynchronous interface.
atm	Asynchronous transfer mode interface.
bri	Integrated services digital network (ISDN). Basic Rate Interface (BRI).
ethernet	Ethernet 10-Mbps interface.
fastethernet	Fast Ethernet 100-Mbps interface.
fddi	Fiber-distributed data interface.
hssi	High-speed serial interface.
serial	Serial interface.
tokenring	Token-ring interface.
vg-anylan	100-Mbps VG-AnyLAN port adapter.

Figure 2-15 Listing of the serial terminal lines you can configure.

```
CISCO7500(config)#line ?
  <0-6>    First Line number
  aux      Auxiliary line
  console  Primary terminal line
  vty      Virtual terminal
```

ROUTER SUBCOMMANDS

Router subcommands configure IP routing protocol parameters and follow the use of the router command. The top portion of Figure 2-16 illustrates the use of the router command followed by the ? command to display a list of router subcommands supported by the router used at this point in time.

Once again, note that you can drill down to obtain information about a particular router command by entering that command and then entering that command with the ? command parameter, as illustrated in the lower portion of Figure 2-16.

Figure 2-16   List of `router` commands and specific information on RIP subcommands.

```
CISCO7500(config)#router ?
  bgp        Border Gateway Protocol (BGP)
  egp        Exterior Gateway Protocol (EGP)
  eigrp      Enhanced Interior Gateway Routing Protocol (EIGRP)
  igrp       Interior Gateway Routing Protocol (IGRP)
  isis       ISO IS-IS
  iso-igrp   IGRP for OSI networks
  mobile     Mobile routes
  ospf       Open Shortest Path First (OSPF)
  rip        Routing Information Protocol (RIP)
  static     Static routes

CISCO7500(config)#router rip
CISCO7500(config-router)#?
Router configuration commands:
  default-metric          Set metric of redistributed routes
  distance                Define an administrative distance
  distribute-list         Filter networks in routing updates
  exit                    Exit from routing protocol configuration mode
  help                    Description of the interactive help system
  maximum-paths           Forward packets over multiple paths
  neighbor                Specify a neighbor router
  network                 Enable routing on an IP network
  no                      Negate or set default values of a command
  offset-list             Add or subtract offset from IGRP or RIP
                          metrics
  passive-interface       Suppress routing updates on an interface
  redistribute            Redistribute information from another routing
                          protocol
  timers                  Adjust routing timers
  validate-update-source  Perform sanity checks against source
                          address of routing updates
```

Abbreviating Commands

It is often not necessary to type the entire word for the router to accept a command. Generally, three or four letters of the command are enough for the router to discern the command being requested and perform the desired action. For example, the following command:

```
Router# show interface serial0
```

could be abbreviated as

```
Router# sh int s0
```

which is certainly much easier to type! When in doubt, try abbreviating the command to the first three letters. If the first three letters are not

enough for the router to determine the command, you will get an
ambiguous command error at the router prompt. You can then use the
router's context-sensitive help by typing the first three letters with a question mark at the end. The router will display all of the commands that
match the first three letters and then you can add as many characters as
necessary to distinguish the command you want.

Remember, the ? is your friend. By using the built-in context-sensitive
help, even a Cisco novice can determine the correct syntax of a command.

General Console Operations

Now that we have a general understanding of router configuration operations, let's look at specific operations. In this section we first examine how
to control router general operations, such as assigning a hostname, generating a banner message, and setting the day and date. Once this is accomplished, we examine how to tune our console and, if desired, log
messages.

HOSTNAME ASSIGNMENT

The assignment or reassignment of a name to your router is accomplished
through the use of the hostname command. The hostname command is a
configuration command so you must be in the privilege-user mode to set
or reset the hostname. Figure 2-17 illustrates entering the privilege-user
mode followed by the use of the configure command, the hostname
command, and the ? parameter to obtain online assistance on the use of

Figure 2-17   Using the hostname command to set and reset the name assigned to a
router.

```
User Access Verification

Password:
router>enable
Password:
router#configure
Configuring from terminal, memory, or network [terminal]?
Enter configuration commands, one per line.  End with CNTL/Z.
router(config)#hostname ?
  WORD  This system's network name

router(config)#hostname beverly
beverly(config)#hostname gilbert
gilbert(config)#hostname Macon7500
Macon7500(config)#exit
```

each command. Note that online assistance informs you that you need to enter a word which will be used as the system's network name. In Figure 2-17 we assume that no hostname was previously assigned, so the default name of router was assigned. The hostname command was then followed by the word beverly to change the name to beverly. Next, the hostname command was followed by the word gilbert to change the name of the router to gilbert. While these changes are nice for the ego of one author and his wife, in reality hostnames should be meaningfully assigned, especially when you have a complex network. The last use of the hostname command in Figure 2-17 illustrates the use of a more meaningful name, with Macon7500 used, as this better describes the location and type of router. Although Figure 2-17 shows the use of the enable command to enter the privilege mode, in subsequent examples we assume we made our point about the use of the enable command and simply show the # prompt after a hostname to indicate we are in privilege mode.

BANNER CREATION

A *banner* is a message displayed when a certain type of initial activity is performed. In a Cisco router environment several types of banner messages can be displayed. Figure 2-18 illustrates the use of the banner configuration command followed by the ? parameter to display a list of the types of banner messages supported on the authors' router. In Figure 2-18 note that LINE is not a banner option, but the manner by which you enter a banner-text message. For example, to display the message Welcome you enter it within a pair of delimiting characters, such as the pound (#) sign, so the line entry becomes #Welcome#. Carefully select your delimiter character as that character cannot be used in the banner message.

The banner exec command is used to display a message when a line is activated, an incoming vty connection occurs, or a similar EXEC process

Figure 2-18 Using the banner command to display the types of banner messages supported by a router.

```
Cisco7500#configure
Configuring from terminal, memory, or network [terminal]?
Enter configuration commands, one per line.  End with CNTL/Z.
Cisco7500(config)#banner ?
  LINE            c banner-text c, where 'c' is a delimiting character
  exec            Set EXEC process creation banner
  incoming        Set incoming terminal line banner
  login           Set login banner
  motd            Set Message of the Day banner
  prompt-timeout  Set Message for login authentication timeout
  slip-ppp        Set Message for SLIP/PPP
```

occurs. In comparison, the banner login command results in the display of a message when you connect to a router facility that requires a login such as a telnet connection. Thus, the banner login command results in a message display before the result of any banner exec command message. Other banner command options listed in Figure 2-18 include incoming, motd, prompt-timeout, and slip-ppp.

A banner incoming message results in the display of a message when an incoming connection initiated from the network side of a router occurs. The motd subcommand permits you to specify a message of the day. A motd banner will be displayed whenever any type of connection to the router occurs. Thus, you should consider its use when you have information to convey that affects all users. For example, the command banner motd #Router will be taken offline from 21:00 to 23:00 tonight for hardware upgrade# would represent a common type of use for this banner.

The prompt-timeout subcommand displays a message if a login authentication process times out. Finally, the slip-ppp subcommand results in the display of a message for access via those protocols.

Note that banners are displayed in a particular order regardless of the sequence of commands you use to set banners. The banner motd, if set, will be displayed first. That banner will be followed, if previously configured, by the banner incoming. If a user login occurs, the banner exec, if configured, will then be displayed.

Figure 2-19 illustrates the creation and display of two messages. The upper portion shows the use of two banner commands. The first com-

Figure 2-19 Using the banner command to configure text displays at login and when an EXEC process occurs.

```
Macon(config)#banner exec #Welcome#
Macon(config)#banner login #Hello#
Macon(config)#exit
Macon#exit



Hello

User Access Verification

Password: Welcome
Macon>enable
Password:
Macon#configure
Configuring from terminal, memory, or network [terminal]?
Enter configuration commands, one per line.  End with CNTL/Z.
```

mand, banner exec, associates the message Welcome with the occurrence of an EXEC process. The second command, banner login, associates the message Hello with an incoming connection. The results of the two banner commands are illustrated in the lower portion of Figure 2-19.

Before moving on, a word about misconfiguration of messages and their erasure is warranted. If you use an improper delimiter, such as cWelcomec, you will not obtain the correct message display. Because of the manner by which Cisco routers buffer data, it is sometimes not a simple solution to just redo the message. Instead, it is far better to use the no version of a banner command to delete the previous entry. For example, entering a no banner exec command followed by no banner login command suppresses the previous entries. In terms of commands, a no version of each command is usually available to enter to either return a router parameter to its default or alleviate the effect of a previously issued command.

DAY/TIME SETTINGS

Cisco routers support several commands that affect the system calendar and system clock. You can use the calendar set command to set a 7000 or 4500 series system calendar by entering the command followed by the time and date in either of the following two formats:

```
hh:mm:ss day month year
hh:mm:ss month day year
```

You enter the day as a numeric and the month by full name, allowing the operating system to automatically distinguish between the two formats. Once you set the system calendar, you can configure your router to be the authoritative time source for a network. To do so, you would use the clock calendar-valid global command.

A second date/time-related command to note is the clock set command. This command has the same format for parameter entries as the calendar set command. Instead of setting the system calendar, the clock set command sets the system clock.

Figure 2-20 provides several examples of the use of the clock and calendar commands. The first two examples simply list options supported for each command. A show calendar command was then used to display the system calendar, which was found to be rather dated. Next, the calendar set command was used to update the system calendar and another show command verified our setting. We then used the clock read-calendar command to read the hardware calendar values into the system clock and used two additional show commands to display our results.

Depending on your router, other date/time commands may be available. Some commands will enable your system to automatically switch to

Figure 2-20 Setting the system calendar and system clock.

```
Cisco7500#clock ?
  read-calendar    Read the hardware calendar into the clock
  set              Set the time and date
  update-calendar  Update the hardware calendar from the clock

Cisco7500#calendar ?
  set  Set the time and date

Cisco7500#show calendar
18:38:24 UTC Wed Aug 6 1997

Cisco7500#calendar set 10:55:00 28 september 1999
Cisco7500#show calendar
10:55:09 UTC Tue Sep 28 1999

Cisco7500#clock read-calendar
Cisco7500#show clock
10:58:23.415 UTC Tue Sep 28 1999
Cisco7500#show calendar
10:59:18 UTC Tue Sep 28 1999
```

daylight savings time, while another command allows you to perform a reverse of the clock read-calendar. That is, the clock update-calendar command enables Cisco 7500 or 4500 routers' calendars to be set from the system clock.

TERMINAL CUSTOMIZATION

Similar to the way we feel about food, products, and other topics, no one terminal setting makes everyone happy. Recognizing this, you can change terminal parameters to meet your specific preference through the use of the terminal command.

Once you connect to your router, you can obtain information about the current terminal line through the show terminal command. Figure 2-21 is an example of the use of the show terminal command and its resulting display. By carefully examining the entries in the display, you can determine not only information about the setting of your terminal parameters but also information about system settings. For example, you will note from Figure 2-21 that idle session disconnect warning is not set at the system level. Thus, it might be a good idea to give users a warning.

You can easily display a list of commands to change the hardware and software parameters of the current terminal line by using the command terminal ?, as illustrated in Figure 2-22.

Figure 2-21   Using the show terminal command to display information about the terminal configuration parameters for the current line.

```
Cisco7500>show terminal
Line 2, Location: "", Type: "vt100"
Length: 24 lines, Width: 80 columns
Baud rate (TX/RX) is 9600/9600
Status: PSI Enabled, Ready, Active, No Exit Banner
Capabilities: none
Modem state: Ready
Special Chars: Escape  Hold  Stop  Start  Disconnect  Activation
               ^^x     none   -     -      none
Timeouts:      Idle EXEC    Idle Session   Modem Answer  Session
Dispatch
               00:10:00     never                        none     not
set
                            Idle Session Disconnect Warning
                              never
                            Login-sequence User Response
                            00:00:30
                            Autoselect Initial Wait
                              not set
Modem type is unknown.
Session limit is not set.
Time since activation: 00:06:27
Editing is enabled.
History is enabled, history size is 10.
DNS resolution in show commands is enabled
Full user help is disabled
Allowed transports are pad v120 mop telnet.  Preferred is telnet.
No output characters are padded
No special data dispatching characters
Cisco7500>
```

To illustrate some common examples of terminal parameter alteration let's assume you wish to set the terminal width to 132 columns and the number of lines to 32. First you use the terminal width command, followed by the number of columns for your setting. Thus, your entry would be as follows:

```
Router>terminal width 132
```

To set the number of lines on the screen to 32 you use the terminal length command, indicating the number of lines you desire in the command as follows:

```
Router>terminal length 32
```

Figure 2-22 Displaying a list of commands that affect the hardware and software parameters of the current terminal line.

```
Cisco7500#terminal ?
  data-character-bits     Size of characters being handled
  databits                Set number of data bits per character
  default                 Set a command to its defaults
  domain-lookup           Enable domain lookups in show commands
  download                Put line into 'download' mode
  editing                 Enable command line editing
  escape-character        Change the current line's escape character
  exec-character-bits     Size of characters to the command exec
  flowcontrol             Set the flow control
  full-help               Provide help to unprivileged user
  help                    Description of the interactive help system
  history                 Enable and control the command history
                          function
  international           Enable international 8-bit character support
  ip                      IP options
  length                  Set number of lines on a screen
  monitor                 Copy debug output to the current terminal line
  no                      Negate a command or set its defaults
  notify                  Inform users of output from concurrent
                          sessions
  padding                 Set padding for a specified output character
  parity                  Set terminal parity
  rxspeed                 Set the receive speed
  special-character-bits  Size of the escape (and other special)
                          characters
  speed                   Seet the transmit and receive speeds
  start-character         Define the start character
  stop-character          Define the stop character
  stopbits                Set async line stop bits
  terminal-type           Set the terminal type
  transport               Define transport protocols for line
  txspeed                 Set the transmit speeds
  width                   Set width of the display terminal
```

For both commands the no prefix (terminal no width, terminal no length) will restore applicable settings to a default of 80 columns and 24 lines.

Some of the terminal parameters are rather dated and represent an era of electromechanical devices. For example, the terminal padding command governs the generation of null bytes after a specified character. The generation of nulls was commonly used during the 1980s when many terminals required extra time for an electromechanical printhead to move back to the left-most position on the next line. However, unless your organization uses antiquated equipment in an era of CRT displays, it is doubtful you would ever use this parameter setting. Similarly, many other settings are interesting but may not be applicable to most readers.

LOGGING

The ability to observe the changing condition of a router through its message logging facility is an important capability often overlooked by many persons. In this section we review message logging and the commands associated with this facility.

Message logging is controlled through the EXEC privilege mode. Once in the EXEC privilege mode, you can use one or more logging subcommands within the global configuration command. Figure 2-23 illustrates the display of logging subcommand options supported by a particular router. Note that we are in the privilege mode (#) and first entered the command configure to display the prompt config which allowed us to enter logging ? to display the various logging options supported.

To enable or disable message logging you enter the logging on command or its no version, respectively. The two commands are shown here and although they appear simple, they require a bit of explanation:

```
logging on
no logging on
```

The logging on command enables message logging to all supported destinations other than the console. The no logging on command reverts logging to the console terminal and turns off logging to a prior selected destination other than the console.

In examining the message logging options listed in Figure 2-23 note that logging to a specified hostname results in messages being sent to a syslog server host. For those not familiar with the terminology, a *syslog server* is a UNIX host that captures and saves messages. Thus, you would enter logging hostname or an IP address to specify the UNIX host to be used as a syslog server. Like most EXEC commands, the no logging hostname command deletes the prior operation, removing the syslog server with the specified address from the list of syslogs.

Figure 2-23 Logging subcommand options.

```
Cisco7500#configure
Configuring from terminal, memory, or network [terminal]?
Enter configuration commands, one per line.  End with CNTL/Z.
CISCO4000(config)#line vty 0 4
CISCO4000(config-line)#login
CISCO4000(config-line)#password bad4you
CISCO4000(config-line)#exit
:CISCO4000(config)#exit
Cisco7500(config)#logging ?
```

Figure 2-24 Observing `logging message` options.

```
-OCisco7500 (config)#logging buffered ?
  <4096-2147483647>  Logging buffer size
  alerts             Immediate action needed
  critical           Critical conditions
  debugging          Debugging messages
  emergencies        System is unusable
  errors             Error conditions
  informational      Informational messages
  notifications      Normal but significant conditions
  warnings           Warning conditions
  <cr>
```

The `logging buffered` configuration command permits messages to be written to memory. Figure 2-24 illustrates the various options available using this command which are also applicable to the `logging console`, `monitor`, `history`, and `trap` subcommands. In examining Figure 2-24 note that you can use the `logging buffered` command to set logging to memory and assign an amount of memory for message logging. Also note that you can specify eight types of messages to be logged. Earlier versions of IOS used both level numbers and different keywords to allow you to limit logging messages to be sent to the console or another area. Last but not least, once again the `no` version of the command cancels the use of the buffer and reverts message writing to the console terminal.

The `logging trap` command limits the amount of messages transmitted to a syslog server. You need to follow the command with one of the keywords listed in Figure 2-24, which limits logging messages transmitted to those with a level at or above the level of the keyword.

The `logging monitor` subcommand is similar to the `trap` subcommand, since it limits messages sent to terminal lines that are referred to as monitors. Messages are logged based on being at or above the keyword entered after the command. The keywords in Figure 2-24 that are applicable for a `trap` are also applicable for the `monitor` command.

You can also set up monitoring for a specific interface by using the `logging source-interface` subcommand. You specify an interface after the command, such as serial0.

One nifty feature of logging is the ability to log messages of a particular area of interest such as the authorization system. To accomplish this you use the `logging facility` subcommand, followed by the facility type you want to log.

Our overview of monitoring will conclude with a discussion of an additional monitoring-related command: the `show logging` command, which lets you view the state of logging. The use of this command is

Figure 2-25   Viewing the state of logging on the router.

```
Cisco7500#show logging
Syslog logging: enabled (0 messages dropped, 0 flushes, 0 overruns)
    Console logging: level debugging, 97 messages logged
    Monitor logging: level debugging, 0 messages logged
    Buffer logging: disabled
    Trap logging: level informational, 105 message lines logged
Cisco7500#configure
Configuring from terminal, memory, or network [terminal]?
Enter configuration commands, one per line. End with CNTL/Z.
Cisco7500(config)#logging buffer
Cisco7500(config)#end
Cisco7500#show logging
Syslog logging: enabled (0 messages dropped, 0 flushes, 0 overruns)
    Console logging: level debugging, 98 messages logged
    Monitor logging: level debugging, 1 messages logged
    Buffer logging: level debugging, 1 messages logged
    Trap logging: level informational, 106 message lines logged

Log Buffer (65536 bytes):
4d01h: %SYS-5-CONFIG_I: Configured from console by vty0 (198.78.46.8)
```

shown in Figure 2-25 where we first used the show logging command and then observed that buffer logging is disabled. Next, we entered the configure command and used the logging buffer command to initiate recording messages to memory. After we exited the config mode, we used another show logging and observed that buffer logging is enabled. Note that toward the bottom of Figure 2-24 the log buffer by default is assigned 65,536 bytes of storage. As previously noted, there are limits to the minimum and maximum buffer area that can be used.

Now that we have a general understanding of the basic hardware and software components of a router and its EXEC command modes, this chapter will conclude by focusing on router security management issues.

Security Management Considerations

Regardless of the manner by which you intend to use a router, several key security-related areas must be considered. Those areas include establishing passwords to secure access to your router and the development of appropriate access lists to govern the flow of acceptable data through the router.

PASSWORD MANAGEMENT

You can control access to your router, access to the use of privileged EXEC commands, and even access to individual lines through the use of passwords by using one or more of the commands listed in Table 2-4.

Table 2-4   Security Management Commands

Command	Operational effect
`line console 0`	Establishes a password on the console terminal.
`line vty 0 4`	Establishes a password for telnet connections.
`enable-password`	Establishes a password for access to the privileged EXEC mode.
`Enable secret`	Establishes an `enable secret` password using MD5 encryption.
`service password-encryption`	Protects the display of passwords from the use of the `show running-config` command.

Figure 2-26 illustrates the use of the configure `line` and `password` commands to change a previously established password which controls access from the console terminal. Note that this new password contains a numeric character which is used to separate two conventional alphabetic portions of a password. In general, it is highly recommended that you consider using a mixture of alphanumerics in your passwords to minimize the potential that a hacker might successfully employ a dictionary attack.

ACCESS LISTS

A second area of security management involves controlling the flow of packets through the router. To do so you can configure one or more access lists and apply those lists to one or more router interfaces. Chapter 6 focuses on this topic, so we will defer a discussion of this topic here.

Figure 2-26   Changing a previously established password for virtual terminal access so it consists of alphanumerics.

```
Cisco7500#configure
Configuring from terminal, memory, or network [terminal]?
Enter configuration commands, one per line.  End with CNTL/Z.
CISCO4000(config)#line vty 0 4
CISCO4000(config-line)#login
CISCO4000(config-line)#password bad4you
CISCO4000(config-line)#exit
CISCO4000(config)#exit
```

CHAPTER 3

Working
with the
Internet Protocol

T his chapter focuses on the *Internet protocol* (IP) and reviews a number of IP-related topics for the successful configuration and operation of a router. The fields within the IP header, IP addressing, and,
because ICMP messages are transported via IP, the Internet control message protocol (ICMP) are discussed.

As part of the examination of IP addressing, the use of secondary
addressing and subnet zero are covered. As noted later in this book, filtering of IP packets can be based on IP addresses as well as ICMP message
types and control field values. Thus, this chapter also provides a founda-
tion for understanding the operation of filtering functions based upon IP
addresses and ICMP message types and control field values.

Once we understand IP addressing and ICMP, we review the role of the
address resolution protocol (ARP) and router commands available to view
entries in the ARP cache and to store static entries in the cache, followed
by another addressing-related topic, broadcasting. The discussion of
broadcasting will examine how to create a broadcast address different
from the well-known sequence of hex Fs, and the rationale for carefully
considering whether or not to allow directed broadcasts onto your network. This chapter concludes by reviewing layer 4 and examining TCP
and UDP.

0	4	8		16		31
Vers	Hlen	Service Type		Total Length		
Identification				Flags	Fragment Offset	
Time to Live		Protocol		Header	Checksum	
Source IP Address						
Destination IP Address						
Options + Padding						

Figure 3-1   The IP header.

The IP Header

Figure 3-1 shows the fields contained in the IP header. In Figure 3-1, note that the header contains a minimum of 20 bytes of data, and the width of each field is shown with respect to a 32-bit word. To understand the functions performed by the IP header, let's examine the functions of the fields in the header.

Vers Field

The Vers field consists of four bits. The value of those bits identifies the version of the IP protocol used to create the datagram. The current version of the IP protocol is 4, and the next generation IP protocol will be version 6.

Hlen and Total Length Fields

The Hlen field is 4 bits in length. This field, which follows the Vers field, indicates the length of the header in 32-bit words. In comparison, the total length field indicates the total length of the datagram, including its header and higher-layer information. Since 16 bits are used for this field, an IP datagram can be up to 2^{16}, or 65,535, octets in length.

Service Type Field

The service type field indicates how the datagram is processed. Three of the 8 bits in this field are used to denote the precedence or level of importance assigned by the sender. Thus, this field provides a priority mechanism for the routing of IP datagrams.

Identification and Fragment Offset Fields

The identification field identifies each datagram or fragmented datagram. If a datagram is fragmented into two or more pieces, the fragment offset field specifies the offset in the original datagram of the data being transported. Thus, this field indicates where a fragment belongs in the complete message. The actual value in this field is an integer which corresponds to a unit of 8 octets, providing an offset in 64-bit units. It is important that security devices be able to recognize all fragments as members of the same datagram. Some recent attacks have exploited holes in firewalls and router code which block the initial fragment of a data packet but allow the remaining fragments to pass through. This type of attack takes advantage of the fact that the layer 4 header information is contained *only* in the first datagram fragment. Once this fragment is blocked, if the blocking device does not keep a record of the discarded initial packet, it may mistakenly allow subsequent unauthorized fragments through. While an actual application connection cannot be established without the layer 4 header information in the initial fragment, an attacker might be able to create a denial of service attack by sending many fragmented datagrams to a particular host. The host must hold the fragments in memory while it waits for all fragments to arrive, consuming valuable resources.

Time to Live Field

The *time to live* (TTL) field specifies the maximum time that a datagram can exist. This field is used to prevent a misaddressed datagram from endlessly wandering the Internet or a private IP network. Since an exact time is difficult to measure, it is commonly used as a hop count field, that is, routers decrease the value of this field by 1 as a datagram flows between networks. If the value of the field reaches 0, the datagram is discarded.

Flags Field

The flags field contains two bits used to denote how fragmentation occurs, with a third bit in the field presently unassigned. The setting of 1 of the two fragmentation bits can be used as a direct fragment control mechanism since a value of 0 indicates the datagram can be fragmented, while a value of 1 indicates the datagram should not fragment. The second bit is set to 0 to indicate that a fragment in a datagram is the last fragment, while a value of 1 indicates more fragments follow.

Protocol Field

The protocol field identifies the higher-level protocol used to create the message carried in the datagram. For example, a value of decimal 6 would indicate TCP, while a value of decimal 17 would indicate UDP.

The 8-bit protocol field enables protocols to be uniquely defined under IP version 4. Table 3-1 lists the current assignment of Internet protocol numbers. Note that although TCP and UDP represent by far the vast majority of Internet traffic, other protocols can also be transported and a large block of protocol numbers are currently unassigned. Under the evolving IP version 6, the protocol field is named the Next Header field.

Table 3-1   Assigned Internet Protocol Numbers

Decimal	Keyword	Protocol
0	HOPOPT	IPv6 hop-by-hop option
1	ICMP	Internet control message
2	IGMP	Internet group management protocol
3	GGP	Gateway-to-gateway
4	IP	IP in IP (encapsulation)
5	ST	Stream
6	TCP	Transmission control protocol
7	CBT	CBT
8	EGP	Exterior gateway protocol
9	IGP	Any private interior gateway (used by Cisco for their IGRP)
10	BBN-RCC-MON	BBN RCC monitoring

Decimal	Keyword	Protocol
11	NVP-II	Network voice protocol version 2
12	PUP	PUP
13	ARGUS	ARGUS
14	EMCON	EMCON
15	XNET	Cross-net debugger
16	CHAOS	Chaos
17	UDP	User datagram
18	MUX	Multiplexing
19	DCN-MEAS	DCN measurement subsystems
20	HMP	Host monitoring
21	PRM	Packet radio measurement
22	XNS-IDP	XEROX NS IDP
23	TRUNK-1	Trunk-1
24	TRUNK-2	Trunk-2
25	LEAF-1	Leaf-1
26	LEAF-2	Leaf-2
27	RDP	Reliable data protocol
28	IRTP	Internet reliable transaction
29	ISO-TP4	ISO transport protocol class 4
30	NETBLT	Bulk data transfer protocol
31	MFE-NSP	MFE network services protocol
32	MERIT-INP	MERIT internodal protocol
33	SEP	Sequential exchange protocol
34	3PC	Third-party connect protocol
35	IDPR	Interdomain policy routing protocol
36	XTP	XTP
37	DDP	Datagram delivery protocol
38	IDPR-CMTP	IDPR control message transport protocol

(Continued)

55

Table 3-1 (*Continued*)

Decimal	Keyword	Protocol
39	TP++	TP++ transport protocol
40	IL	IL transport protocol
41	IPv6	Ipv6
42	SDRP	Source demand routing protocol
43	IPv6-Route	Routing header for IPv6
44	IPv6-Frag	Fragment header for IPv6
45	IDRP	Interdomain routing protocol
46	RSVP	Reservation protocol
47	GRE	General routing encapsulation
48	MHRP	Mobile host routing protocol
49	BNA	BNA
50	ESP	Encap security payload for IPv6
51	AH	Authentication header for IPv6
52	I-NLSP	Integrated net layer security
53	SWIPE	IP with encryption
54	NARP	NBMA address resolution protocol
55	MOBILE	IP mobility
56	TLSP	Transport layer security protocol (using Kryptonet key management)
57	SKIP	SKIP
58	IPv6-ICMP	ICMP for IPv6
59	IPv6-NoNxt	No next header for IPv6
60	IPv6-Opts	Destination options for IPv6
61		Any host internal protocol
62	CFTP	CFTP
63		Any local network
64	SAT-EXPAK	SATNET and backroom EXPAK

Decimal	Keyword	Protocol
65	KRYPTOLAN	Kryptolan
66	RVD	MIT remote virtual disk protocol
67	IPPC	Internet pluribus packet core
68		Any distributed file system
69	SAT-MON	SATNET monitoring
70	VISA	VISA protocol
71	IPCV	Internet packet core utility
72	CPNX	Computer protocol network executive
73	CPHB	Computer protocol heart beat
74	WSN	Wang span network
75	PVP	Packet video protocol
76	BR-SAT-MON	Backroom SATNET monitoring
77	SUN-ND	SUN ND PROTOCOL-temporary
78	WB-MON	WIDEBAND monitoring
79	WB-EXPAK	WIDEBAND EXPAK
80	ISO-IP	ISO Internet protocol
81	VMTP	VMTP
82	SECURE-VMTP	SECURE-VMPT
83	VINES	VINES
84	TTP	TTP
85	NSFNET-IGP	NSFNET-IGP
86	DGP	Dissimilar gateway protocol
87	TCF	TCF
88	EIGRP	EIGRP
89	OSPFIGP	OSPFIGP
90	Sprite-RPC	Sprite RPC protocol
91	LARP	Locus address resolution protocol
92	MTP	Multicast transport protocol
93	AX.25	AX.25 frames

(Continued)

Table 3-1 (Continued)

Decimal	Keyword	Protocol
94	IPIP	IP-within-IP encapsulation protocol
95	MICP	Mobile internetworking control protocol
96	SCC-SP	Semaphore Communications Sec. protocol
97	ETHERIP	Ethernet-within-IP encapsulation
98	ENCAP	Encapsulation header
99		Any private encryption scheme
100	GMTP	GMTP
101	IFMP	Ipsilon flow management protocol
102	PNNI	PNNI over IP
103	PIM	Protocol independent multicast
104	ARIS	ARIS
105	SCPS	SCPS
106	QNX	QNX
107	A/N	Active networks
108	IPPCP	IP payload compression protocol
109	SNP	Sitara networks protocol
110	Compaq-Peer	Compaq peer protocol
111	IPX-in-IP	IPX in IP
112	VRRP	Virtual router redundancy protocol
113	PGM	PGM reliable transport protocol
114		Any 0-hop protocol
115	L2TP	Layer 2 tunneling protocol
116	DDX	D-II data exchange (DDX)
117-254		Unassigned
255		Reserved

Source and Destination Address Fields

The source and destination address fields are each 32 bits in length. Each address represents a network and a host computer on the network. It is extremely important to understand the composition and formation of IP addresses to correctly configure devices connected to an IP network, so this topic is examined next. Once we understand IP addressing, we review the address-resolution process required to enable layer 3 packets that use IP addresses to be correctly delivered via layer 2 addressing.

IP Addressing

This section looks at the mechanism which enables TCP and UDP packets to be transmitted to unique or predefined groups of hosts. That mechanism is the addressing method used by the Internet protocol, commonly referred to as *IP addressing*. The current version of the Internet protocol is 4. The next generation Internet protocol, which is currently being operated on an experimental portion of the Internet, is version 6, or IPv6. There are significant differences in the method of addressing used by each version of the Internet protocol, so both versions are covered in this section, beginning with the addressing used by IPv4 and then IPv6. By first covering the addressing used by IPv4, we can discuss address compatibility methods that allow IPv6 addresses to be used to access devices configured to respond to IPv4 addresses.

Overview

IP addresses are used by the Internet protocol to identify distinct device interfaces such as interfaces that connect hosts, routers, and gateways to networks and to route data to those devices. Each device interface in an IP network must be assigned to a unique IP address so that it can receive communications addressed to it. This means that a multiport router will have one IP address for each of its network connections.

IPv4 uses 32-bit binary numbers to identify the source and destination addresses in each packet. This address space provides 2,294,967,296 distinct addressable devices, which exceeded the world's population when the Internet was initially developed. However, the proliferation of personal computers, the projected growth in the use of cable modems which require individual IP addresses, and the fact that every interface on a gateway or router must have a distinct IP address has contributed to a rapid depletion of available IP addresses. Recognizing that hundreds of millions of Chinese and Indians may eventually be connected to the Internet, and also recognizing the potential for cell phones and even pacemakers to communicate via the Internet, the *Internet Activities Board* (IAB) began work on a replacement for the current version of IP during 1992. Although the addressing limitations of IPv4 was of primary concern, the efforts of the IAB resulted in a new protocol with a number of significant improvements over IPv4, including the use of 128-bit addresses for source and destination devices. This new IP version referred to as IPv6, was finalized during 1995 and is currently being evaluated on an experimental portion of the Internet. Since this section is concerned with IP addressing, we cover the addressing schemes, address notation, host address restrictions, and special addresses associated with both IPv4 and IPv6.

IPv4

The IP was officially standardized in September 1981. Included in the standard was a requirement that each host connected to an IP-based network be assigned a unique 32-bit address value for each network connection. This requirement resulted in some networking devices, such as routers and gateways, that have interfaces to more than one network and host computers with multiple connections to the same or different networks being assigned a unique IP address for each network interface. Figure 3-2 shows two bus-based Ethernet LANs connected by a pair of routers. Note that each router has two interfaces, one represented by a connection to a LAN and the second represented by a connection to a serial interface. That interface provides router-to-router connectivity via a wide area network. Thus, each router will have two IP addresses, one

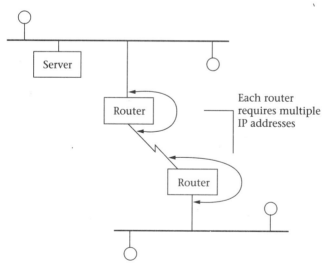

Figure 3-2 IP network addressing requires a unique 32-bit network number for each device network interface. ◯ = Workstations.

assigned to its LAN interface and the other assigned to its serial interface. Assignment of addresses to each specific device interface enables correct routing of packets when a device has two or more network connections.

THE BASIC ADDRESSING SCHEME

When the IP was developed, it was recognized that hosts would be connected to different networks and that those networks would be interconnected to form an Internet. Thus, in developing the IP addressing scheme, it was also recognized that a mechanism would be required to identify a network, as well as a host, connected to a network. This recognition resulted in the development of a two-level addressing hierarchy illustrated in Figure 3-3.

Under the two-level IP addressing scheme, all hosts on the same network must be assigned the same network prefix but must have a unique host address to differentiate one host from another. The 32-bit IP address is subdivided into network and host portions. The first 4 bits specify whether the network portion is 1, 2, or 3 bytes in length, with the result that the host portion is 3, 2, or 1 bytes in length. Similarly, two hosts on different networks must be assigned different network prefixes; however, the hosts can have the same host address. This concept is similar to your telephone number. No one in your area code can have exactly the same phone number as yours, but it's likely that somewhere the same phone number exists in a different area code.

ADDRESS CLASSES

When IP was standardized, it was recognized that the use of a single method of subdivision of the 32-bit address into network and host portions would be wasteful with respect to the assignment of addresses. For example, if all addresses were split evenly, resulting in 16 bits for a network number and 16 bits for a host number, the result would allow a maximum of 65,534 ($2^{16} - 2$) networks with up to 65,534 hosts per network. Then, the assignment of a network number to an organization that only had 100 computers would result in a waste of 65,434 host addresses that could not be assigned to another organization. As a result, the designers of IP subdivided the 32-bit address space into five different address classes, referred to as class A through class E.

Class A addresses are for very large networks, while class B and C addresses are for medium-sized and small networks, respectively. Class A,

Figure 3-3   The two-level IP addressing hierarchy.

B, and C addresses incorporate the two-level IP addressing structure illustrated in Figure 3-3. Class D addresses are used for IP multicasting, where a single message is distributed to a group of hosts dispersed across a network. Class E addresses are reserved for experimental use. Neither class D nor class E addresses incorporates the two-level IP addressing structure used by class A to C addresses.

Figure 3-4 illustrates the five IP address formats, including the bit allocation of each 32-bit address class. In Figure 3-4, note that the address class can easily be determined through the examination of the values of one or more of the first 4 bits in the 32-bit address. Once an address class is identified, the subdivision of the remainder of the address into the network and host address portions is automatically noted. To learn about the use of each address class, let's examine the composition of the network and host portion of each address when applicable, because this examination provides basic information on how such addresses are used. In terms of the allocation of IP addresses, specific class addresses are assigned by the InterNIC.

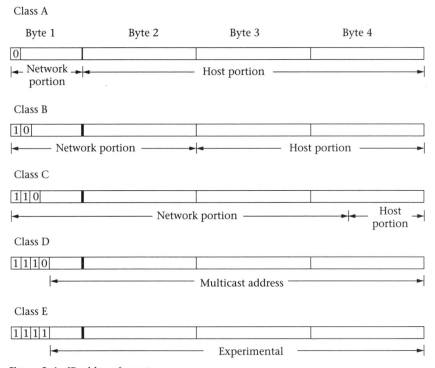

Figure 3-4 IP address formats.

Class A

A class A IP address is defined by a 0-bit value in the high-order bit position of the address. This class of addresses uses 7 bits for the network portion and 24 bits for the host portion of the address. As a result of this subdivision, 128 networks can be defined, with approximately 16.78 million hosts capable of being addressed on each network. Due to the relatively small number of class A networks that can be defined and the large number of hosts that can be supported per network, class A addresses are primarily assigned to large organizations and countries that have national networks.

Class B

A class B network is defined by setting the two high-order bits of an IP address to 10. The network portion of a class B address is 14 bits wide, while the host portion is 16 bits wide. As a result, class B addresses can be assigned to 16,384 networks, with each network able to support up to 65,534 hosts. Due to the manner by which class B addresses are subdivided into network and host portions, such addresses are normally assigned to relatively large organizations with tens of thousands of employees.

Class C

A class C address is identified by setting the first 3 bits in the IP address to 110. As a result, the network portion of the address has 21 bits, while the host portion of the address is limited to 8-bit positions.

The use of 21 bits for a network address enables support of approximately 2 million distinct networks by the class C address class. Since 8 bits are used for the host portion of a class C address, each class C address can, theoretically, support up to 256 hosts. However, an address of all 0's and an address of all 1's cannot be used, reducing the number of host addresses to $2^8 - 2$ or 254. Due to the subdivision of network and host portions of class C addresses, they are primarily assigned for use by relatively small networks such as an organizational LAN. Since it is quite common for many organizations to have multiple LANs, multiple class C addresses are often assigned to organizations that require more than 254 host addresses but are not large enough to justify a class B address. Although class A through C addresses are commonly assigned by the InterNIC to Internet service providers for distribution to their customers, class D and E addresses represent special types of IP addresses.

Class D

In a class D IP address the value 1110 is assigned to the first 4 bits in the address. The remaining bits are used to form what is referred to as a *multicast address*. Thus, the 28 bits used for that address enable approximately 268 million possible multicast addresses.

Multicast is an addressing technique that allows a source to send a single copy of a packet to a specific group through the use of a multicast address. By use of a membership registration process, hosts can dynamically enroll in multicast groups. Thus, the use of a class D address enables up to 268 million multicast sessions to occur simultaneously throughout the world.

Until recently, the use of multicast addresses was relatively limited; however, its use is increasing considerably since it facilitates conservation of bandwidth, which is becoming a precious commodity.

To understand how class D addressing conserves bandwidth, consider a digitized audio or video presentation routed from the Internet onto a private network where users working at 10 hosts on the network wish to receive the presentation. Without a multicast transmission capability, 10 separate audio or video streams containing individual repetitions of an audio or video presentation stream would be transmitted onto the private network, with each stream consisting of packets with 10 distinct host destination addresses. In comparison, with the use of a multicast address, one data stream would be routed to the private network.

An audio or video stream can require a relatively large amount of bandwidth in comparison to interactive query-response client-server communications, so elimination of multiple data streams via multicast transmission can prevent networks from being saturated. This capability can also result in the avoidance of session time-outs when client-server sessions are delayed due to high LAN utilization levels.

Class E

The fifth address class defined by the IP address specification is a reserved address class known as class E. In a class E address the first 4 bits in the 32-bit IP address have the value of 1111, with the remaining 28 bits capable of supporting approximately 268.4 million addresses. Class E addresses are restricted for experimentation.

DOTTED-DECIMAL NOTATION

Since direct use of 32-bit binary addresses is both cumbersome and unwieldy, a more acceptable technique was developed. That technique is referred to as *dotted-decimal notation* because the technique for expressing IP addresses occurs via the use of four decimal numbers separated from one another by decimal points.

Dotted-decimal notation divides the 32-bit Internet protocol address into four 8-bit (1 byte) fields, with the value of each field specified as a decimal number. That number can range from 0 to 255 in bytes 2, 3, and 4. In the first byte of an IP address the setting of the first 4 bits in the byte used to denote the address class limits the range of decimal values that can be assigned to that byte. For example, from Figure 3-4, a class A

Table 3-2 Class A through C Address
Characteristics

Class	Length of Network Address (Bits)	First Number Range (Decimal)
A	8	0-127
B	16	128-191
C	24	192-223

address is defined by the setting of the first bit position in the first byte to 0. Thus, the maximum value of the first byte in a class A address is 127. Table 3-2 summarizes the numeric ranges for class A through class C IP addresses.

To illustrate the formation of a dotted-decimal number, let's focus on the decimal relationship of the bit positions in a byte. Figure 3-5 indicates the decimal values of the bit positions within an 8-bit byte. The decimal value of each bit position corresponds to 2^n, where n is the bit position that ranges from 0 to 7. Using the decimal values of the bit positions shown in Figure 3-5, let's assume the first byte in an IP address has its bit positions set to 01100000. Then, the value of that byte expressed as a decimal number becomes 64 + 32, or 96. Now let's assume that the second byte in the IP address has the bit values 01101000. From Figure 3-5 the decimal value of that binary byte is 64 + 32 + 8 or 104. Let's further assume that the last two bytes in the IP address have the bit values 00111110 and 10000011. Then, the third byte would have the decimal value 32 + 16 + 8 + 4 + 2 or 62, while the last byte would have the decimal value 128 + 2 + 1, or 131.

Based upon this, the dotted-decimal number 96.104.62.131 is equivalent to the binary number 01100000011010000011111010000011. Obviously, it is easier to work with, as well as remember, four decimal numbers separated by dots than a string of 32 bits.

RESERVED ADDRESSES

Three blocks of IP addresses were originally reserved for networks that would not be connected to the Internet. Those address blocks were

128	64	32	16	8	4	2	1

Figure 3-5 Decimal values of bit positions in a byte.

Table 3-3   Reserved IP Addresses
for Private Internet Use

Address Blocks
10.0.0.0–10.255.255.255–
172.16.0.0–172.31.255.255
192.168.0.0–192.168.255.255

defined in RFC 1918, Address Allocation for Private Internets and the ones summarized in Table 3-3.

Security considerations, as well as difficulty in obtaining large blocks of IP addresses, resulted in many organizations using some of the addresses listed in Table 3-3 to connect their networks to the Internet. Since the use of any private Internet address by two or more organizations connected to the Internet would result in addressing conflicts and unreliable delivery of information, those addresses are not directly used. Instead, organizations commonly install a proxy firewall that provides address translation between a large number of private Internet addresses used on the internal network and a smaller number of assigned IP addresses. Not only does this technique allow organizations to connect large internal networks to the Internet without being able to obtain relatively scarce class A or class B addresses, it also hides internal addresses from the Internet community, providing a degree of security since any hacker who attempts to attack a host on your network has to attack your organization's proxy firewall.

As an alternate to a proxy firewall, a router with *network address translation* (NAT) can be used. NAT also hides your organization's internal IP addresses from the Internet community and helps to economize on valuable IP addresses.

One area of RFC 1918 addresses warrants mention, that is, the need to consider filtering such addresses in an access list. One common hacker technique is to use an RFC 1918 address in a denial of service attack or in attempting to perform other dubious activities. By filtering packets with an RFC 1918 source address, you can discard such packets as they arrive at your router's serial interface. Later in this book we illustrate the applicable access-list statements that will send packets with RFC 1918 source addresses to the great bit bucket in the sky.

NETWORKING BASICS

As previously noted, each IP network has a distinct network prefix and each host on an IP network has a distinct host address. When two IP net-

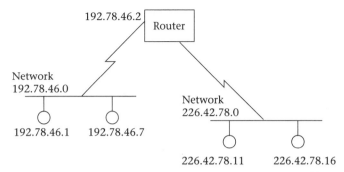

Figure 3-6 Router connections to networks require an IP address for each connection. ○ = Hosts.

works are interconnected by a router, each router port that represents an interface is assigned an IP address that reflects the network to which it is connected. Figure 3-6 illustrates the connection of two networks via a router, indicating possible address assignments. The first decimal number (192) of the 4-byte dotted-decimal numbers associated with two hosts on the network on the left portion of Figure 3-6 denotes a class C address because 192 decimal is equivalent to 11000000 binary. The first 2 bits are set to the bit value 11, which indicates, from Figure 3-4, a class C address. Also note that the first 3 bytes of a class C address indicate the network, while the fourth byte indicates the host address. Thus, the network shown in the left portion of Figure 3-6 is denoted as 192.78.46.0, with device addresses that can range from 192.78.46.1 through 192.78.46.254.

In the lower right portion of Figure 3-6 two hosts are shown connected to another network. Note that the first byte for the 4-byte dotted-decimal number assigned to each host and the router port is decimal 226, which is equivalent to binary 11100010. Since the first 2 bits in the first byte are again set to 11, the second network also represents the use of a class C address. Thus, the network address is 226.42.78.0, with device addresses on the network ranging from 226.42.78.01 to 226.42.78.254.

Although it would appear that 256 devices could be supported on a class C network (0 through 255 used for the host address), in actuality the host portion field of an IP address has two restrictions. First, the host portion field cannot be set to all 0 bits because an all 0's host number is used to identify a base network or subnetwork number, a topic that will be discussed shortly. Second, an all 1's host number represents the broadcast address for a network or subnetwork. Due to these restrictions, a maximum of 254 devices can be defined for use on a class C network. Similarly, other network classes have the previously discussed addressing restrictions which reduces the number of distinct addressable devices that can be connected to each type of IP network by 2. Since, as previously explained, an all 0's host number identifies a base network, the two networks shown in Figure 3-6 are numbered 192.78.46.0 and 226.42.78.0.

SUBNETTING

One of the problems associated with the use of IP addresses is the necessity to assign a distinct network address to each network, which can result in wasting many addresses and requiring a considerable expansion in the use of router tables. To appreciate these problems, let's return to Figure 3-6 which illustrated the connection of two class C networks via a router.

Assume each class C network supported 29 workstations and servers. Adding an address for the router port, each class C network would use 30 out of 254 available addresses. Thus, the assignment of two class C addresses to an organization with a requirement to support two networks with a total of 60 devices would result in 448 ($254 \times 2 - 60$) available IP addresses being wasted. In addition, routers would have to recognize two network addresses instead of one. When this situation is multiplied by numerous organizations with multiple networks, the effect on routing tables becomes more pronounced, resulting in extended search times as routers sort through their routing tables to determine an appropriate route to a network. As a solution to this problem, RFC 950 became a standard in 1985. That standard defines a procedure to subnet or divide a single class A, B, or C network into subnetworks.

Through the process of subnetting, the two-level hierarchy of class A, B, and C networks shown in Figure 3-4 is turned into a three-level hierarchy. In doing so, the host portion of an IP address is divided into a subnet portion and a host portion. Figure 3-7 shows a comparison between the two-level hierarchy initially defined for class A, B, and C networks and the three-level subnet hierarchy.

By subnetting, a class A, B, or C network address can be divided into different subnet numbers, with each subnet used to identify a different network internal to an organization. Since the network portion of the address remains the same, the route from the Internet to any subnet of a

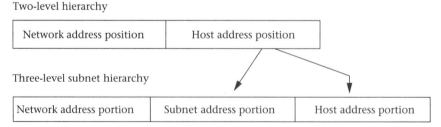

Figure 3-7   Comparison of the three-level subnet hierarchy with the two-level network class hierarchy.

given IP network address is the same. This means that routers within the organization must be able to differentiate between different subnets, but routers outside the organization consider all subnets as one network.

Let's examine the subnet process to learn how it facilitates the use of IP addresses in a less wasteful manner and reduces routing table entries. The concept of masking and the use of the subnet mask, both of which are essential to the extension of the network portion of an IP address beyond its network portion of the address, will be discussed.

To illustrate the concept of subnetting, let's return to the two networks previously illustrated in Figure 3-6, 192.78.46.0 and 226.42.78.0. Let's assume that instead of two networks geographically separated from one another at two distinct locations, we need to establish five networks at one location. Let's further assume that each of the five networks needs to support a maximum of 15 stations. Although your organization could apply for four additional class C addresses, doing so would waste precious IP address space since each class C address supports a maximum of 254 devices. In addition, if your internal network is to be connected to the Internet, entries for four additional networks would be required in a number of routers in the Internet in addition to your organization's internal routers. Instead of requesting four additional class C addresses, let's use subnetting, dividing the host portion of the IP address into a subnet number and a host number. Since we need to support five networks at one location, we must use a minimum of 3 bits from the host portion of the IP address as the subnet number. Note that the number of subnets you can obtain is $2^n - 1$, where n is the number of bits. When $n = 2$, this yields three subnets, which is too few. When $n = 3$, we get seven subnets, which is enough for our example. Since a class C address uses one 8-bit byte for the host identification, a maximum of five bit positions can be used ($8 - 3$) for the host number. Assuming we intend to use the 192.78.46.0 network address for our subnetting effort, we would construct an extended network prefix based upon combining the network portion of the IP address with its subnet number.

Figure 3-8 illustrates the creation of five subnets from the 192.78.46.0 network address. The top entry in Figure 3-8, labeled "Base Network," is the class C network address with a host address byte field set to all 0's. We previously decided to use 3 bits from the host portion of the class C IP address to develop an extended network prefix. Therefore, the five entries in Figure 3-8 below the base network entry indicate the use of 3 bits from the host position in the address to create extended prefixes that identify five distinct subnets created from one IP class C address.

For each subnet there are two addressing restrictions that reduce the number of hosts or, more correctly, interfaces, that can be supported. Those addressing restrictions are the same as for a regular IP network. That is, you cannot use a base subnet address of all 0's or all 1's. Thus, for sub-

Figure 3-8 Creating extended network prefixes via subnetting.

```
Base Network:    11000000.01010000.00101110.00000000 = 192.78.46.0
Subnet #0:       11000000.01010000.00101110.00000000 = 192.78.46.0
Subnet #1:       11000000.01010000.00101110.00100000 = 192.78.46.32
Subnet #2:       11000000.01010000.00101110.01000000 = 192.78.46.64
Subnet #3:       11000000.01010000.00101110.01100000 = 192.78.46.96
Subnet #4:       11000000.01010000.00101110.10000000 = 192.78.46.128
```

net 0 in Figure 3-8, valid addresses would range from 1 to 30. Similarly, for subnet 1, valid addresses would range from 33 to 62. One point of interest is that the zero subnet was, at one point, considered anathema by the Internet community and its use was, and still is, highly discouraged.

Although this viewpoint is no longer widely held, some devices still do not support the use of subnet zero and will not allow configuration of their interface address with an address on the zero subnet. The reason is that confusion can arise between a network and a subnet that have the same address. For example, assume network 129.110.0.0 is subnetted as 255.255.255.9. This would result in subnet zero being written as 129.110.0.0, which is identical to the network address. Cisco routers support the use of subnet zero but this support must be explicitly enabled in the router configuration. To do so you would use the command ip subnet-zero. Without this command, the router will give you an inconsistent network mask error when attempting to configure an interface on subnet zero. Note that even though Cisco provides a way to use the all 0's and 1's subnet, it is discouraged. It is highly encouraged that you test each class of device in your network for support of subnet zero before designing an IP address scheme using this subnet, or just avoid its use.

In our previous example, all five networks appear as the network address 192.78.46.0, with the router at an organization responsible for directing traffic to the appropriate subnet. It is important to note that externally, that is, to the Internet, there is no knowledge that the dotted-decimal numbers shown in the right column represent distinct subnets. This is because the Internet views the first byte of each dotted-decimal number and notes that the first 2 bits are set. This tells routers on the Internet that the address is a class C address for which the first 3 bytes represent the network portion of the IP address and the fourth byte represents the host address. Thus, to the outside world address 192.78.46.32 would not be recognized as subnet 1. Instead, a router would interpret the address as network 192.78.46.0 with host address 32. Similarly, subnet 4 would appear as network address 192.78.46.0 with host address 128. However, internally within an organization, each of the addresses listed in

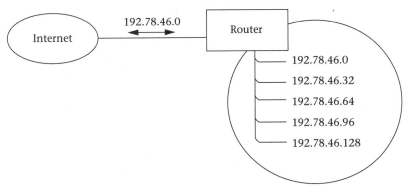

Figure 3-9 Internet versus internal view of subnets.

the right column in Figure 3-8 would be recognized as a subnet. To visualize this dual interpretation of network addresses, see Figure 3-9 which illustrates the Internet versus the private network view of subnets.

As we might logically assume from our prior discussion of class C addresses, any address with the network prefix 192.78.46.0 will be routed to the corporate router. However, although we reviewed how subnet addresses are formed, we have yet to discuss how we assign host addresses to devices connected to different subnets, or how the router can break down a subnet address to correctly route traffic to an appropriate subnet. Thus, a discussion of host addressing on subnets, including the role of the subnet mask, is in order.

HOST ADDRESSES ON SUBNETS

We previously subdivided the host portion of a class C address into a 3-bit subnet field and a 5-bit host field. Since the host field of an IP address cannot contain all 0 bits or all 1 bits, the use of 5 bits in the host portion of each subnet address means that each subnet can support a maximum of $2^5 - 2$ or 30 addresses. Thus, we could use host addresses 1 through 30 on subnet 0, 33 through 62 on subnet 1, and so on. Figure 3-10 illustrates the assignment of host addresses for subnet 3 whose creation was shown in

Figure 3-10 Assigning host addresses by subnet.

```
Subnet #3:  11000000.01010000.00101110.01100000 = 192.78.46.96
Host #1:    11000000.01010000.00101110.01100001 = 192.78.46.97
Host #2:    11000000.01010000.00101110.01100010 = 192.78.46.98
Host #3:    11000000.01010000.00101110.01100011 = 192.78.46.99
Host #30:   11000000.01010000.00101110.01111110 = 192.78.46.126
```

Figure 3-8. In Figure 3-10, we start with the subnet address 192.78.46.96 for which the first 3 bits in the fourth byte are used to indicate the subnet. Then, we use the remaining 5 bits to define the host address on each subnet. Thus, the address 192.78.46.96 represents the third subnet, while addresses 192.78.46.97 through 192.78.46.126 represent hosts 1 through 30 that can reside on subnet 3.

Although we now understand how to create subnets and host addresses on subnets, an unanswered question remains: How do devices on a private network recognize subnet addressing? For example, if a packet arrives at an organizational router with the destination address 192.78.46.97, how does the router know to route that packet onto subnet 3? The answer to this question involves what is known as the subnet mask.

THE SUBNET MASK

The *subnet mask* enables devices on a network to determine the separation of an IP address into its network, subnet, and host portions. To accomplish this, the subnet mask consists of a sequence set to 1 bit that denotes the length of the network and subnet portions of the IP network address associated with a network. For example, let's assume our network address is 192.78.46.96 and we want to develop a subnet mask which can be used to identify the extended network. Since we previously used 3 bits from the host portion of the IP address, the subnet mask would become

```
11111111.11111111.11111111.11100000
```

Similar to the manner by which IP addresses can be expressed using dotted-decimal notation, we can also express subnet masks using that notation. Doing so we can express the subnet mask as

```
255.255.255.224
```

The subnet mask tells the device examining an IP address which bits in the address should be treated as the extended network address consisting of network and subnet addresses. Then, the remaining bits that are not set in the mask indicate the host on the extended network address. However, how does a device determine the subnet of the destination address? Since the subnet mask indicates the length of the extended network, including the network and subnet fields, knowing the length of the network portion of the address enables determination of the number of bits in the subnet field. Once this is accomplished, the device can determine the value of those bits which indicate the subnet. To illustrate this concept, let's use the IP address 192.78.46.97 and the subnet mask 255.255.255.224, with the latter used to define a 27-bit extended network. The relationship between the IP address and the subnet mask is shown in Figure 3-11.

Since the first 2 bits in the IP address are set, a class C address is indi-

| IP address: | 192.78.46.97 | 11000000.01010000.00101110.01100001 |
| Subnet mask: | 255.255.255.244 | 11111111.11111111.11111111.111`00000` |

↖Extended network address

Figure 3-11   The relationship between the IP address and the subnet mask.

cated. Since a class C address consists of 3 bytes used for the network address and 1 byte for the host address, the subnet must be 3 bits in length (27–24). Thus, bits 25 through 27, which are set to 011 in the IP address, identify the subnet as subnet 3. Since the last 5 bits in the subnet mask are set to 0, those bit positions in the IP address identify the host on subnet 3. Since those bits have the value 00001, the IP address references host 1 on subnet 3 on network 192.78.46.0.

To facilitate working with subnets, Table 3-4 provides the number of subnets that can be created for class B and class C networks, their subnet mask, the number of hosts per network, and the total number of hosts supported by a particular subnet mask. Note that the total number of hosts can vary considerably based on the use of different subnet masks and should be carefully considered prior to your subdivision of a network.

CONFIGURATION EXAMPLES

When configuring a workstation or server to operate on a TCP/IP network, most network operating systems require you to enter a minimum of three IP addresses and an optional subnet mask or mask bit setting. The first address is the IP addresses assigned to the workstation or server. The additional addresses are the IP address of the gateway, or router responsible for relaying packets with a destination not on the local network to a different network, and a name resolver, also referred to as the *domain name server* (DNS). The DNS is a computer responsible for translating near-English mnemonic names assigned to computers into IP addresses.

Figure 3-12 shows the first in a series of configuration screens displayed by the Windows 95 TCP/IP Properties dialog box. The IP address screen in Figure 3-12 lets you enter an IP address that is assigned to the workstation or server running Microsoft's TCP/IP protocol stack. The configuration screen also lets you enter the number of subnet mask bits in the form of a dotted-decimal number. Table 3-5 compares the number of subnet bits to host bits and indicates the resulting decimal mask.

In the screen in Figure 3-12, note that clicking on different tabs will display new configuration screens. For example, Figure 3-13 illustrates the DNS Configuration screen that provides a name resolution process. Note that you need to enter the address of one or more DNSs and the name assigned to your host and its DNS domain name. In this example, the host name is shown entered as `gil` while the DNS domain name was entered as

Table 3-4 Subnet Mask Reference

Number of Subnet Bits	Subnet Mask	Number of Subnet Works	Hosts/ Subnet	Total Number of Hosts
Class B				
1	—	—	—	—
2	255.255.192.0	2	16,382	32,764
3	255.255.224.0	6	8,190	49,140
4	255.255.240.0	14	4,094	57,316
5	255.255.248.0	30	2,046	61,380
6	255.255.252.0	62	1,022	63,364
7	255.255.254.0	126	510	64,260
8	255.255.255.0	254	254	64,516
9	255.255.255.128	510	126	64,260
10	255.255.255.192	1,022	62	63,364
11	255.255.255.224	2,046	30	61,380
12	255.255.255.240	4,094	14	57,316
13	255.255.255.248	8,190	6	49,140
14	255.255.255.252	16,382	2	32,764
15	—	—	—	—
16	—	—	—	—
Class C				
1	—	—	—	—
2	255.255.255.192	2	62	124
3	255.255.255.224	6	30	180
4	255.255.255.240	14	14	196
5	255.255.255.248	30	6	170
6	255.255.255.252	62	2	124
7	—	—	—	—
8	—	—	—	—

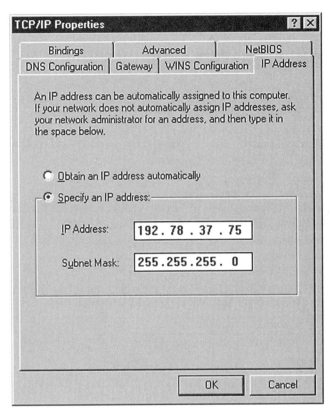

Figure 3-12 The Windows 95 TCP/IP Properties screen lets you set the IP address of the host running the program's TCP/IP protocol stack.

Table 3-5 Subnet Masks

Subnet Bits	Host Bits	Decimal Mask
0	8	0
1	7	28
2	6	192
3	5	224
4	4	240
5	3	248
6	2	252
7	1	254
8	0	255

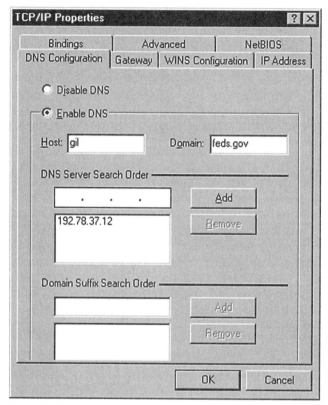

Figure 3-13   The Windows 95 DNS Configuration tab in the TCP/IP Properties dialog box enables configuration of a host so it can be identified by its near-English mnemonic name.

feds.gov. This informs the domain server at the indicated address that requests to access the host with the near-English mnemonic gil.feds.gov should be routed to the IP address previously entered into the IP Configuration screen. Thus, this display screen allows network users to have their computers identified by a name rather than a more cumbersome IP address. The specification of the IP address of at least one domain server also enables the use of near-English mnemonic names to access other computers because the computer now knows to send the name to IP address resolution requests to the indicated domain server IP address.

ROUTER IP ADDRESS ASSIGNMENT

Earlier in this chapter we noted that each router interface must be assigned a distinct IP address. The actual address assignment is performed by using the following interface command:

```
ip address IP-address address-mask
```

Here the address mask identifies the bits that represent the network number in the IP address, which can be either a conventional mask or a subnet mask. Chapter 4 discusses the configuration of different router interfaces and presents several examples of the use of the `ip address` command.

Although prevailing convention is to assign a single IP address to each router interface, Cisco's IOS supports the assignment of multiple IP addresses per interface. Those additional addresses are referred to as secondary IP addresses and are assigned using the previously described `ip address` command with a suffix of `secondary` as shown here:

```
ip address address-mask secondary
```

Perhaps the key reason for assigning multiple IP addresses to a single interface is to overcome IP addressing restrictions. For example, assume you wish to connect your router to a segment with 400 hosts but were assigned class C addresses only capable of supporting a maximum of 254 hosts per logical subnet. By configuring a second IP address on the interface, you can support two logical subnets on one physical subnet. Thus, you could now support up to 508 hosts on the subnet.

CLASSLESS NETWORKING

As previously noted, the use of individual class A, B, and C addresses can result in a significant amount of unused address space, making them very inefficient. As a result of this inefficiency, another method was developed to assign IP addresses to organizations. This alternative method results in a more efficient assignment of IP addresses since it better ties the number of distinct IP addresses to the requirements of an organization. Since the technique does away with network classes, it is commonly referred to as *classless networking*.

Under classless networking an organization is assigned a number of bits to use as the local part of its addresses that best corresponds to the number of addresses it needs. For example, if an organization requires 4000 IP addresses, it would be given 12 bits (4096 distinct addresses) to use as the local part of its address. The remaining 20 bits in the 32-bit address space are then used as a prefix to denote what is referred to as a *supernetwork*. To denote the network part of a classless network, the forward slash (/) is used, followed by the number of bits in the prefix. Thus, the previously mentioned classless network would be denoted as /20.

Currently, address allocations used for classless networking are taken from available class C addresses. Thus, obtaining a 20-bit prefix is equivalent to obtaining 16 continuous class C addresses. Table 3-6 lists the classless address blocks that can be assigned from available class C address space.

In addition to providing a better method for allocating IP addresses, classless addressing enables a router to forward traffic to an organization

Table 3-6   Classless Network Address Assignments

Network Part	Local Bits	Equivalent Number of Class C Addresses	Distinct Addresses
124	8	1	256
123	9	2	512
122	10	4	1,024
121	11	8	2,048
120	12	16	4,096
119	13	32	8,192
118	14	64	16,284
117	15	128	32,768

using a single routing entry. Due to the tremendous growth of the Internet, classless addressing makes it more efficient to locate entries in router tables. This is because one classless entry can replace up to 129 class C addresses, enabling a router to locate entries faster as it searches its routing tables. As a result, the use of classless addressing will increase to extend the availability of IP addresses and enable routers to operate more efficiently as we wait for IPv6 to be deployed.

IPv6

IPv6 was developed to simplify the operation of the Internet protocol. In addition, it allows addition of new operations as they are developed through a header daisy-chain capability, adds built-in security and authentication, and extends source and destination addresses to an address space that could conceivably meet every possible addressing requirement for generations. The latter is accomplished through an expansion of source and destination addresses to 128 bits, which is the focus of this section.

ADDRESS ARCHITECTURE

IPv6 is based upon the same architecture used in IPv4, that is, each network interface requires a distinct IP address. The key differences between IPv6 and IPv4 with respect to addresses are how an interface is identified and the size and composition of the address. Under IPv6, an interface can be identified by several addresses to facilitate routing and management. In comparison, under IPv4 an interface can only be assigned one address. IPv6 uses 128 bits or 96 more bits than an IPv4 address.

ADDRESS TYPES

IPv6 addresses include unicast and multicast, which were included in IPv4. In addition, IPv6 adds a new address category known as *anycast*. Although an anycast address identifies a group of stations similar to a multicast address, a packet with an anycast address is delivered to only one station, the nearest member of the group. The use of anycast addressing will facilitate network restructuring while minimizing the amount of configuration changes required to support a new network structure. This is because you can use an anycast address to reference a group of routers, and the alteration of a network when stations use anycast addressing would enable them to continue to access the nearest router without users having to change the address configuration of their workstations.

ADDRESS NOTATION

Since IPv6 addresses consist of 128 bits, a mechanism is required to facilitate their entry as configuration data. The mechanism used is to replace those bits by the use of eight 16-bit integers separated by colons, with each integer represented by four hexadecimal digits. For example:

```
6ACD:00001:00FC:B10C:0001:0000:0000:001A
```

To facilitate the entry of IPv6 addresses you can skip leading 0's in each hexadecimal component. That is, you can write 1 instead of 0001 and 0 instead of 0000. This suppression of 0's in each hexadecimal component reduces the previous network address to

```
6ACD:1:FC:B10C:1:0:0:1A
```

Under IPv6, a second method of address simplification was introduced, the double-colon (::) convention. Inside an address a set of consecutive null 16-bit numbers can be replaced by two colons (::). Thus, the previously reduced IP address could be further reduced as

```
6ACD:1:FC:B10C:1::1A
```

It is important to note that the double-colon convention can only be used once inside an address because the reconstruction of the address requires the number of integer fields in the address to be subtracted from eight to determine the number of consecutive fields of zero value the double colon represents. Otherwise, the use of two or more double colons would create ambiguity that would not allow the address to be correctly reconstructed.

ADDRESS ALLOCATION

The use of a 128-bit address space provides a high degree of address assignment flexibility beyond that available under IPv4. IPv6 addressing enables identification of Internet service providers, local and global multicast addresses, private site addresses for use within an organization, hierarchical geographical global unicast addresses, and other types of addresses. Table 3-7 lists the initial allocation of address space under IPv6.

The Internet Assigned Numbers Authority (IANA) was assigned the task of distributing portions of IPv6 address space to regional registries around the world, such as the InterNIC in North America, RIPE in Europe, and APNIC in Asia. To illustrate the planned use of IPv6 addresses, let's review what will probably be the most common type of IPv6 address—the *provider-based address*.

Provider-Based Addresses

The first official distribution of IPv6 addresses will be through the use of provider-based addresses. Based on the initial allocation of IPv6 addresses shown in Table 3-7, each provider-based address will have the 3-bit prefix 010. That prefix will be followed by fields that identify the registry that allocated the address, the service provider, and the subscriber. The latter field actually consists of three subfields, a subscriber ID that can represent an organization, and variable network and interface identification fields used in a similar manner to IPv4 network and host fields. Figure 3-14 illustrates the initial structure for a provider-based address.

Special Addresses

Under IPv6 five special types of unicast addresses were defined, of which one deserves special attention. That address is the version 4 address which was developed to provide a migration path from IPv4 to IPv6.

In a mixed IPv4 and IPv6 environment, devices that do not support IPv6 will be mapped to version 6 addresses using the following form:

```
0:0:0:0:0:FFFF:w.x.y.z
```

Here w.x.y.z represents the original IPv4 address. Thus, IPv4 addresses will be transported as IPv6 addresses using the IPv6 version 4 address format. This means that an organization with a large number of workstations and servers connected to the Internet only has to upgrade their router to support IPv6 addressing when IPv6 is deployed. Then, they can gradually upgrade their network on a device-by-device basis to obtain an orderly migration to IPv6. Now that we understand IPv4 and IPv6 addressing, let's look at the address-resolution process and ICMP before concluding with TCP and UDP.

Table 3-7   IPv6 Address Space Allocation

Allocation	Prefix (binary)	Fraction of Address Space
Reserved	0000 0000	1/256
Unassigned	0000 0001	1/256
Reserved for NSAP allocation	0000 001	1/128
Reserved for IPX allocation	0000 010	1/128
Unassigned	0000 011	1/128
Unassigned	0000 1	1/32
Unassigned	0001	1/16
Unassigned	001	1/8
Provider-based unicast address	010	1/8
Unassigned	011	1/8
Reserved for geographic-based unicast address	100	1/8
Unassigned	101	1/8
Unassigned	110	1/8
Unassigned	1110	1/16
Unassigned	1111 0	1/32
Unassigned	1111 10	1/64
Unassigned	1111 110	1/128
Unassigned	1111 1110 0	1/512
Link-local use addresses	1111 1110 10	1/1024
Site-local use addresses	1111 1110 11	1/1024
Multicast addresses	1111 1111	1/256

Prefix	Registry ID	Provider ID	Subscriber ID	Subnet ID	Station ID

Figure 3-14 Provider-based address structure. Prefix: 3 bits set to 010; registry: 5 bits identifies organization that allocated the address; provider: 24 bits, with 16 used to identify ISP and 8 used for future extensions; subscriber: 32 bits, with 24 used to identify the subscriber and 8 for extension; subnet: 16 bits to identify the subnetwork; station: 48 bits to identify the station.

Address Resolution

The physical address associated with a local area network workstation is often referred to as its hardware or *media access control* (Mac) address. In actuality, that address can be formed via software to override the burnt-in address on the network adapter card, a technique referred to as *locally administrated addressing*. When the built-in hardware address is used, this addressing technique is referred to as *universally administrated addressing* since it represents a universally unique address whose creation we will be discussed. For both techniques frames that flow at the data-link layer use 6-byte source and destination addresses formed either via software or obtained from the network adapter.

Figure 3-15 illustrates the formats for both Ethernet and token-ring frames. Both networks were standardized by the Institute of Electrical and Electronics Engineers (IEEE) and use 6-byte source and destination addresses. The IEEE assigns blocks of addresses 6-hex characters in length to vendors that represent the first 24 bits of the 48-bit field used to

Preamble (1)	Start of frame delimiter (7)	Destination address (6)	Source address (6)	Type/ length (2)	Information (46 to 1500)	FCS (4)

(a)

Starting delimiter (1)	Access control (1)	Frame control (1)	Destination address (1)	Source address (6)	Routing information (optional)

Variable Information	FCS (4)	Ending delimiter (1)	Frame status (1)

(b)

Figure 3-15 Ethernet and Token Ring frame formats. FSC = frame check sequence. (*n*) = *n* bytes, representing field length. (*a*) Ethernet. (*b*) Token Ring.

uniquely identify a network adapter card. The vendor then encodes the remaining 24 bits or 6-hex character positions to identify the adapter manufactured by the vendor. Thus, each Ethernet and token-ring adapter has a unique hardware of burnt-in identifiers that denote the manufacturer and the adapter number product by the manufacturer. If an organization decides to override the hardware address, they can do so via software; however, a 48-bit address must still be specified for each station address.

When an Ethernet or token-ring station has data to transmit, it encodes the destination address and source address fields with 48-bit numbers that identify the layer 2 locations on the network to receive the frame and the layer 2 device that is transmitting the frame. In comparison, at the network layer IP uses a 32-bit address that has no relation to the Mac or layer 2 address. Thus, a common problem associated with the routing of an IP datagram to a particular workstation on a local area network involves the delivery of the datagram to its correct destination. This delivery process requires an IP device that needs to transmit a packet via a layer 2 delivery service to obtain the correct Mac or layer 2 address so it can take a packet and convert it into a frame for delivery. In the opposite direction, a workstation must be able to convert a Mac address into an IP address. Both of these address translation problems are handled by protocols developed to provide an address resolution. One protocol, known as the *address resolution protocol* (ARP) translates an IP address into a hardware address. The *reverse address resolution protocol* (RARP), as its name implies, performs a reverse translation or mapping, converting a hardware layer 2 address into an IP address.

Operation

Figure 3-16 illustrates the format of an ARP packet. Note that the numbers in some fields indicate the bytes in a field when a field spans a 4-byte boundary.

The 16-bit Hardware Type field indicates the type of network adapter. For example, a value of 1 indicates 10-Mbps Ethernet, 6 indicates an IEEE 802 network, and 16 indicates *asynchronous transmission mode* (ATM). Similarly, the 16-bit Protocol Type field indicates the protocol for which an address resolution process is being performed. For IP the Protocol Type field has a value of hex 0800. The Hardware Length field denotes the number of bytes in the hardware address. The value of this field is 6 for both Ethernet and Token Ring. The Protocol Length field is similar to the Hardware Length field, indicating the length of the address for the protocol to be resolved. For IPv4 the value of this field is 4. The Operation field has a value of 1 for an ARP Request. When a target station responds, the value of this field is changed to 2 to denote an ARP replay.

0	8	16	31

Hardware type		Protocol type	
Hardware length	Protocol length	Operation	
SENDER HARDWARE ADDRESS (0–3)			
SENDER HARDWARE ADDRESS (4–5)		SENDER IP ADDRESS (0–1)	
SENDER IP ADDRESS (2–3)		TARGET HARDWARE ADDRESS (0–1)	
TARGET HARDWARE ADDRESS (2–5)			
TARGET IP ADDRESS			

Figure 3-16 The ARP packet format.

The Sender Hardware Address field is 6 bytes in length and indicates the hardware address of the station generating the ARP Request or ARP Reply. That address is followed by a 4-byte Sender IP Address field. This field, as its name implies, indicates the IP address of the originator of the packet. The next to last field, Target Hardware Address, is originally set to zero in an ARP Request. The last field, Target IP Address, is set to the IP address for which the originator needs a hardware address.

For a basic understanding of the operation of ARP, let's assume one computer user located on an Ethernet network wants to transmit a datagram to another computer located on the same network. The first computer would transmit an ARP packet that would be carried as an Ethernet broadcast frame to all stations on the network. Thus, the packet would be transported to all devices on the Ethernet LAN. The packet would contain the destination IP address which is known, since the computer is transmitting the IP address to a known location. Another field in the ARP packet used for the target hardware address would be set to all 0's as the transmitting station does not know the destination hardware address. Each device on the Ethernet LAN will read the ARP packet as it is transmitted as a broadcast frame. However, only the station that recognizes that it has the destination field's IP address will copy the frame off the network and respond to the ARP request. When it does, it will transmit an ARP reply in which its physical address is inserted in the ARP Target Hardware Address field that was previously set to 0.

To alleviate constant transmission of ARP packets, as well as to lower the utilization level of the LAN, the originator will record received infor-

3-17 Using the show arp command to view the contents of the ARP cache.

```
7500#show arp
col   Address           Age (min)   Hardware Addr    Type    Interface
net   205.131.175.100       134     0050.544d.73ff   ARPA    FastEthernet1/0
rnet  205.131.175.123         6     00c0.4fb0.d10d   ARPA    FastEthernet1/0
rnet  205.131.175.124       137     00c0.4fb0.d206   ARPA    FastEthernet1/0
rnet  205.131.176.85          1     0060.9725.040d   ARPA    Ethernet4/1/1
rnet  205.131.176.80          5     00c0.4fc5.c866   ARPA    Ethernet4/1/1
ernet 205.131.175.90        131     00c0.4fd8.fb7a   ARPA    FastEthernet1/0
ernet 205.131.175.33        139     00a0.c99d.9333   ARPA    FastEthernet1/0
ernet 205.131.175.32        144     00c0.4fc2.3c31   ARPA    FastEthernet1/0
ernet 205.131.175.35          9     00c0.4fb6.6386   ARPA    FastEthernet1/0
ternet 205.131.175.37         8     0090.2751.41a5   ARPA    FastEthernet1/0
ternet 205.131.175.36         3     00c0.4f68.4c94   ARPA    FastEthernet1/0
ternet 205.131.175.38        46     0090.279a.9292   ARPA    FastEthernet1/0
ternet 205.131.175.45       181     00a0.c95c.a124   ARPA    FastEthernet1/0
ternet 205.131.175.47       176     00a0.c95c.a124   ARPA    FastEthernet1/0
nternet 205.131.175.48      205     00a0.c95c.a124   ARPA    FastEthernet1/0
nternet 205.131.175.53       93     00a0.c96b.38c3   ARPA    FastEthernet1/0
nternet 205.131.175.52       18     00a0.c99d.9333   ARPA    FastEthernet1/0
Internet 205.131.175.55      93     00a0.c96b.38c3   ARPA    FastEthernet1/0
Internet 205.131.175.54     156     0060.0837.7417   ARPA    FastEthernet1/0
Internet 205.131.175.56       5     0090.2771.c20f   ARPA    FastEthernet1/0
Internet 205.131.175.1      118     0050.e2b4.1b00   ARPA    FastEthernet1/0
Internet 205.131.174.1        3     0000.f651.9074   SNAP    TokenRing4/0/0
Internet 205.131.175.3        0     00a0.c96b.38c3   ARPA    FastEthernet1/0
Internet 205.131.174.2        -     0008.9e6c.1501   SNAP    TokenRing4/0/0
Internet 205.131.175.2        -     0010.7936.a820   ARPA    FastEthernet1/0
Internet 205.131.175.5        6     0010.4b72.160c   ARPA    FastEthernet1/0
Internet 205.131.174.4      168     0000.f615.f1cf   SNAP    TokenRing4/0/0
Internet 205.131.174.5       19     0006.29aa.f78c   SNAP    TokenRing4/0/0
Internet 205.131.175.4      150     00a0.c96b.38c3   ARPA    FastEthernet1/0
Internet 205.131.175.11      91     00a0.c96b.38c3   ARPA    FastEthernet1/0
I
```

contains the protocol, IP address, age expressed in minutes since the address was resolved, the MAC hardware address, and the type of encapsulation and interface. In this example all entries are associated with the IP protocol, however, if your router is supporting a mixture of protocols you can use the show ip arp command to restrict the resulting display to IP entries.

DYNAMIC VERSUS STATIC ENTRIES

The ARP process provides a dynamic mapping of 32-bit IP addresses to 48-bit MAC addresses. Because the amount of memory allocated to the ARP cache is finite, each entry placed into memory is time stamped to provide a mechanism to age the entry. The age of each ARP entry is by default set to 4 h or 14,400 s. When the age of the entry reaches 0, it is purged from cache, providing space for a new entry.

mation in a table known as an ARP cache. The use
quick transmission of subsequent datagrams with
respondences between IP addresses and MAC addre
hardware address on the network.

The standard also calls for devices on the networ,
ARP table with the MAC and IP address pair of the *sen*
Additionally, when a device initializes its network co
boot process, it issues a `gratuitous arp`, which is ar.
own IP address. This is how a station determines if an
network is using its assigned IP address and becomes awa

Finally, there is a feature in the standard called *pro*
allows a device to answer an ARP request on behalf of an
reason this might be necessary is that the device whi
intended recipient of the ARP request might not reside on
ical subnet as the originator of the request. Since the ARP r
2 broadcast, it will be blocked at the router interface.

If, for example, the originating device had a standard (
mask, the device would assume that any address within
resided on its own physical network and would expect it to r
ARP request. However, if the network had actually been sub
two parts, some of the hosts would reside on the other side of a
the ARP request would not be seen on the second subnet. The
originating host might not have the correct subnet mask could
limitations of the operating system or a misconfiguration.

In this scenario, the router is aware of both subnets and can a
ARP request for other devices on the second subnet by supplying
MAC address. The originating device will enter the router's MAC
in its ARP cache and will correctly send packets destined for the e
to the router. This feature is enabled by default on Cisco routers.

An additional use of this feature is that with most operating syste
you enter your own IP address as your default gateway address on
host, the host will issue an ARP request for every destination, even t
it knows to be on remote networks. This is beneficial because if there
multiple routers on the subnet or the router address is unknown, y
ARP request will automatically be answered via the proxy ARP feat
without configuring a single, static default gateway. Thus, ARP provide:
well-thought out methodology for equating physical hardware address
to IP's logical addresses and allows IP addressing at layer 3 to occur inde
pendently from LAN addressing at layer 2.

Cisco ARP Operations

Figure 3-17 illustrates the use of the `show arp` command to view the contents of a Cisco router's ARP cache. In Figure 3-17 note that the ARP cache

Most applications work quite well under dynamic ARP, however, under certain situations you may wish to have permanent entries in the ARP cache. For example, a voice gateway where milliseconds of delay could distort reproduced sound might be a candidate for a static ARP entry. Perhaps recognizing such situations Cisco routers support the arp configuration command given here:

```
arp ip-address hardware-address type [alias]
```

where the ip-address and hardware-address represent the dotted-decimal IP address and the 48-bit hardware address, respectively, with the latter entered as three sequences of 4-hex characters, with a dot used to separate each sequence. The type field entry is an encapsulation description, with arpa used for Ethernet interfaces. For fiber-distributed data interface (FDDI) and Token Ring the type field is always set to snap.

Before illustrating the use of the arp configuration command, a slight digression concerning IOS version 12 is in order. If you enter the arp command followed by a question mark, you will receive the following display, which indicates *incorrectly* that you only need to enter ARP followed by only an IP address:

```
Cisco7500(config)#arp ?
  A.B.C.D IP address of ARP entry
```

THE arp COMMAND

Returning to the use of the arp configuration command, the following example illustrates the correct use of the command. In this example we are configuring a static entry that associates the IP address of 205.131.175.11 with the MAC hardware address of 00a0.c96b.38c for an Ethernet interface:

```
Cisco7500(config)#arp 205.131.175.11 00a0.c96b.38c3 arpa
```

Three additional ARP-related commands warrant attention: arp, arp timeout, and clear arp-cache. The arp command is an interface command, with timeout one of its options. The following example illustrates the ARP options available under IOS version 12:

```
Cisco7500(config-if)#arp ?
  arpa         Standard arp protocol
  frame-relay  Enable ARP for a frame relay interface
  probe        HP style arp protocol
  snap         IEEE 802.3 style arp
  timeout      Set ARP cache timeout
```

The use of the arpa subcommand sets ARP to support standard Ethernet frames. In comparison, when configuring a token-ring or FDDI interface, you would normally select the snap option. The probe subcommand results in resolution occurring using the Probe protocol, as well as ARP, to communicate with a version of the IEEE 802.3 network supported by Hewlett-Packard.

THE timeout OPTION

Perhaps the most frequently used arp command option is the timeout option. The arp timeout command is used to configure the length of time an entry will remain in the ARP cache. This command is also an interface command which is set during configuration of a router's interface. The format of this command is

    arp timeout seconds

where seconds represents the time-out. As previously mentioned, by default entries are set to 4 h. A value of 0 s results in no time-out, with the current cache entries, in effect, becoming static entries that cannot be cleared. Because only certain types of interfaces, such as different versions of Ethernet, use ARP, this command is ignored when an interface does not use the technology. If you decide to restore the default time-out, you can do so by entering the no arp timeout command.

Another ARP-related command is the clear arp-cache command. Entering this command deletes all dynamic entries from the ARP cache, leaving static entries.

You can view the settings of interfaces that use ARP by using the show interfaces command. Figure 3-18 illustrates the use of this command to view the settings associated with an Ethernet interface. In Figure 3-18 note that the ARP type is ARPA, with the ARP time-out of 4 h the default value. Many times it is a good idea to view interface settings and carefully review such settings to alleviate potential problems. For example, a multi-operating adapter can be set to operate at a bandwidth (indicated by the term BW in Figure 3-18) of 10,000 kbit or 100,000 kbit. Obviously you want a correct data rate compatible with the switch or hub port to which the router's Ethernet interface will be connected.

Broadcasts

A *broadcast* is a packet (layer 3) or frame (layer 2) destined for all hosts on a particular physical network. The use of broadcasts facilitates discovery of addresses as illustrated previously when we discussed ARP. In addition, broadcasts are commonly used at layer 2 so servers can periodically advertise their presence on a network. In a Cisco router environment two types of broadcasts are available: directed broadcasts and flooding. A *directed broadcast* is a packet transmitted to a specific network containing an IP address that represents the broadcast address of the specific network. For example, consider the class C network 205.131.176.0. Its conventional

Figure 3-18   Using the show interfaces command to view ARP settings associated with a specific interface.

```
Cisco7500#show interfaces ethernet4/1/4
Ethernet4/1/4 is administratively down, line protocol is down
  Hardware is cxBus Ethernet, address is 0010.7936.a88c (bia
0010.7936.a88c)
  MTU 1500 bytes, BW 10000 Kbit, DLY 1000 usec,
      reliability 255/255, txload 1/255, rxload 1/255
  Encapsulation ARPA, loopback not set
  Keepalive set (10 sec)
  ARP type: ARPA, ARP Timeout 04:00:00
  Last input never, output never, output hang never
  Last clearing of "show interface" counters never
  Queueing strategy: fifo
  Output queue 0/40, 0 drops; input queue 0/75, 0 drops
  5 minute input rate 0 bits/sec, 0 packets/sec
  5 minute output rate 0 bits/sec, 0 packets/sec
      0 packets input, 0 bytes, 0 no buffer
      Received 0 broadcasts, 0 runts, 0 giants, 0 throttles
      0 input errors, 0 CRC, 0 frame, 0 overrun, 0 ignored
      0 input packets with dribble condition detected
      122594394 packets output, 2898147213 bytes, 0 underruns
      0 output errors, 0 collisions, 1 interface resets
      0 babbles, 0 late collision, 0 deferred
      0 lost carrier, 0 no carrier
      0 output buffer failures, 0 output buffers swapped out
CiISCO7500#
```

broadcast address is 205.131.176.255. Let's assume the class C network is an Ethernet LAN. Upon the arrival of this directed broadcast, the router would convert it into a layer 2 broadcast, resulting in up to 254 LAN stations receiving a copy of the packet within an Ethernet frame. In comparison, a *flooding broadcast* results in packets transmitted to every network. One common example of flooding is at layer 2 when a bridge receives a frame with an unknown destination address. When this occurs, the bridge forwards the frame onto all ports other than the port on which it was received, resulting in the flooding of the frame.

Directed Broadcasts

In an IP environment, directed broadcasts are commonly used by hackers to initiate a denial of service attack. For example, a hacker could set up a workstation to continuously ping the broadcast address of an IP network such as 205.131.176.255. The router would then transmit the ping to each station on the network, resulting in up to 254 responses. As bad as this seems, it can get worse. Suppose the hacker sets his or her workstation's address to the address of a station on a different network. This would result in the continuous string of pings to the 205.131.176.255 address, resulting in up to 254 responses flowing to the spoofed IP address. Because of this problem it is highly recommended that you turn off directed broadcasts on your router by using the following command:

```
no ip directed broadcasts
```

Use of Nonstandard Broadcast Address

If your organization needs to associate a broadcast address for an interface, you can consider the use of a nonstandard address. For example, Cisco routers by default support an all 1's default broadcast address. You can use the ip broadcast-address interface configuration command to set a different IP broadcast address. For example, to specify an IP broadcast address of 205.131.176.20 for your network you would use the following command entry:

```
ip broadcast-address 205.131.176.20
```

Once you configure this address as your network broadcast address, packets with that address arriving at your router would be converted to a layer 2 broadcast. To restore the default IP broadcast address you would use the no form of the command, that is:

```
no ip broadcast-address
```

Now that we understand ARP and broadcasts, lets continue our examination of the Internet protocol by discussing ICMP.

Internet Control Message Protocol (ICMP)

ICMP is an error-reporting mechanism transported via IP datagrams. The format of an ICMP message and its relationship to an IP datagram is illustrated in Figure 3-19. Note that although each ICMP message has its own format, each begins with the same three fields: an 8-bit Type field, an 8-bit Code field, and a 16-bit Checksum field.

The ICMP Type Field

The ICMP Type field defines the meaning of the message and its format. Perhaps the two most familiar ICMP messages are type 0 and type 8. A Type field value of 8 is an echo request, while a Type 0 ICMP message denotes a reply. Although their official names are Echo Reply and Echo Request, most persons are more familiar with the term *ping* which is used to reference both the request and reply. Table 3-8 lists the values of ICMP Type fields that currently identify specific types of ICMP messages.

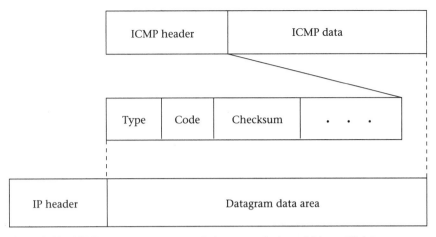

Figure 3-19 ICMP messages transported via encapsulation within an IP datagram.

Table 3-8 ICMP Type Field Values

Type	Name
0	Echo reply
1	Unassigned
2	Unassigned
3	Destination unreachable
4	Source quench
5	Redirect
6	Alternate host address
7	Unassigned
8	Echo request
9	Router advertisement
10	Router selection
11	Time exceeded
12	Parameter problem
13	Time stamp
14	Time stamp reply

(Continued)

Table 3-8 (*Continued*)

Type	Name
15	Information request
16	Information reply
17	Address mask request
18	Address mask reply
19	Reserved (for security)
20—29	Reserved (for robustness experiment)
30	Traceroute
31	Datagram conversion error
32	Mobile host redirect
33	IPv6 where-are-you
34	IPv6 I-am-here
35	Mobile registration request
36	Mobile registration reply
37	Domain name request
38	Domain name reply
39	SKIP
40	Photuris
41—255	Reserved

The ICMP Code Field

The second field common to each ICMP header is the Code field. The Code field provides additional information about the message and may not be meaningful for certain messages. For example, both Type field values of 0 and 8 always have a Code field value of 0. In comparison, a Type field value of 3 (destination unreachable) can have one of 16 possible Code field values which further define the problem. Table 3-9 lists the Code field values presently assigned to ICMP messages based upon their Type field values. As we will note when we examine ICMP filtering, Cisco uses similar but different names for many ICMP message types and

Table 3-9 ICMP Code Field Values Based on Message Type

Message Type	Code Field Values
3	Destination unreachable
	Codes:
	0 Net unreachable
	1 Host unreachable
	2 Protocol unreachable
	3 Port unreachable
	4 Fragmentation needed and don't fragment was set
	5 Source route failed
	6 Destination network unknown
	7 Destination host unknown
	8 Source host isolated
	9 Communication with destination network is administratively prohibited
	10 Communication with destination host is administratively prohibited
	11 Destination network unreachable for type of service
	12 Destination host unreachable for type of service
	13 Destination host unreachable for type of service
	14 Communication administratively prohibited
	15 Precedence cutoff in effect
5	Redirect
	Codes:
	0 Redirect datagram for the network (or subnet)
	1 Redirect datagram for the host
	2 Redirect datagram for the type of service and network
	3 Redirect datagram for the type of service and host

(Continued)

93

Table 3-9 (*Continued*)

Message Type	Code Field Values
6	Alternate host address
	Codes:
	0 Alternate address for host
11	Time exceeded
	Codes:
	0 Time to live exceeded in transit
	1 Fragment reassembly time exceeded
12	Parameter problem
	Codes:
	0 Point indicates the error
	1 Missing a required option
	2 Bad length
40	Photuris
	Codes:
	0 Reserved
	1 Unknown security parameters index
	2 Valid security parameters, but authentication failed
	3 Valid security parameters, but decryption failed

Control field values. However, their effect is that a router can examine the contents of IP datagrams transporting ICMP messages and perform filtering based on the values of ICMP Type and Code fields.

ICMP is a very simple but powerful protocol. One of the more powerful features allows messages to be sent to devices that redirect them to different next hop IP addresses for certain destinations. If this message were sent to a router, an attacker could conceivably redirect packets to flow over a different path that the attacker controlled where the packets could be sniffed at leisure. Additionally, since the use of ICMP echo and echo-reply packets (ping) is almost a universal troubleshooting tool and are allowed through most firewalls, programs have been written to exploit the use of these messages to create denial of service attacks through the use of directed broadcast pings. As previously noted, a directed broadcast ping is a ping to all hosts on a network or subnet. When we examine the creation of access lists, we will also focus on methods to limit echo and echo-reply packet flows.

TCP and UDP

Both TCP and UDP are layer 4 transport protocols that add a header that identifies the type of data being transported. Thus, as layer 4 data obtain a layer 3 header, both the destination in the form of an IP address and the type of data in the form of a port number permit support of different applications by a common host. Although both TCP and UDP are similar in that they identify the type of data being transported, the differences between the functionality of each transport protocol are significant. TCP is a connection-oriented, reliable transport protocol that creates a virtual circuit for the transfer of information. In comparison, UDP is a connectionless, unreliable transport protocol where routers forward datagrams without requiring setup of a session between originator and recipient. This method of transmission is a best-effort forwarding method and does not require the handshaking process used by TCP to establish and maintain a communications session. This also means that you can consider a comparison of TCP and UDP as a trade-off between reliability and performance. Now that we've reviewed the general differences between TCP and UDP, let's look at the format of their headers, including their port number fields which are used in conjunction with IP address fields by workstations and servers to identify particular traffic addressed to hosts and by routers and firewalls to filter packets.

The TCP Header

At the transport layer TCP accepts application data in chunks up to 64 kbytes in length. Those chunks are fragmented into a series of smaller pieces that are transmitted as separate IP datagrams, typically 512 or 1024 bytes in length. The actual selection of the length of a datagram depends on the length supported by source and destination networks and any intermediate networks. That is, TCP's at each end denote the maximum datagram length they support and select the smallest mutually supported size.

Since no IP guaranteed mechanism exists to ensure datagrams will be correctly received—both content and sequence—the TCP header has to provide the mechanism for reliable and orderly delivery of data. To do so the TCP header includes a field that is used for the sequencing of datagrams and a Checksum field for reliability. Since traffic from different applications, such as FTP and HTTP, can flow from or to a common host,

0	16	31
Source Port	Destination Port	
Length	Checksum	

Figure 3-20 The TCP header.

a way to differentiate the type of data carried by each datagram is needed. This data differentiation is accomplished by the use of a Destination Port field which contains a numeric that identifies the process or application in the datagram. In actuality, the TCP header plus data is referred to as a *segment*, so the port number identifies the type of data in the segment and the IP header is added to the TCP header to form the datagram that will contain the source and destination IP address. Now that we understand the TCP header and its relationship to the application process and IP header, let's look at the fields in the TCP header (see Figure 3-20).

SOURCE AND DESTINATION PORT FIELDS

The Source and Destination Port fields are each 16 bits in length. Each field identifies a user process or application, with the first 1024 (0 to 1023) out of 65,536 available port numbers standardized with respect to the type of traffic transported using a specific numeric value. The Source Port field is optional and when not used is set to a value of zero. In actuality, the use of TCP and UDP source and destination port numbers depends upon the user program using the transport layer protocol. That is, if the user program operates quiesently waiting for requests, it is designed to look for a specific port number, such as 21 for a Destination Port when FTP is used. For user programs that originate traffic such programs commonly use random port numbers for the source port. For example, when you first open FTP to transfer a file, port number 1234 might be used as the source port number, while later in the day when you open up an FTP application to transmit another file source, port number 2048 might be used. However, for all FTP usage the destination port would be fixed at 21 which is the standardized port number for an FTP server. When the server responds, it will place the source port number in the Destination Port field which enables the file originator to correctly identify the response to its datagram. As we will note later in this section, each datagram has a sequence number which enables the opposite end of the transmission to ensure that datagrams are received in their correct order and none is lost. The term *well-known port*, which is commonly used to denote an application layer protocol or process, actually references a port address at or below 1023. Both TCP and UDP headers contain fields for identifying source and destination ports. For example, telnet, which is transported by

TCP, uses the well-known port number 23, while *simple network management protocol* (SNMP), which is transported by UDP, uses the well-known port number 161.

PORT NUMBERS

Port numbers transported by TCP and UDP can vary from a value of 0 through 65,535. This universe of port numbers is divided into three ranges: well-known ports, registered ports, and dynamic or private ports. Well-known ports are those whose values range from 0 through 1023. Registered ports are those whose values range from 1024 through 49,151. Dynamic or private ports are those whose values range from 49,152 through 65,535.

Well-known ports are assigned by the *Internet Assigned Numbers Authority* (IANA) and are used to indicate the transportation of standardized processes. Where possible, the same well-known port number assignments are used with TCP and UDP. Ports used with TCP are normally used to provide connections that transport long-term conversations. In some literature well-known port numbers are specified as being in the range of values from 0 through 255. While that range was correct several years ago, the range for assigned ports managed by the IANA were recently expanded to the range of values from 0 through 1023.

Although the vast majority of TCP/IP applications use well-known port values, not all applications do. Many new applications not yet standardized, such as Internet telephony applications, use proprietary port assignments. Most of those port numbers are in the range 49,152 through 65,535 and represent dynamic or private ports. However, the authors have also encountered products that use registered port values in the range 1024 through 49,151. Table 3-10 provides a summary of some of the more popular well-known ports, including the service supported by a particular port and the type of port, TCP or UDP, for which the port number is primarily used.

SEQUENCE AND ACKNOWLEDGMENT NUMBER FIELDS

The Sequence Number field is 32 bits in length and assures the sequentiality of the data stream. The Acknowledgment Number field, which is also 32 bits in length, verifies the receipt of data.

The Acknowledgment Number field informs the recipient that the datagram transmitted arrived at its destination. Because it would be inefficient to have to acknowledge each datagram, a variable window is supported by the protocol. That is, returning an Acknowledgment field value of 7 would indicate the receipt of all data up through the seventh datagram. To ensure lost datagrams or lost acknowledgments do not place this transport protocol in an infinite waiting period, the originator will retransmit data if a response is not received within a predefined period of time. The previously described use of the Acknowledgment field is

Table 3-10   Well-Known TCP and UDP Services and Port Use

Keyword	Service	Port Type	Port Number
TCPMUX	TCP port service multiplexer	TCP	1
RJE	Remote job entry	TCP	5
ECHO	Echo	TCP, UDP	7
DAYTIME	Daytime	TCP, UDP	13
QOTD	Quote of the day	TCP	17
CHARGEN	Character generator	TCP	19
FTD-DATA	File transfer (default data)	TCP	20
FTP	File transfer (control)	TCP	21
TELNET	Telnet	TCP	23
SMTP	Simple mail transfer protocol	TCP	25
MSG-AUTH	Message authentication	TCP	31
TIME	Time	TCP	37
NAMESERVER	Host name server	TCP, UDP	42
NICNAME	Who is	TCP	43
DOMAIN	Domain name server	TCP, UDP	53
BOOTPS	Bootstrap protocol server	TCP	67
BOOTPC	Bootstrap protocol client	TCP	68
TFTP	Trivial file transfer protocol	UDP	69
FINGER	Finger	TCP	79
HTTP	World Wide Web	TCP	80
KERBEROS	Kerberos	TCP	88
RTELNET	Remote telnet service	TCP	107
POP2	Post office protocol version 2	TCP	109
POP3	Post office protocol version 3	TCP	110
NNTP	Network news transfer protocol	TCP	119
NTP	Network time protocol	TCP, UDP	123

Keyword	Service	Port Type	Port Number
NETBIOS-NS	NetBIOS name server	UDP	137
NETBIOS-DGM	NetBIOS datagram service	UDP	138
NETBIOS-SSN	NetBIOS session service	UDP	139
NEWS	News	TCP	144
SNMP	Simple network management protocol	UDP	161
SNMTTRAP	Simple network management protocol traps	UDP	162
BGP	Border gateway protocol	TCP	179
HTTPS	Secure HTTP	TCP	413
RLOGIN	Remote login	TCP	513
TALK	Talk	TCP, UDP	517

referred to as *positive acknowledgment or retransmission* (PAR). PAR requires that each unit of data be explicitly acknowledged. If a unit of data is not acknowledged by the time the originator's time-out period is reached, the previous transmission is retransmitted. When the Acknowledgment field is in use, a flag bit referred to as the ACK flag in the Code field will be set. We will shortly discuss the 6 bits in that field.

Hlen Field
The Hlen field is 4 bits in length. This field, which is also referred to as the Offset field, contains a value that indicates where the TCP header ends and the Data field starts, specified as a number of 32-bit words. This field is required because the inclusion of options can result in a variable length header. Since the minimum length of the TCP header is 20 bytes, the minimum value of the Hlen field would be five 32-bit words.

Code Bits Field
The Code Bits field is also referred to as a Flags field as it contains 6 bits, each of which is used as a flag to indicate whether a function is enabled or disabled. Two-bit positions indicate whether or not the Acknowledgment and Urgent Pointer fields are significant. The purpose of the urgent bit or flag is to recognize an urgent or priority activity, such as when a user presses the CTRL-BREAK key combination. Then the application will set the Urgent flag which results in TCP immediately transmitting everything it

URG	ACK	PSH	RST	SYN	FIN

Figure 3-21 The flags in the Code Bit field. URG: urgent pointer field significant. ACK: acknowledgment field significant. PSK: push function. RST: reset connection. SYN: synchronize sequence numbers. FIN: release connection.

has for the connection. The setting of the urgent bit or flag also indicates that the Urgent Pointer field is in use. Here the Urgent Pointer field indicates the offset in bytes from the current sequence number where the urgent data is located. Other bits or flags include a PSH (push) bit that requests the receiver to immediately deliver data to the application and forgo any buffering, an RST (reset) bit to reset a connection, a SYN (synchronization) bit used to establish connections, and a FIN (finish) bit which signifies the sender has no more data and the connection should be released. Figure 3-21 illustrates the relationship of each of the six 1-bit flags to one another within the Code Bit field.

Window Field

The Window field is 2 octets in length and it controls the flow of data (flow control) between source and destination. This field is used to indicate the maximum number of blocks of data the receiving device can accept. A large value can significantly improve TCP performance since it permits the originator to transmit a number of blocks without having to wait for an acknowledgment, while permitting the receiver to acknowledge the receipt of multiple blocks with one acknowledgment.

Since TCP is a full-duplex transmission protocol, both ends of a communications session can insert values in the Window field to control the flow of data. By reducing the value of the Window field, one end, in effect, informs the other end to transmit less data. Thus, the Window field provides a bidirectional flow control capability.

Checksum Field

The Checksum field is 2 octets in length and is included in the header so TCP can provide an error-detection and correction capability. Instead of actually computing a checksum over the entire TCP header, the field is primarily concerned with ensuring that key fields are validated. To do so the checksum calculation occurs over what is referred to as a 12-octet pseudoheader. This pseudoheader includes the 32-bit Source and Destination Address fields in the IP header, the 8-bit Protocol field, and a Length field that denotes the length of the TCP header and data transported within the TCP segment. Thus, the checksum can be used to ensure data arrived at its correct destination and the receiver has no doubt about the address of the originator or the length of the header and application data transported by TCP.

Options and Padding Fields

The last two fields in the TCP header are the Options and Padding fields which actually represent an Options field with, when necessary, a variable number of 0's added as pads to ensure the header ends on a 32-bit boundary. The Options field is variable in length and is added as an even multiple of octets. This field specifies options required by the TCP protocol operating on a host, such as the protocol's segment size support, which indicates to the receiver the amount of data the originator is willing to accept. Table 3-11

Table 3-11   TCP Option Numbers

Number	Length	Meaning
0	—	End-of-option list
1	—	No operation
2	4	Maximum segment size
3	3	WSOPT—window scale
4	2	SACK permitted
5	N	SACK
6	6	Echo (made obsolete by option 8)
7	6	Echo reply (made obsolete by option 8)
8	10	TSOPT—time stamp option
9	2	Partial-order connection permitted
10	3	Partial-order service profile
11		CC
12		CC.NEW
13		CC.ECHO
14	3	TCP alternate checksum request
15	N	TCP alternate checksum data
16		Skeeter
17		Bubba
18	3	Trailer checksum option
19	18	MD5 signature option

(Continued)

Table 3-11   (*Continued*)

TCP Alternate Checksum Numbers	
Number	**Description**
0	TCP checksum
1	8-bit Fletchers' algorithm
2	16-bit Fletchers' algorithm
3	Redundant checksum avoidance

lists the presently defined TCP option numbers. In Table 3-11 note that an option value of 2 indicates that a Maximum Segment Size field follows as the Option field. Also note that this field is 4 octets in length. In terms of options 0 and 1, they are exactly 1 octet in length. All other options have a 1-octet value field followed by a Length field that transports the option.

Now that we understand the TCP header, let's review the second transport layer protocol supported by the TCP/IP protocol suite, the *user data protocol* (UDP).

The UDP Header

The user datagram protocol (UDP) is the second transport layer protocol supported by the TCP/IP protocol suite. Through the use of UDP an application can transport data in the form of IP datagrams without first establishing a connection to the destination. Thus, UDP is a connectionless protocol. This also means that when transmission occurs via UDP, there is no need to release a connection, simplifying the communications process. This, in turn, results in a header that is greatly simplified and much smaller than TCPs.

Figure 3-22 illustrates the composition of the UDP header consisting of 64 bytes followed by actual user data. In comparing the TCP and UDP headers you will note the simplicity of the latter. Since UDP is a connectionless protocol that does not require the acknowledgment of datagrams or a sequence of datagrams to be treated as an entity, the Sequence and Acknowledgment fields of UDP can be eliminated. Similarly, because UDP does not consider a sequence of datagrams as an entity, a Window field is not needed. As a result of the best effort, connectionless nature of UDP, a relatively small header is required for this transport layer protocol. Similar to TCP, an IP header will prefix the UDP header, with the resulting message consisting of the IP header, UDP header, and user data—referred to as a UDP datagram.

0	16	31
Source Port	Destination Port	
Length	Checksum	

Figure 3-22 The UDP header.

SOURCE AND DESTINATION PORT FIELDS

The Source and Destination Port fields are each 2 octets in length and function in a similar manner to their counterparts in the TCP header. That is, the Source Port field is optional and a value is either randomly selected or it is filled with 0's when not used, while the destination port contains a numeric which identifies the destination application or process. Since UDP is commonly used by several Internet telephony products that do not use standardized port numbers, this situation must be considered when developing access lists. For example, you must determine the port used by a specific product. Then you will probably have to reprogram your organization's router access list to enable UDP datagrams using ports previously blocked to transport Internet telephony data onto your private network via the Internet.

LENGTH FIELD

The Length field indicates the length of the UDP datagram to include header and user data. This 2-octet field has a minimum value of eight that represents a UDP header without data.

CHECKSUM FIELD

The Checksum field is 2 octets in length. The use of this field is optional and is filled with 0's if the application does not require a checksum. If a checksum is required, it is calculated on what is referred to as a pseudo-header. This new logically formed header consists of the source and destination addresses and the Protocol field from the IP header. By verifying the contents of the two address fields through its checksum computation, the pseudoheader assures that the UDP datagram is delivered to the correct destination network and host on the network. However, this does not verify the contents of the datagram.

Router Access-List Considerations

Since an IP header will prefix TCP and UDP headers, four addresses can be used for enabling or disabling the flow of datagrams. Those addresses are the source and destination IP addresses contained in the IP header and the source and destination port numbers contained in the TCP and UDP headers. Cisco routers include a packet-filtering capability which enables users to program access lists to permit or deny packets from flowing between two private networks from the Internet onto a private network or in the reverse direction. Although routers are very flexible and permit a high degree of user configuration, they do not look into the contents of data being transported or allow you to authenticate remote users, encrypt transmission, or perform proxy services. Thus, many organizations will program router access lists as a first line of defense and use firewalls to enhance the security of their private networks.

CHAPTER 4

Interface Configuration

This chapter provides detailed information about the configuration process associated with different router interfaces by examining the procedures for configuring a router interface. Once this is accomplished, the actual process required to configure various types of interfaces, including LAN interfaces and different types of WAN interfaces, is reviewed.

In examining each type of router interface, numerous examples of the use of configuration commands are provided. Examples that follow a discussion when there are only one or a few lines of commands are shown in boldface, while a series of commands are incorporated into a referenced figure. As in other chapters, the numerous examples are provided to help easily tailor those examples to different operational environments.

Working with the `interface` Command

The key to correctly configuring a router interface is obtained using the `interface` command. Since the `interface` command lets you change the settings of a router, you must first access the router's privilege mode of operation. Once this is done, you then enter the `configuration` command, since `interface` is actually a subcommand supported by the `configuration` command.

The `interface` Command Options

Figure 4-1 shows how to enter a router's privilege mode, followed by the entry of the `configuration` command, which can be abbreviated as `config`, and the use of the `interface ?` command to display a list of

105

Figure 4-1 Configuration of a router interface requires you to be in the privilege mode of operation.

```
Cisco7500>enable
Password:
Cisco 7500#configure
Configuring from terminal, memory, or network [terminal]?
Enter configuration commands, one per line.  End with CNTL/Z.
Cisco7500(config)#interface ?
  Async              Async interface
  BVI                Bridge-Group Virtual Interface
  Dialer             Dialer interface
  Ethernet           IEEE 802.3
  FastEthernet       FastEthernet IEEE 802.3
  Group-Async        Async Group interface
  Lex                Lex interface
  Loopback           Loopback interface
  Multilink          Multilink-group interface
  Null               Null interface
  Port-channel       Ethernet Channel of interfaces
  Serial             Serial
  TokenRing          IEEE 802.5
  Tunnel             Tunnel interface
  Virtual-Template   Virtual Template interface
  Virtual-TokenRing  Virtual TokenRing
```

interfaces supported by one of the routers used by the authors. If you examine the display of interfaces shown in Figure 4-1, note the omission of ATM and HSSI as well as a few additional interfaces. Since many Cisco routers are modular devices customized through the addition of different modular interfaces, most only support a subset of all available interfaces. Since the IOS recognizes the modules installed in a router, it does not display a particular interface for configuration if the router lacks hardware support for that interface. This explains, for example, the omission of ATM and HSSI interfaces in the display shown in Figure 4-1, since those interfaces were not installed in the router the authors were working with at this particular time.

In examining Figure 4-1, the prompt Cisco7500(config)# indicates you are in the privilege configuration mode. At this time, you can begin the configuration of one or more router interfaces. The remainder of this chapter reviews the configuration of different types of LAN and WAN interfaces, beginning with local area network interfaces.

LAN Interface Configuration

This section examines the configuration of three types of local area network interfaces: Ethernet, Fast Ethernet, and Token Ring. The interface configuration command is used for the configuration of each interface. When we enter the interface command, followed by an applicable interface, the config prompt changes to config-if, indicating we are configuring an interface.

The general format of the interface command is shown here:

```
interface <type> <connector>
```

where <type> identifies the interface type, such as serial, Ethernet, Fast Ethernet, or Token Ring, while <connector> indicates the port where the interface resides and may follow one of two general formats discussed next. The use of the interface command to configure an Ethernet interface follows one of these two formats:

```
interface ethernet s/m/p
interface ethernet s/p
```

where m is the module number installed in a slot, s represents a slot number, and p represents a port number on the module. For example, to configure an Ethernet interface located in slot 3 on port 2, you would enter the following interface command:

```
interface ethernet3/2
```

Since the configuration of Ethernet and Fast Ethernet interfaces are similar, both are examined in the next section, indicating, when appropriate, the differences between the two.

Ethernet and Fast Ethernet

To illustrate the configuration of an Ethernet or Fast Ethernet interface, let's do things a bit backward and use the show interfaces command to view a particular Ethernet interface because we can then note the parameters we may wish to configure. Once this is done, we use the interface configuration command to illustrate the manner by which we can configure either type of Ethernet interface.

Figure 4-2 illustrates the resulting display in response to a show interface ethernet command. This example shows the Ethernet interface built into port 0 of module 4 installed in slot 1 in our router. This particular interface is noted as being "administratively down."

Interface status

When configuring a router interface, it's a good idea to ensure the interface is first shut down so you can configure the interface without adversely affecting other equipment and review your settings prior to activating the interface. To disable an interface, use the shutdown interface

Figure 4-2   Viewing an Ethernet interface.

```
Ethernet4/1/1 is up, line protocol is up
Hardware is cxBus Ethernet, address is 0010.7936.a889 (bia 0010.7936.a889)
Internet address is 205.131.176.1/24
MTU 1500 bytes, BW 10000 Kbit, DLY 1000 usec,
    reliability 255/255, txload 3/255, rxload 32/255
Encapsulation ARPA, loopback not set
Keepalive set (10 sec)
ARP type: ARPA, ARP Timeout 04:00:00
Last input 00:00:09, output 00:00:04, output hang never
Last clearing of "show interface" counters 23:25:03
Queueing strategy: fifo
Output queue 0/40, 0 drops; input queue 0/75, 0 drops
5 minute input rate 1267000 bits/sec, 176 packets/sec
5 minute output rate 119000 bits/sec, 165 packets/sec
    8211063 packets input, 3077628431 bytes, 0 no buffer
    Received 24620 broadcasts, 0 runts, 0 giants, 0 throttles
    13 input errors, 13 CRC, 0 frame, 0 overrun, 0 ignored
    0 input packets with dribble condition detected
    7619221 packets output, 680642075 bytes, 0 underruns
    6 output errors, 6 collisions, 0 interface resets
    0 babbles, 0 late collision, 253299 deferred
    0 lost carrier, 0 no carrier
    0 output buffer failures, 0 output buffers swapped out
```

subcommand. To restart a previously disabled interface, use the no
shutdown interface subcommand. For example, to bring down the
Ethernet interface on port 2 installed in slot 1 in your router, enter the following commands:

```
interface ethernet1/2
shutdown
```

Similarly, to bring up the previously disabled interface, enter the following commands:

```
interface ethernet1/2
no dhutdown
```

In Figure 4-2 the second line indicates the layer 2 Mac address of the
Ethernet interface and the third line indicates the IP address assigned to
the interface. While the Mac address, by default, represents the burnt-in
address of the interface, you can override that address through the use of
the mac-address interface command, which is examined shortly. For
the few organizations that use locally administrated addressing this command lets you override the burnt-in hardware address.

The second address, which is the IP address, is set through the use of
the ip interface configuration command, which is also examined
later in this section.

Continuing our tour of the interface in Figure 4-2, line 4 denotes the settings for the *Maximum transmission unit* (MTU), *bandwidth* (BW), and *delay* (DLY). By default, the Ethernet MTU is 1500 for both Ethernet and Fast Ethernet and cannot be reset to a different value. This fixed MTU value may be changed by the time you read this book since the tagging associated with *virtual LANs* (vLANs) results in the MTU exceeding 1500 bytes.

Since many Ethernet ports are now manufactured as dual-speed devices, such ports can be set to one of two speeds. In Figure 4-2 the port is set to a 10-Mbps operating rate. Since Fast Ethernet operates at 100 Mbps the bandwidth of a Fast Ethernet port or a dual-speed Ethernet/Fast Ethernet port would be set to 100 Mbps when operating as a Fast Ethernet LAN connection. The third value, DLY, indicates the delay of the interface in microseconds.

The next line in Figure 4-2 displays reliability, txload, and rxload, all as fractions of 255. All three parameters are calculated as an exponential average over 5 min. For reliability, you want a value of 255/255, which indicates no problems. Observation of txload and rxload, which indicates the transmit and receive load, respectively, provides an indication of whether or not the interface is on the verge of being saturated. That is, as the fraction value increases toward unity, the value indicates a heavier transmit or receive load on the interface. For both versions of Ethernet a good rule of thumb on shared media is to consider an upgrade after a prolonged level of utilization exceeds 50 percent. This would be equivalent to a load of 127/255. Although you cannot directly control the counters, you can use the c l e a r command to reset their values.

If we look down a few lines in Figure 4-2, note that encapsulation is set to ARPA and loopback is not set. As discussed in Chapter 3 three Ethernet encapsulation methods are available to specify: ARPA for standard Ethernet version 2.0, iso1 for IEEE 802.3 encapsulation, and snap for IEEE 802.2 Ethernet. As we note shortly, we can easily configure the encapsulation method, as well as turn loopback on and off, hopefully ensuring it is off if we are not doing testing and require an operational interface.

Again continuing our tour of the display of the Ethernet interface, note a value for keepalive, followed by an ARP type and ARP time-out value on the following line. The term keepalive references whether or not the router transmits keepalive frames after a period of LAN inactivity. As indicated in Figure 4-2, keepalives are set, with a period of 10 s of inactivity, resulting in a keepalive signal being transmitted.

The default ARP method is ARPA and its default cache table entry time-out value is 4 h. Thus, the ARP type and time-out value shown in Figure 4-2 represent interface default settings.

If you look at the line in Figure 4-2 that begins Queuing strategy, note the term *fifo*, a mnemonic for first-in, first-out. Unless you are running

Ethernet to a switch port that supports the IEEE 802.3p priority queuing scheme, you will probably accept the default queuing of fifo. If you use 802.3p and transport real-time data, such as voice and video, you will probably change the queuing default to prioritize your real-time traffic. Since the remaining portion of Figure 4-2 provides performance information about the interface that is not adjustable via the interface command, although important, we will not cover such data in this chapter.

Now that we understand the display of a typical Ethernet interface, let's look at how we control the parameters just discussed. In doing so, we also examine some additional interface parameters that may be useful when you configure an Ethernet or Fast Ethernet interface.

The interface configuration **Commands**

You can view the available interface configuration commands by entering the question mark (?) after you enter privilege mode and then enter the command interface followed by a particular interface. An example of this procedure, which results in the display of a list of interface configuration commands, is illustrated in Figure 4-3.

Figure 4-3 Displaying a list of Ethernet interface configuration commands.

```
Password:
Cisco7500>enable
Password:
Cisco7500#config
Configuring from terminal, memory, or network [terminal]?
Enter configuration commands, one per line.  End with CNTL/Z.
Cisco7500(config)#interface ethernet4/1/0
Cisco7500(config-if)#?
Interface configuration commands:
  access-expression    Build a bridge boolean access expression
  appletalk            Appletalk interface subcommands
  arp                  Set arp type (arpa, probe, snap) or timeout
  backup               Modify backup parameters
  bandwidth            Set bandwidth informational parameter
  bgp-policy           Apply policy propogated by bgp community string
  bridge-group         Transparent bridging interface parameters
  carrier-delay        Specify delay for interface transitions
  cdp                  CDP interface subcommands
  cmns                 OSI CMNS
  custom-queue-list    Assign a custom queue list to an interface
  decnet               Interface DECnet config commands
  default              Set a command to its defaults
  delay                Specify interface throughput delay
  description          Interface specific description
  dspu                 Down Stream PU
  exit                 Exit from interface configuration mode
  fair-queue           Enable Fair Queuing on an Interface
  fras                 DLC Switch Interface Command
  help                 Description of the interactive help system
```

Figure 4-3   *(Continued)*

```
Interface configuration commands:
  hold-queue           Set hold queue depth
  ip                   Interface Internet Protocol config commands
  ipx                  Novell/IPX interface subcommands
  keepalive            Enable keepalive
  lan-name             LAN Name command
  llc2                 LLC2 Interface Subcommands
  load-interval        Specify interval for load calculation for an
                       interface
  locaddr-priority     Assign a priority group
  logging              Configure logging for interface
  loopback             Configure internal loopback on an interface
  mac-address          Manually set interface MAC address
  mls                  mls router sub/interface commands
  mop                  DEC MOP server commands
  mpoa                 MPOA interface configuration commands
  mtu                  Set the interface Maximum Transmission Unit (MTU)
  multilink-group      Put interface in a multilink bundle
  netbios              Use a defined NETBIOS access list or enable name-
                       caching
  no                   Negate a command or set its defaults
  ntp                  Configure NTP
  priority-group       Assign a priority group to an interface
  random-detect        Enable Weighted Random Early Detection (WRED) on
                       an Interface
  rate-limit           Rate Limit
  sap-priority         Assign a priority group
  shutdown             Shutdown the selected interface
  smrp                 Simple Multicast Routing Protocol interface
                       subcommands
  sna                  SNA pu configuration
  snapshot             Configure snapshot support on the interface
  snmp                 Modify SNMP interface parameters
  standby              Hot standby interface subcommands
  timeout              Define timeout values for this interface
  traffic-shape        Enable Traffic Shaping on an Interface or Sub-
                       Interface
  transmit-buffers     configure transmit-buffers policies
  transmit-interface   Assign a transmit interface to a receive-only
                       interface
  transmitter-delay    Set dead-time after transmitting a datagram
  tx-burst-deferral    Sets maximum number of back-to-back packets other
                       stations can transmit before the EIP attempts to
                       acquire carrier
  tx-queue-limit       Configure card level transmit queue limit
```

In Figure 4-3 note the list is applicable to several types of interfaces such as Ethernet and Fast Ethernet. If fact, if you entered the command `interface serial0/1/1` followed by the question mark, you would obtain the same display shown in Figure 4-3. However, because Token Ring has some slightly different commands, its interface list of commands differs slightly from that in Figure 4-3 as we note later in this chapter. Since, hopefully, we realize that LANs are quite different from WANs, we should also realize that only a subset of the commands listed in Figure 4-3 is applicable to specific types of interfaces. The remainder of this section provides an alphabetical summary of the `interface` commands in Figure 4-3 that are applicable to both Ethernet and Fast Ethernet interfaces.

ARP

The `arp interface` command is used to set the ARP type and, if applicable, a time-out for cache entries different from the 4-hour default value. The following example illustrates the display of ARP options and the setting of the ARP type to ARPA. If you wish to set a time-out value different from the 4-hour default, you would have to enter the `arp timeout interface` command followed by a value, in seconds, between 1 and 4294967.

```
Cisco7500(config-if)#arp ?
  arpa          Standard arp protocol
  frame-relay   Enable ARP for a frame relay interface
  probe         HP style arp protocol
  snap          IEEE 802.3 style arp
  timeout       Set ARP cache timeout

Cisco7500(config-if)#arp arpa
```

Bandwidth

The `bandwidth interface configuration` command lets you set bandwidth informational parameters. The following example illustrates the potential to set the interface up to 1 Gbps. Next, the `bandwidth interface configuration` command is used to set the bandwidth to 10 Mbps. For Fast Ethernet, which operates at 100 Mbps, you would set the bandwidth to 100 Mbps.

```
Cisco7500(config-if)#bandwidth ?
  <1-10000000>  Bandwidth in kilobits

Cisco7500(config-if)#bandwidth 10000000
```

Delay

The `delay interface` command is used to set a delay value for an interface in tens of microseconds. Certain higher-level protocols can use this information to make operating decisions. For example, the setting can be used to differentiate between satellite and terrestrial circuits as well as between LANs and WANs. For Ethernet a default value of 1000 msec is used while Fast Ethernet has a default delay one-tenth of Ethernet or 100 msec. In comparison, serial ports connected to terrestrial circuits have a default setting of 20,000 msec. The following example illustrates the display of the `delay interface` command help information as well as the use of the command.

```
Cisco7500(config-if)#delay ?
  <1-16777215>  Throughput delay (tens of microseconds)

Cisco7500(config-if)#delay 1000
```

Description

The description interface command permits you to assign up to an 80-character label to the interface for display purposes. If you have a large number of interfaces, it is easy to become confused as to what interface supports particular networks. By using the description, as well as a lan-name interface command, which we will examine shortly, you can reduce or eliminate potential errors associated with configuring the incorrect interface. The following example illustrates the display of the description command followed by its use to assign the text "Web server connection" to the interface.

```
Cisco7500(config-if)#description ?
  LINE  Up to 80 characters describing this interface

Cisco7500(config-if)#description Web server connection
```

Hold-Queue

Each router interface has a limited amount of storage for data packets. That limit is referred to as a hold-queue, and its value determines the amount of storage for inbound and outbound packets. If too little storage is specified under a moderate packet arrival rate, the interface will reject new packets, resulting in an increase in retransmissions. If too much storage is specified, a lower amount of packets will be rejected, however, the delay through the buffer area will increase, which could adversely affect real-time transmission. You can specify the hold-queue limit of an interface for both inbound and outbound directions. To do so, use the following command format:

```
Hold-queue length {in|out}
```

where length is the maximum number of packets that can be placed in the queue prior to newly arriving packets being lost. The default input queue value is 75 packets, while the default output queue value is 40 packets. The following example illustrates the display of hold-queue command information followed by two examples of the use of the command. Note that the display of assistance information is misleading as it does not tell you that you must specify the queue direction in the command.

```
Cisco7500(config)#interface ethernet4/1/0
Cisco7500(config-if)#hold-queue ?
  <0-4096>  Queue length

Cisco7500(config-if)#hold-queue 80 in
Cisco7500(config-if)#hold-queue 80 out
```

IP

The use of the IP interface command opens up a wonderful world of numerous IP commands. However, while important, a discussion of most of those commands will be deferred because other commands deal with setting up access lists discussed in Chapter 5 or are more applicable to the serial interface, which is described later in this chapter, or reference routing, which is described in another chapter. Thus, for our purpose at present, which is to configure an Ethernet or Fast Ethernet interface to operate in an IP environment, we focus our attention on assigning an IP address to the interface. The following example illustrates the use of the ip address command to assign an IP address to the interface we are configuring.

```
Cisco7500(config-if)#ip address ?
  A.B.C.D  IP address
Cisco7500(config-if)#ip address 192.131.176.1 255.255.255.0
```

The lan-name Command

The lan-name command is similar to the description interface configuration command in that you can use it to assign a text label for display purposes. The following example illustrates that this command allows the assignment of up to eight characters as a LAN designator and provides an example of the use of the command.

```
Cisco7500(config-if)#lan-name ?
  WORD  Up to 8 characters lan name
Cisco7500(config-if)#lan-name CHICAGO
```

Logging

You can use the logging interface command to record the change to the status of an interface. The following example shows the options available through its use:

```
Cisco7500(config)#interface ethernet4/1/2
Cisco7500(config-if)#logging ?
  event  Interface events
Cisco7500(config-if)#logging event ?
  link-status        UPDOWN and CHANGE messages
  subif-link-status  Sub-interface UPDOWN and CHANGE messages
```

Loopback

The loopback command lets you test an interface. The use of this command ties transmitter to receiver, in effect looping back data transmitted to the interface. Since the IP ping program lets you test an interface, the lookback command is normally used for connections that do not support ping.

The loopback command is entered simply by typing loopback. To restore the interface to its normal mode of operation, enter the command no loopback.

For testing an Ethernet or Fast Ethernet interface used in a non-IP environment, you first set the interface into loopback. Next, you would use test equipment or a station on a connected network with appropriate software to test the interface.

The mac-**Address**

As previously discussed, you can override the burnt-in hardware address assigned to an Ethernet or token-ring interface by using the mac-address interface subcommand. The following example shows the format for entering a mac address, followed by the actual use of the command to assign the address 0010.7936.a88a to an interface:

```
Cisco7500(config-if)#mac-address ?
  H.H.H  MAC address

Cisco7500(config-if)#mac-address 0010.7936.a88a
Cisco7500(config-if)#
```

Now that we understand the use of interface commands applicable to Ethernet and Fast Ethernet, let's look at Token Ring.

Token Ring

We begin our examination of Token Ring by turning our attention to the display of a token-ring interface. Figure 4-4 displays the status of the

Figure 4-4   Viewing the settings of a token-ring interface.

```
TokenRing4/0/0 is up, line protocol is up
  Hardware is cxBus Token Ring, address is 0008.9e6c.1501 (bia
0008.9e6c.1501)
  Internet address is 205.131.174.2/24
  MTU 4464 bytes, BW 16000 Kbit, DLY 630 usec,
     reliability 255/255, txload 2/255, rxload 1/255
  Encapsulation SNAP, loopback not set
  Keepalive set (10 sec)
  ARP type: SNAP, ARP Timeout 04:00:00
  Ring speed: 16 Mbps
  Duplex: half
  Mode: Classic token ring station
  Single ring node, Source Route Transparent Bridge capable
  Group Address: 0x00000000, Functional Address: 0x08000000
  Ethernet Transit OUI: 0x000000
  Last Ring Status 1w0d <Soft Error> (0x2000)
  Last input 00:00:00, output 00:00:00, output hang never
  Last clearing of "show interface" counters 23:24:47
  Queueing strategy: fifo
  Output queue 0/40, 0 drops; input queue 0/75, 0 drops
  5 minute input rate 46000 bits/sec, 45 packets/sec
  5 minute output rate 131000 bits/sec, 37 packets/sec
     2145190 packets input, 601021512 bytes, 0 no buffer
     Received 1568 broadcasts, 0 runts, 0 giants, 0 throttles
     0 input errors, 0 CRC, 0 frame, 0 overrun, 0 ignored, 0 abort
     2112792 packets output, 945892185 bytes, 0 underruns
     0 output errors, 0 collisions, 0 interface resets
     0 output buffer failures, 0 output buffers swapped out
     0 transitions
```

token-ring interface on port 2 on module 0 installed in slot 4 of our router.

In comparing the display of the token-ring interface to the Ethernet interface previously shown in Figure 4-2, note that the MTU, BW, and DLY settings are different. This difference results from the fact that Token Ring is a different type of network. In addition, just as different versions of Ethernet are available, there are also different versions of Token Ring. If you look at the value for BW in Figure 4-4, note a setting of 16 Mbps, which represents one of two types of token-ring operating rates supported by Cisco routers, with the other operating rate supported being 4 Mbps. At the time this book was prepared, a new version of Token Ring that operates on a dedicated switch connection at 100 Mbps was standardized, but Cisco router token-ring modules do not yet support this third version of Token Ring.

The `interface configuration` Commands

Just as for Ethernet, you use the `interface configuration` command to configure a token-ring interface as the following two formats show:

```
interface tokenring s/m/p
interface tokenring s/p
```

where m is the module number installed in a slot, s represents a slot number, and p represents a port number on the module. For example, to configure a token-ring interface located in slot 3 on port 2 , enter the following `interface` command.

```
interface tokenring3/2
```

Now that we understand how to specify a token-ring interface for configuration, look at the applicable commands needed in an IP environment. Figure 4-5 illustrates the `interface` commands applicable to a token-ring interface. If you compare the contents of Figure 4-5 to the Ethernet `interface` commands previously listed in Figure 4-3, note they are very similar, with Token Ring having a few additional `interface` commands such as `early-token-release` and `ring-speed`. Since all of the previously covered commands are essentially applicable to Token Ring, we will primarily focus our attention on new interface commands or the modified use of previously discussed commands for configuring a token-ring interface in this section.

ARP

By default, the encapsulation method defined for Token Ring is SNAP. Thus, it is not necessary to use the `arp` command to configure an encapsulation method for Token Ring.

Figure 4-5 Token-ring interface commands.

```
Cisco7500(config)#interface tokenring4/0/1
Cisco7500(config-if)#?
Interface configuration commands:
  access-expression    Build a bridge boolean access expression
  appletalk            Appletalk interface subcommands
  arp                  Set arp type (arpa, probe, snap) or timeout
  backup               Modify backup parameters
  bandwidth            Set bandwidth informational parameter
  bgp-policy           Apply policy propogated by bgp community string
  bridge-group         Transparent bridging interface parameters
  carrier-delay        Specify delay for interface transitions
  cdp                  CDP interface subcommands
  cmns                 OSI CMNS
  custom-queue-list    Assign a custom queue list to an interface
  decnet               Interface DECnet config commands
  default              Set a command to its defaults
  delay                Specify interface throughput delay
  description          Interface specific description
  dspu                 Down Stream PU
  early-token-release  Enable early token release
  ethernet-transit-oui Token-ring to Ethernet OUI handling
  exit                 Exit from interface configuration mode
  fair-queue           Enable Fair Queuing on an Interface
  fras                 DLC Switch Interface Command
  full-duplex          Configure full-duplex operational mode
  half-duplex          Configure half-duplex and related commands
  help                 Description of the interactive help system
  hold-queue           Set hold queue depth
  ip                   Interface Internet Protocol config commands
  ipx                  Novell/IPX interface subcommands
  keepalive            Enable keepalive
  lan-name             LAN Name command
  llc2                 LLC2 Interface Subcommands
  lnm                  IBM Lan Manager
  load-interval        Specify interval for load calculation for an
                       interface
  locaddr-priority     Assign a priority group
  logging              Configure logging for interface
  mac-address          Manually set interface MAC address
  mls                  mls router sub/interface commands
  mpoa                 MPOA interface configuration commands
  mtu                  Set the interface Maximum Transmission Unit (MTU)
  multilink-group      Put interface in a multilink bundle
  multiring            Enable RIF usage for a routable protocol
  netbios              Use a defined NetBIOS access list or enable
                       name-caching
  no                   Negate a command or set its defaults
  ntp                  Configure NTP
  port                 Enable concentrator port mode
  priority-group       Assign a priority group to an interface
  random-detect        Enable Weighted Random Early Detection (WRED) on an
                       Interface
    rate-limit           Rate Limit
```

(Continued)

Figure 4-5 (*Continued*)

```
ring-speed            Set the token ring speed
sap-priority          Assign a priority group
shutdown              Shutdown the selected interface
smrp                  Simple Multicast Routing Protocol interface
                      subcommands
sna                   SNA pu configuration
snapshot              Configure snapshot support on the interface
snmp                  Modify SNMP interface parameters
source-bridge         Configure interface for source-route bridging
standby               Hot standby interface subcommands
timeout               Define timeout values for this interface
traffic-shape         Enable Traffic Shaping on an Interface or Sub-
                      Interface
transmit-buffers      configure transmit-buffers policies
transmit-interface    Assign a transmit interface to a receive-only
                      interface
transmitter-delay     Set dead-time after transmitting a datagram
tx-queue-limit        Configure card level transmit queue limit
```

Bandwidth

Most recent Cisco token-ring modules can automatically adjust to the applicable ring speed. For older equipment use the ring-speed interface command described later in this section.

Delay

The default delay for a 16-Mbps token-ring interface is 630 μsec. The use of this interface command is the same as previously described when we covered Ethernet.

Description

Similar to the use of this command when configuring an Ethernet interface, description allows you to assign up to an 80-character label to a token-ring interface.

Early-Token-Release

One feature of 16-Mbps token-ring networks is that a station can release a new token immediately after the station transmits a frame. This feature is referred to as *early token release* and its use enhances the efficiency of a token-ring network. This feature is supported on certain Cisco token-ring modules by using the early-token-release interface subcommand. By default, early token release is disabled. To enable this feature, enter the following command:

```
early-token-release
```

Hold-Queue

As previously discussed when we examined the setting of an Ethernet interface, each router interface has a limited amount of storage for data packets referred to as a *hold-queue* whose value determines the amount of storage for inbound and outbound packets. If too little storage is specified under a moderate packet arrival rate, the interface rejects new packets, resulting in an increase in retransmissions. If too much storage is specified, a lower amount of packets is rejected; however, the delay through the buffer area will increase, which could adversely affect real-time transmission.

You can specify the hold-queue limit of an interface for both inbound and outbound directions. To do so, use the following command format:

```
Hold-queue length {in|out}
```

where `length` is the maximum number of packets that can be placed in the queue prior to newly arriving packets being lost. The default input queue value is 75 packets, while the default output queue value is 40 packets. The following example illustrates the display of `hold-queue` command information followed by two examples of the use of the command. Once again, note that the display of assistance information is misleading as it does not tell you that you must specify the queue direction in the command.

```
Cisco7500(config)#interface tokenring4/0/2
Cisco7500(config-if)#hold-queue ?
  <0-4096>  Queue length

Cisco7500(config-if)#hold-queue 80 in
Cisco7500(config-if)#hold-queue 80 out
```

IP

The primary use of the `ip` subcommand for a token-ring interface is to associate a layer 3 address with the interface. In doing so, use the `ip` command as illustrated here:

```
Cisco7500(config-if)#ip address ?
  A.B.C.D  IP address
Cisco7500(config-if)#ip address 192.131.176.1 255.255.255.0
```

Note you must enter both the IP address and subnet mask for the entry to be accepted by your router.

The `lan-name` Interface Command Function

The `lan-name interface` command functions the same for both Token Ring and Ethernet. That is, you use it to assign up to an eight-character descriptor to the network to be connected. The following example illustrates the use of the command:

```
Cisco7500(config-if)#lan-name ?
  WORD  Up to 8 characters lan name

Cisco7500(config-if)#lan-name engineer
```

The mac-address **Interface**

Similar to Ethernet, you can override the burnt-in token-ring layer 2 media access control (Mac) address. To do so, use the mac-address interface subcommand followed by three groups of four hex characters, each separated by a dot (.) as indicated here;

```
Cisco7500(config-if)#mac-address ?
  H.H.H  MAC address

Cisco7500(config-if)#mac-address 0008.9e6c.1541
Cisco7500(config-if)#
```

MTU

The maximum transmission unit (MTU) of a token-ring interface considerably exceeds that of an Ethernet interface. For example, at 4 Mbps, the token-ring default MTU is 4464 bytes, while all versions of Ethernet use an MTU of 1500 bytes. The setting of an MTU is important if you are performing layer 2 bridging. For example, if you were bridging token-ring and Ethernet LANs, you would set the token-ring MTU to 1500 bytes. The following example illustrates the possible MTU settings and how you could set the MTU of a token-ring interface to 1500 bytes.

```
Cisco7500(config-if)#mtu ?
  <64-17979>  MTU size in bytes

Cisco7500(config-if)#mtu 1500
```

However, because IP has the built-in capability to fragment packets at layer 3, you do not normally need to consider setting the token-ring MTU when you are operating at layer 3 and performing routing.

The ring-speed **Interface Command**

Modern Cisco router token-ring interfaces automatically adjust to either 4 or 16 Mbps. On older Cisco equipment you must use the ring-speed interface command to set the interface to either 4 or 16 Mbps. The format of the command is shown here:

```
ring-speed speed
```

where speed is either 4 or 16 to represent a 4- or 16 -Mbps operating rate. For example, to set the operating rate of token-ring port 1 to 4 Mbps, enter the following commands:

```
interface tokenring 1
ring-speed 4
```

Now that we understand the interface configuration commands associated with Ethernet and token-ring LANs, let's look at the wide area network and examine the commands used for configuring different types of serial interfaces.

WAN Interface Configuration

This section reviews the interface commands required to configure different types of serial interfaces. First, we examine the interface commands required to configure a standard serial interface. After that, we look at several specialized types of serial interfaces, examining the interface commands required to configure HSSI.

Standard Serial Port Configuration

The standard serial port used on Cisco routers provides support for four different types of connections, including RS-232, V.35, RS-449, and X.21. The RS-232 interface is typically used to support data rates up to 33.6 kbps, while the V.35 interface supports data rates up to approximately 6 Mbps. Normally, the RS-232 interface is used to support modem connections, while the V.35 interface enables the router to be connected to different types of digital transmission facilities such as 56-kbps to 1.544-Mbps circuits.

In actuality, the V.35 connection allows the router to connect to a service unit, and the service unit is then connected to the digital transmission facility. The RS-449 interface is another high-speed transmission interface, however, it is not as popular as the V.35 interface. Finally, the X.21 interface is an intelligent interface where codes are used to define transitions. Although popular in Europe, the X.21 interface has never achieved any significant usage in North America.

Interface Specification

As with other router interfaces, you can specify a serial interface in several ways, with the manner of specification based on the type of serial card and how the card is installed in a router. That is, the serial card can have two or four interfaces. Depending on the type of router, the interface card could be installed in a slot or in a module that is installed in a slot in the router.

The use of the interface command to configure a standard serial interface follows one of these two formats:

```
interface serial s/m/p
interface serial s/p
```

where m is the module number installed in a slot, s represents a slot number, and p represents a port number on the module. For example, to configure a serial interface located in slot 3 on port 2, enter the following interface command.

```
interface serial3/2
```

Serial interface configuration **Commands**

Figure 4-6 lists the serial interface commands supported under IOS version 12.0. If you examine those commands and compare them to the

Figure 4-6 Serial interface configuration commands.

```
Cisco7500>enable
Password:
Cisco7500#config
Configuring from terminal, memory, or network [terminal]?
Enter configuration commands, one per line.  End with CNTL/Z.
Cisco7500(config)#interface serial0/0/0
Cisco7500(config-if)#?
Interface configuration commands:
  access-expression         Build a bridge boolean access expression
  appletalk                 Appletalk interface subcommands
  arp                       Set arp type (arpa, probe, snap) or timeout
  asp                       ASP interface subcommands
  autodetect                Autodetect Encapsulations on Serial interface
  backup                    Modify backup parameters
  bandwidth                 Set bandwidth informational parameter
  bgp-policy                Apply policy propogated by bgp community string
  bridge-group              Transparent bridging interface parameters
  bsc                       BSC interface subcommands
  bstun                     BSTUN interface subcommands
  carrier-delay             Specify delay for interface transitions
  cdp                       CDP interface subcommands
  clock                     Configure serial interface clock
  compress                  Set serial interface for compression
  crc                       Specify CRC word-size
  custom-queue-list         Assign a custom queue list to an interface
  dce-terminal-timing-enable Enable DCE terminal timing
  decnet                    Interface DECnet config commands
  default                   Set a command to its defaults
  delay                     Specify interface throughput delay
  description               Interface specific description
  dialer                    Dial-on-demand routing (DDR) commands
  dialer-group              Assign interface to dialer-list
  down-when-looped          Force looped serial interface down
  dspu                      Down Stream PU
  dxi                       ATM-DXI configuration commands
  encapsulation             Set encapsulation type for an interface
  exit                      Exit from interface configuration mode
  fair-queue                Enable Fair Queuing on an Interface
  fras                      DLC Switch Interface Command
    full-duplex               Configure full-duplex operational mode
```

Figure 4-6 (*Continued*)

```
half-duplex            Configure half-duplex and related commands
help                   Description of the interactive help system
hold-queue             Set hold queue depth
idle-character         Set idle character type
ignore-dcd             ignore dcd
invert                 Serial invert modes
ip                     Interface Internet Protocol config commands
ipx                    Novell/IPX interface subcommands
keepalive              Enable keepalive
lan-name               LAN Name command
llc2                   LLC2 Interface Subcommands
load-interval          Specify interval for load calculation for an
                       interface
locaddr-priority       Assign a priority group
logging                Configure logging for interface
loopback               Configure internal loopback on an interface
mac-address            Manually set interface MAC address
mls                    mls router sub/interface commands
mop                    DEC MOP server commands
mpoa                   MPOA interface configuration commands
mtu                    Set the interface Maximum Transmission Unit
                       (MTU)
multilink-group        Put interface in a multilink bundle
netbios                Use a defined NETBIOS access list or enable
                       name-caching
no                     Negate a command or set its defaults
nrzi-encoding          Enable use of NRZI encoding
ntp                    Configure NTP
ppp                    Point-to-Point Protocol
priority-group         Assign a priority group to an interface
pulse-time             Enables pulsing of DTR during resets
random-detect          Enable Weighted Random Early Detection (WRED)
                       on an Interface
rate-limit             Rate Limit
sap-priority           Assign a priority group
sdllc                  Configure SDLC to LLC2 translation
serial                 serial interface commands
shutdown               Shutdown the selected interface
smds                   Modify SMDS parameters
smrp                   Simple Multicast Routing Protocol interface
                       subcommands
sna                    SNA pu configuration
snapshot               Configure snapshot support on the interface
snmp                   Modify SNMP interface parameters
stun                   STUN interface subcommands
timeout                Define timeout values for this interface
traffic-shape          Enable Traffic Shaping on an Interface or
                       Sub-Interface
transmit-buffers       configure transmit-buffers policies
transmit-interface     Assign a transmit interface to a receive-only
                       interface
transmitter-delay      Set dead-time after transmitting a datagram
tx-queue-limit         Configure card level transmit queue limit
```

commands supported by Ethernet and token-ring interfaces, note the many similarities between the two. However, you will also notice some key differences as well as the fact that there are many more possible serial interface commands to consider than either of the two LAN interface commands we previously covered.

The reason why there are more serial interface commands is because the serial port can be used to provide more connection options. For example, the serial port can be configured to provide access into several types of packet networks. In addition, the serial port can be used to provide access to an IBM SNA network or used to support access to a special type of network referred to as *switched multimegabit data services* (SMDS) offered by several *regional Bell operating companies* (RBOCs).

Although the number of serial interface commands is quite extensive, in actuality, only a small number of commands are required to support most connections of a router to transport IP. Only when you wish to really fine-tune a network and employ queuing, data compression, and a few additional techniques will you require the use of more than a handful of serial interface configuration commands. To illustrate how you can use just a few commands to appropriately configure a serial interface, look at Figure 4-7 which illustrates the status of a serial interface to an *Internet service provider* (ISP) via a 1.544-Mbps T1 transmission facility.

In Figure 4-7 the third line contains a description of the line connection. While not necessary, this illustrates a practical use of the description command to define the circuit to which the serial port is connected. Following the description is the Internet IP address, which means we must use the ip address command to set the IP address of the interface. Following the IP address is a line that shows the setting of the MTU, bandwidth, and delay.

After the display of three performance metrics, the following line denotes the encapsulation type, crc, and loopback. As we will shortly see, the primary configuration of a serial line in an IP environment is for encapsulation as *higher-level data-link control* (HDLC). However, frame relay is also a popular access into ISPs and you can also use SMDS if it is supported in your area. Thus, you need to specify an encapsulation method. In addition, you can consider the setting of a *cyclic redundancy check* (crc), loopback, and keepalive if you do not wish to accept the defaults. About halfway down the display of Figure 4-7 note a queuing strategy, which is denoted as weighted fair. As previously discussed, in certain instances you may wish to develop a more sophisticated queuing strategy, especially if your organization is attempting to transport real-time applications along with other data through a common serial interface. Now that we understand the major settings for a serial interface, let's look at the serial configuration commands needed to use to affect the settings. In doing so, we again discuss the commands in alphabetical order.

Figure 4-7   Examining the status of a serial connection to an ISP.

```
Serial0/0/0 is up, line protocol is up
  Hardware is cyBus Serial
  Description: MCI MGBC673F00010002
  Internet address is 4.0.156.2/30
  MTU 1500 bytes, BW 1544 Kbit, DLY 20000 usec,
     reliability 255/255, txload 168/255, rxload 18/255
  Encapsulation HDLC, crc 16, loopback not set
  Keepalive set (10 sec)
  Last input 00:00:01, output 00:00:00, output hang never
  Last clearing of "show interface" counters 4d00h
  Input queue: 0/75/0 (size/max/drops); Total output drops: 4476
  Queuing strategy: weighted fair
  Output queue: 0/1000/64/4476 (size/max total/threshold/drops)
     Conversations  0/43/256 (active/max active/max total)
     Reserved Conversations 0/0 (allocated/max allocated)
  5 minute input rate 113000 bits/sec, 140 packets/sec
  5 minute output rate 1018000 bits/sec, 142 packets/sec
     15022335 packets input, 1488986356 bytes, 0 no buffer
     Received 0 broadcasts, 0 runts, 0 giants, 0 throttles
     165 input errors, 165 CRC, 0 frame, 0 overrun, 0 ignored, 0 abort
     16580786 packets output, 635392803 bytes, 0 underruns
     0 output errors, 0 collisions, 0 interface resets
     0 output buffer failures, 3746887 output buffers swapped out
     0 carrier transitions
     RTS up, CTS up, DTR up, DCD up, DSR up
```

Bandwidth

The bandwidth command is used to set the operating rate of the serial interface. The following example illustrates the use of the bandwidth interface configuration command to set the bandwidth to 1.544 Mbps, which is the operating rate of a T1 line:

```
Cisco7500(config-if)#bandwidth ?
  <1-10000000>  Bandwidth in kilobits

Cisco7500(config-if)#bandwidth 1544000
```

Delay

The delay interface configuration command is used to specify the delay, in microseconds. For a WAN connect a delay of 2000 μsec is a practical setting. The following example illustrates the display of the delay interface command help information as well as the use of the command:

```
Cisco7500(config-if)#delay ?
  <1-16777215>  Throughput delay (tens of microseconds)

Cisco7500(config-if)#delay 2000
```

Encapsulation

The encapsulation serial interface command is used to define the protocol used to transport data across the wide area network. The following example illustrates the encapsulation methods supported by the serial interface and the setting of the encapsulation method to HDLC:

```
Cisco7500(config-if)#encapsulation ?
  atm-dxi         ATM-DXI encapsulation
  bstun           Block Serial tunneling (BSTUN)
  frame-relay     Frame Relay networks
  hdlc            Serial HDLC synchronous
  lapb            LAPB (X.25 Level 2)
  ppp             Point-to-Point protocol
  sdlc            SDLC
  sdlc-primary    SDLC (primary)
  sdlc-secondary  SDLC (secondary)
  smds            Switched Megabit Data Service (SMDS)
  stun            Serial tunneling (STUN)
  x25             X.25

Cisco7500(config-if)#encapsulation hdlc
```

IP

The serial interface that connects to the outside world consists of two IP interface configuration commands.

IP Address

The first is the address command, which enables you to assign a layer 3 IP address to the interface, as illustrated here:

```
Cisco7500(config-if)#ip address ?
  A.B.C.D  IP address
Cisco7500(config-if)#ip address 192.131.176.1 255.255.255.0
```

Once again, note that you must include a subnet mask to successfully assign an IP address to an interface.

The no directed-broadcast Command

The second delay interface command is not necessary but, for security reasons, highly recommended. That configuration command is no directed-broadcasts. The use of this command prevents directed broadcasts and may prevent considerable aggravation resulting from a hacker attack. For example, if a hacker sets a station to issue continuous pings to your network's broadcast address, the inbound ping would be transported to each workstation on your network. This, in turn, would result in every active station on your network responding to each ping, in effect saturating your network and the outbound side of your serial port. To compound a bad situation, if the hacker spoofed the source IP address, the responses would flow to the spoofed address, adversely affecting two networks! The following example illustrates how you would turn off directed broadcasts:

```
Cisco7500(config-if)#no ip directed-broadcast
```

Loopback

Similar to our discussion covering other types of interfaces, you normally want to ensure loopback is not set, unless you wish to disable the interface for testing. Thus, for normal operations you would use the no loopback serial interface command to change the status of a previously set loopback.

Keepalive

For most serial interfaces the default setting of 10 s for keepalive signals should be sufficient. Thus, most readers will not have to use the keepalive serial interface to specify a different value.

Queuing

In Figure 4-7 note the queuing strategy is listed as weighted fair. This is a default setting which, in effect, informs us there is no priority associated with different data resulting in data flowing into predefined queues and extracted based on some metric. Cisco routers support priority queuing which enables certain types of data to be output prior to other types of data. To accomplish this, assign data based on a certain characteristic such as protocol or application defined by port number to a particular priority queue. When the router is ready to transmit a packet, it scans the priority queues from highest to lowest, transmitting packets in the highest-priority queues prior to transmitting packets in the lower-priority queues.

While you can establish priority queuing on any router interface, for most applications it only makes sense to do so on a serial interface. This is because the serial interface normally operates at a much lower data rate than a LAN interface and is more susceptible to congestion.

There are four priority queues: high, medium, normal, and low. As you might expect, data placed in the high queue has the highest priority for extraction, while data in the low queue has the lowest priority.

You can assign a priority to packets by protocol, including application carried through the use of the priority-list global configuration command. The format of this command is

```
Priority-list list# protocol protocol-name queue-keyword [options]
```

where list# is an integer between 1 and 16 that identifies the priority list you are creating. The protocol-name, such as IP, defines the protocol, while the queue-keyword defines one of the four priority queue names: high, medium, normal, or low.

Several options are supported by the priority-list command. Those options are described in Table 4-1.

To illustrate the use of the priority-list command, let's assume you want to assign a medium priority to Web traffic. Since Web traffic is carried via TCP on port 80, you would enter the following command.

```
Priority-list 1 protocol ip medium tcp 80
```

Table 4-1   The `priority-list` Command Options

Option	Description
gt byte-count	Specifies the priority level assignment. Goes into effect when the packet length exceeds the specified value.
lt byte-count	Specifies the priority level assignment. Goes into effect when the packet length is less than the specified value.
list list-number	Assigns traffic priorities based on a specific IP access list number assigned by the access-group interface command.
tcp port	Assigns priority based on TCP port number
udp port	Assigns priority based on UDP port number

As a second example, assume you implemented a voice over IP application that uses UDP port 6232 to transport digitized voice. To assign such packets to a high priority, you would use the following `priority-list` command.

```
priority-list 2 protocol ip high udp 6232
```

If you only want to assign a priority to Web and digitized voice traffic, all other traffic would be, by default, assigned to the normal queue. However, you could use a simplifier version of the `priority-list` `global configuration` command to assign all other traffic to a default priority. To do so, use the keyword `default` in the `priority-list` command, as illustrated in the following:

```
priority-list list# default queue-keyword
```

For example, to assign all other traffic to the low-priority queue, enter the following command:

```
priority-list 2 default low
```

Similar to any queue, Cisco router priority queues have a finite length. By default, the maximum queue size for high-, medium-, normal-, and low-priority queues are 20, 40, 60, and 80 packets, respectively. You can use another version of the `priority-list global configuration` command to change the default size of one or more priority queues, however, you should carefully consider the data handled by a queue prior to doing so. This is because there is a trade-off between packet loss and delay when you change a queue length, with a larger queue reducing packet loss but increasing the time for data to flow through the queue. This can be harmful if you are transmitting real-time data such as digitized voice. In any event, to change a queue limit, use the `queue-limit` keyword in the `priority-list` command. The format to use is

```
priority-list list# queue-limit high-limit, medium-limit, normal-limit
   low-limit
```

For example, to set the maximum number of packets for the high-priority queue to 30 while retaining 40, 60, and 80 for the other types of priority queues, enter the following command:

```
priority-list 2 30 40 60 80
```

The last step you must consider involves assigning a priority list to a particular interface. To accomplish this task, use the `priority-group` `interface` subcommand. The format of this command is shown here:

```
priority-group list#
```

where the `list#` is the priority list number assigned to an interface.

We can put the preceding information together and apply our previously created priority list to the `serial0/0/0` interface. To conclude this section, let's do so. The following statements indicate how packets flowing outbound on the interface `serial0/0/0` are classified and extracted by priority list 2.

```
Interface serial0/0/0
Priority-group 2
Priority-list 2 protocol ip medium tcp 80
Priority-list 2 protocol ip medium tcp 80
priority-list 2 default low
priority-list 2 30 40 60 80
```

High-Speed Serial Interfaces (HSSI)

The previous section discussed the use of the standard serial interface on Cisco routers. Standard serial interfaces can support up to 4 Mbps of traffic, which is a high enough data rate for many organizations. However, there are times when more bandwidth is desired, and this is why the *high-speed serial interface* (HSSI) specification is needed. HSSI interfaces are capable of supporting speeds of up to OC-1 (52 Mbps). Additionally, it can support lower-speed specifications such as T3 (approximately 45 Mbps) and E3 (approximately 34 Mbps) and fractions thereof. The actual speed of the link in use is determined by the CSU/DSU that terminates the physical line from the telephone company. The clocking rate is passed to the HSSI interface by the CSU/DSU by an electrical signal so that the interface knows the true rate of the line.

HSSI interfaces are very useful when an organization wants to support a WAN link in excess of T1 speeds. While a standard serial interface is capable of handling up to two full T1s (approximately 3 Mbps), it is not capable of handling much more than this. The only real alternative to HSSI for high-speed WAN links is ATM interfaces. However, HSSI interfaces support many different kinds of encapsulations other than ATM. In fact, as we will see in the next section, HSSI interfaces can support every encapsulation that a standard serial interface supports except X.25.

HSSI Interface Specification

Physically, an HSSI interface resembles a *small computer systems interface 2* (SCSI-2) and has a 50 pin D-shaped connector. However, despite the physical similarities, the electrical specifications are different and are incompatible. The HSSI cable specifications can support 52-Mbps data rates at cable runs of up to 50 ft, which should be more than adequate for most requirements.

As with serial router interfaces, you can specify an HSSI interface in several ways, based on the type of HSSI card and how the card is installed in a router. Typically, there is only a single HSSI interface per slot due to the high bandwidth demands of the interface. Depending on the type of router, the HSSI card could be installed in a slot or in a module that is installed in a slot in the router.

The use of the interface command to configure an HSSI interface follows one of these two formats:

```
interface hssi s/p
interface hssi s
```

where s represents a slot number and p represents a port number in the slot. For example, to configure an HSSI interface located in slot 0 on port 0, enter the following interface command:

```
interface hssi 0/0
```

This type designation is the most common for HSSI interfaces since they are likely to be found in higher-end routers such as the 7200 and 7500 series. However, they are also supported on the 4700 series routers, in which case there is only a slot designation:

```
Interface hssi 0
```

HSSI Interface Configuration Commands

With the exception that they do not support X.25 encapsulation, HSSI interfaces are configured in exactly the same manner as standard serial interfaces. A sample output from a show interface command is displayed here:

```
Hssi0 is up, line protocol is up
  Hardware is MXT
  Internet address is 192.168.5.1/30
  MTU 4470 bytes, BW 6176 Kbit, DLY 200 usec, rely 255/255, load 11/255
  Encapsulation HDLC, loopback not set, keepalive set (10 sec)
  Last input 00:00:00, output 00:00:00, output hang never
  Last clearing of "show interface" counters never
  Queueing strategy: fifo
  Output queue 0/40, 0 drops; input queue 1/75, 1 drops
  5 minute input rate 4436000 bits/sec, 872 packets/sec
  5 minute output rate 289000 bits/sec, 234 packets/sec
     8428113 packets input, 944764468 bytes, 0 no buffer
     Received 3420 broadcasts, 0 runts, 0 giants, 1 throttles
             0 parity
     13 input errors, 1 CRC, 0 frame, 1 overrun, 0 ignored, 11 abort
     2282006 packets output, 382710178 bytes, 0 underruns
     0 output errors, 0 applique, 1 interface resets
     0 output buffer failures, 0 output buffers swapped out
     0 carrier transitions    TM=down  CA=up  LC=down
```

By now, the fields in this output should be familiar to you. They are similar, if not identical, to the output produced by a standard serial interface. Since we have already covered the commands available on serial interfaces, we will not duplicate that effort in this section. As noted, with the exception that they do not support X.25 encapsulation, HSSI interfaces support all of the options supported on standard serial interfaces. Configuring an HSSI interface is therefore no different than configuring a standard serial interface. The same queuing and other features discussed apply equally well to HSSI interfaces. In fact, it can be said that if you are familiar with standard serial interfaces, you are already familiar with HSSI interfaces, the only real difference being the physical characteristics of the interface.

CHAPTER 5

Configuring and Applying Access Lists

This chapter provides an overview of the different types of access lists, their general formats, the use of different keywords within an access list, and how access lists are applied to an interface. After these topics are covered, we discuss specific types of relatively new access lists supported in IOS versions 11.3 through 12.0. Those new access lists, which are features added to traditional access lists, include dynamic access lists, time-based access lists, reflexive access lists, and TCP Intercept.

Overview

An access list is an ordered set of statements that permits or denies the flow of packets across an interface based on matching criteria of access-list parameters and information contained in packets. This definition does not mention anything about security nor does it mention that an access list can be used to establish a security policy or implement the flow of data based on certain parameters within a packet.

Purpose

While access lists perform each of these functions and more, their *primary* purpose is to permit or deny the flow of packets based on established criteria. Thus, your packet-filtering criteria will result in an access list that implements a specific policy even though an access doesn't represent a policy. For example, assume an access list is created to prohibit employees on a LAN connected to the Internet from being able to surf the Web during business hours. In this situation you construct an access list incorporating certain parameters which, when applied to a router's interface, enable implementation of this organizational policy.

Application

In terms of router interfaces, for an access list to be in effect it must be created and applied to an interface. Since the flow of data across an interface is bidirectional, an access list is applied to a specific direction on an interface, either inbound or outbound. Here the term *inbound* refers to the flow of data toward a router, while *outbound* refers to the flow of data away from a router.

Figure 5-1 shows a router with one serial and two Ethernet ports. In this sample network schematic, the serial port provides a connection to the Internet, while ports E0 and E1 provide connectivity for two Ethernet LANs.

In Figure 5-1 the dual arrows are associated with each interface. Arrows pointed inbound toward the router indicate the inbound direction on an interface, while arrows pointing away from a router indicate the outbound direction associated with each router interface.

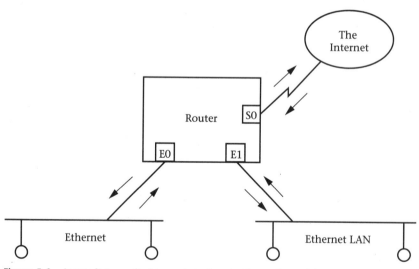

Figure 5-1 Access lists applied to an interface in the outbound (arrows pointed away from the router) or inbound (arrows pointed toward the router) direction. E0 = Ethernet0 and E1 = Ethernet1 interfaces. S0 = Serial0 interface.

Types of Access Lists

Two types of access lists are supported by Cisco routers: standard and extended. A *standard access list* is limited in functionality since it only allows filtering based on source address. In comparison, an *extended access list*, as its name implies, provides extended packet filtering, so you can filter packets based on source and destination address and upper-layer application data. This section examines both types of access lists, with special attention on *Internet protocol* (IP) access lists since IP is the only protocol supported for Internet transmission.

Standard IP Access Lists

The format of a standard IP access list is shown here:

```
access-list[list number][permit|deny][source address][wildcard-mask][log]
```

Note that, in this format, the horizontal bar (|) between two items is an identifier that means you must select one of the choices on each side of the bar.

In examining the format of the standard IP access list, certain items require explanation. First, the term `access-list` has a hyphen between the two words. Second, the list number is a numeral between 1 and 99 that identifies the access-list statements belonging to a common access list. In addition, any number between 1 and 99 informs the IOS that the access list is associated with the IP protocol. Thus, the list number has a dual function: it defines the protocol on which the access list operates and it informs the IOS to treat all access-list statements with the same list number as a single entity.

In actuality, Cisco supports a reference to protocols in an access list both by name and by number. Table 5-1 is a list of protocols supported both by name and number. Since the primary focus of this chapter is upon IP-related access lists, most of our discussion will focus on those access lists within the ranges 1 to 99 and 100 to 199.

Keywords

The keyword `permit` and the keyword `deny` let you specify whether or not packets that match an access-list entry are allowed to flow through an interface or are filtered. The keyword `permit` allows packets to flow through the interface, while the keyword `deny` results in packets matching the specified source address within a standard IP access list being sent to the great bit bucket in the sky.

Table 5-1 Protocols with Access Lists Specified by Names and Numbers

Protocols with Access List Specified by Name	
Apollo domain	
IP	
IPX	
ISO CLNS	
NetBIOS IPX	
Source-routing bridging NetBIOS	
Protocols with Access List Specified by Numbers	
IP	1–99
Extended IP	100–199
Ethernet type code	200–299
Ethernet address	700–799
Transparent bridging (protocol type)	200–299
Transparent bridging (vendor code)	700–799
Extended transparent bridging	1100–1199
DECnet and extended DECnet	300–399
XNS	400–499
Extended XNS	500–599
AppleTalk	600–699
Source-route bridging (protocol type)	200–299
Source-route bridging (vendor code)	700–799
IPX	800–899
Extended IPX	900–999
IPX SAP	1000–1099
IPX SAP SPX	1000–1099
Standard VINES	1–100
Extended VINES	101–200
Simple VINES	201–300

Source Address

For a standard IP access list the source address is the IP address of a host or group of hosts specified using dotted-decimal notation. In actuality, the specification of a group of hosts is based on the use of the `wildcard-mask`. Thus, let's look at the `wildcard-mask` and, after a brief examination, consider several examples that show how to specify a range of IP addresses.

The `wildcard-mask`

The `wildcard-mask` supported by Cisco access lists functions in a reverse manner to a subnet mask, that is, the access-list mask uses a binary 0 to represent a match and a binary 1 to represent a don't care condition.

To illustrate the operation of a `wildcard-mask`, let's assume your organization has the class C network address 198.78.46.0. Assuming you did not employ subnets, when you configure each station on that network, you would enter a subnet mask of 255.255.255.0. In this situation a 1 bit is a match, while a 0 bit is a don't care condition. Thus, by specifying 255 in each of the first three positions of the four-position subnet mask field, the TCP/IP protocol stack matches the network address in each packet and doesn't care about the host address. Since the Cisco `wildcard-mask` is the opposite of a subnet mask, the following standard IP access-list statement is used to all packets on the network with a source network address of 198.78.46.0:

```
access-list 1 permit 198.78.46.0 0.0.0.255
```

In this access-list statement the `wildcard-mask` of 0.0.0.255 is the compliment of the subnet mask. Thus, another technique for specifying an access-list `wildcard-mask` is to determine the subnet mask and take its inverse.

Other Keywords

Although most access-list keywords are only applicable to extended access lists, three are applicable to standard IP access lists that warrant consideration. Those keywords are `host`, `any`, and `log`. The first two keywords, `host` and `any`, are alternative methods for specifying an IP address and host mask as a single entity and are not included in the previously presented access format.

Host

`Host` signifies an exact match and is the `wildcard-mask` of 0.0.0.0. For example, assume you want to permit packets from source address 198.78.46.8. You could code the following access-list statement:

```
access-list 1 permit 198.78.46.8 0.0.0.0
```

Because the keyword host signifies an exact match, you could recode the previous access-list statement as follows:

```
access-list 1 permit host 198.78.46.8
```

Thus, host is an abbreviation for a wildcard-mask of 0.0.0.0.

Any

In a standard access list the keyword any is used as an abbreviation for a source address and wildcard-mask of 0.0.0.0 255.255.255.255. For example, assume you wish to deny packets from source address 198.78.46.8 and permit packets from all other addresses. The standard access-list statements to accomplish this would be as follows:

```
access-list 1 deny host 198.78.46.8
access-list 1 permit any
```

Note the order of the two statements. Access-list statements are processed in a top-down order. This means that if we reversed the order and placed the permit statement before the deny statement, we could not bar or filter packets from host address 198.78.46.8 since the permit statement would allow all packets. Thus, unlike a classroom where order may be disruptive, in an access list the order of statements can be dangerous because improperly ordered statements can create security loopholes into a network or allow users to avoid compliance with organizational policies.

Log

The keyword log is applicable to IOS version 11.3. When included in an access list, this keyword results in the logging of packets that match permit and deny statements in the access list. Thus, another term for an access list that contains the keyword log is a *logged access list*.

When you apply a logged access list to an interface, the first packet that triggers the access list causes an immediate logging message. Subsequent packets examined over 5-min periods are then displayed on the console or logged to memory, with the manner by which messages are logged controlled by the IOS logging console command.

Logged messages include the access-list number, whether the packet was permitted or denied, the source IP address, and the number of packets matched during 5-min intervals after the first match is displayed. For example, assume the following standard IP access list:

```
access-list 1 permit 198.78.46.0 0.0.0.0 log
```

Now let's assume the preceding access list resulted in 10 packets being matched over a 5-min period. When the first match occurs, the following display would appear:

```
list 1 permit 198.78.46.1 1 packet
```

Then, 5 min later, the following display would appear:

```
list 1 permit 198.78.46.8 9 packets
```

Use of the keyword log to effect console logging provides you with a testing and alert capability. Logging can be used to test the development of different access lists by observing the resulting match of packets as different activities are attempted. When used as an alert facility, you would scan the display to locate repeated attempts to perform an activity an access-list statement was developed to deny. In this situation, repeated attempts to perform an activity an access-list statement is configured to deny would more than likely indicate a potential hacker attack.

Extended IP Access Lists

An *extended IP access* extends the ability to filter packets. Use of an extended IP access list permits you to filter packets based on source and destination address, protocol, source and destination port, and a variety of options that allow comparison of specific bits in certain packet fields. The general format of an extended IP access list is shown here:

```
access-list[list number][permit|deny][protocol|protocol keyword][source
   address source-wildcard][source port][destination address]
   [destination-wildcard][destination port][log][options]
```

Field Overview

This section briefly examines each field in an extended IP access list and provides an overview of the use of each field and some of the options supported by this type access list.

List Number

Similar to a standard IP access list, the list number identifies an extended IP access list. Numbers 100 through 199 can be used to define 100 unique extended IP access lists.

Permit/Deny

The use of either permit or deny lets you specify whether or not packets that match an access-list statement are allowed to flow through an interface or are filtered. Again, this provides the same function as their use in a standard IP access list.

Protocol

The protocol entry defines the protocol to be filtered, such as IP, TCP, UDP, ICMP, and so on. When entering a protocol, it is important to remember the relationship of protocols within the TCP/IP protocol suite that form datagrams. That is, an IP header is used to transport ICMP, TCP, UDP, and various routing protocols. This means that if you specify IP as the protocol to be filtered, all matches against other fields will cause the packet to be either permitted or denied regardless of whether the packet is an application transported by TCP or UDP or an ICMP message. Thus, if you wish to filter based on a specific protocol, you should specify that protocol. In addition, you should place more specific entries ahead of less specific entries. For example, if you code a statement permitting IP for a specific address followed by denying TCP for that address, the second statement would never take effect. However, reversing the order would allow you to bar TCP to the address while permitting all other protocols to that address.

Source Address and Wildcard-Mask

The source address and wildcard-mask function in the same manner as previously described for a standard IP access list. Thus, you can use the term host followed by a specific IP address to specify a specific host, the term any to represent a source address and wildcard-mask of 0.0.0.0 255.255.255.255, or an IP address and wildcard-mask to specify a network range. As a brief review, remember that the wildcard-mask supported by Cisco access lists functions in a reverse manner to a subnet mask, with a binary 0 used to represent a match and a binary 1 used to represent a don't care condition.

Occasionally, when you configure an access list and subsequently use the IOS show command to view the list, you can become confused about your prior entry because when a wildcard-mask bit is set to 1 (don't care), IOS converts the bit in the IP address portion of the access-list entry to a binary 0. For example, the following series of IOS commands creates an extended IP access list and displays the contents of the list:

```
router # config terminal
router (config) # access-list 101 permit IP 198.78.46.20 0.0.0.255
   host 205.131.172.1
router (config) # exit
router # show access-list 101
Extended IP access list 101
permit IP 198.78.46.0 0.0.0.255 host 205.131.175.1
```

In this example station 20 on network 198.78.46.0 is automatically converted to the network address since the wildcard-mask in the host portion of the class C address was set to all 1's (255).

Although not shown, it is important to note that each access list has an implicit deny all built into the bottom of the list. Thus, the previously constructed access list has the following statement implicitly added to the end of the list:

```
access-list 101 deny 0.0.0.0 255.255.255.255
```

Source Port Number

The source port number can be specified in several ways. First, it can be specified explicitly, either as a numeral or as a recognized mnemonic. For example, you could use either 80 or http to specify the Web's HyperText transmission protocol. For TCP and UDP you can use the keyword operators lt (less than), gt (greater than), eq (equal), and neq (not equal).

Destination Address and Wildcard-Mask

The destination address and wildcard-mask have the same structure as for the source address and wildcard-mask. This also means you can use such keywords as any and host to specify any destination address and a specific address without having to specify a mask.

Destination Port Number

The destination port can be specified in the same manner as for a source port. That is, you can specify a number, mnemonic, or use an operator with a number or mnemonic to specify a range. The following examples illustrate the use of operators in access-list statements:

```
access-list 101 permit tcp any host 198.78.46.8 eq smtp
access-list 101 permit tcp any host 198.78.46.3 eq www
```

The first statement permits TCP from any host to the specific host 198.78.46.8 as long as the packet conveys SMTP data. The second statement permits TCP packets from any host to the specific host 198.78.46.3 as long as the destination port is Web traffic. In this example the mnemonic www is the same as http and equals numeric 80.

Options

A wide range of options is supported by an extended IP access list. One commonly used option is log which was described earlier. A second commonly used option is established. This option is only applicable to the TCP protocol and restricts TCP traffic in one direction as a response to sessions initiated in the opposite direction. To do so, an access-list statement with the established option examines each TCP packet to determine if its ACK or RST bit is set. If so, this indicates that the packet is a part of a previously established conversation. For example, consider the following extended IP access-list statement:

```
access-list 101 permit tcp any host 198.78.46.8 established
```

This access-list statement allows any TCP packet from any source address to flow to the specific host 198.78.46.8 only if the packet's ACK or RST bit is set. This means that the host 198.78.46.8 must have previously initiated the TCP session.

Keywords

Table 5-2 contains a list of commonly used access-list keywords and a brief description of their use. Keywords such as any, established, host, precedence, remark, and tos are directly placed in an access list. The other keywords are fields within an access list where a numeral or mnemonic is substituted for the keyword. Although we examine the use of many keywords in this chapter, one deserves special mention at this

Table 5-2 Access-List Keywords

Keyword	Utilization
any	Abbreviation for an address and wildcard-mask value of 0.0.0.0 255.255.255.255. Applicable to source and destination fields.
established	Filters if ACK or RST bits are set (TCP only).
host	Abbreviation for a wildcard-mask of 0.0.0.0. Applicable to both source and destination.
icmp-type	Filtering by ICMP message type. You can also specify the ICMP message code (0 to 255).
port	Defines the decimal number or name of a TCP or UDP port.
protocol	Defines the protocol for filtering. Can include one of the keywords eigrp, gre, icmp, igmp, igrp, ip, ipinip, nos, ospf, tcp, or udp, or an integer between 0 and 255 representing an IP protocol.
precedence *precedence*	Filtering by the precedence level name or number (0 to 7).
remark	Adding text comments to an access list.
TOS *tos*	Filtering by service level specified by a number (0 to 15) or name.

time since its use facilitates including remarks about your entries in an access list. That keyword is `remark`.

Commented IP Access-List Entries

Beginning in version 12.0, the `remark` keyword applies to both standard and extended IP access lists. The keyword `remark` is placed after the access-list number in a separate access-list statement followed by the comment or remark to be entered. The statement with the remark can be placed before or after the actual `permit` or `deny` statement you wish to describe; however, for legibility you should be consistent with respect to the location of your remarks. The following example illustrates the use of two remarks within a common access list.

```
access-list 101 remark allow traffic to Gil's PC
access-list 101 permit ip any host 198.78.46.8
access-list 101 remark allow only Web traffic to Web server
access list 101 permit tcp any host 198.78.46.12 eq 80
```

Creating and Applying an Access List

An access list can be created directly from the console or with a word processor or text editor, first storing the file in ASCII text. In the case of ASCII text, the PC on which you sorted the file functions as a server, requiring the installation of a tftp program on the computer. Once this is accomplished, the router acts as a client and retrieves the file.

Initially, we will create relatively small access lists with a limited number of statements, so we will illustrate the entry of statements from the console. However, as access lists become more complex, you will more than likely want to enter your statements into a file that would be loaded using tftp.

Three items are required to apply an access list to an interface: an access list, an interface to apply the access list to, and a method to define the direction the access list is applied to on the interface. Standard and extended IP access lists have already been discussed, so let's look at the interface and interface direction on which the access list is applied.

Specifying an Interface

To specify an interface use the `interface` command. For example, to apply an access list to serial port 0, first we have to define the interface with the following command:

```
interface serial0
```

Similarly, to apply an access list to a router port connected to an Ethernet LAN, first we must define the port with the following command, assuming the port was Ethernet0:

```
interface ethernet0
```

Since you can abbreviate many keywords in a command, you could also specify the following command:

```
interface e0
```

Using the `ip access-group` Command

The third part of the three-step process is to define the direction of the interface to which the access list is applied by using the `ip access-group` command shown here:

```
ip access-group[list number][in|out]
```

The list number identifies the access list, while the use of the keyword `in` or `out` identifies the direction to which the access list will be applied. The direction indicates whether packets are examined as they arrive (in) or leave (out) a router interface.

The following example puts all three steps together:

```
interface serial0
ip access-group 107 in
access-list 107 remark allow traffic to Gil's PC
access-list 107 ip any host 198.78.46.8
access-list 107 remark allow only Web traffic to Web server
access-list 107 tcp any host 198.78.46.12 eq 80
access-list 107 remark block everything else
access-list 107 deny ip any any
```

This example first used the `interface` command to define serial port 0. Next, we used the `ip access-group` command to apply the access-list statements entered as access-list number 107 in the inbound direction on the serial interface. Finally, we entered six access-list statements that form the access list, with three statements using the keyword `remark` so we can provide comments about subsequent statements in the list. Note that the last statement in the access list is only for a "doubting Thomas" because it represents the implicit `deny all` setting associated with every access list and does not appear unless needlessly explicitly typed. If you wanted to enter the commands and statements previously described directly from a terminal connected to the router's console port, you would first use the privileged EXEC command. An example of the terminal session is shown here:

```
router # config terminal
Enter configuration commands, one per line. End with CTRL/Z.
interface serial0
router (config-if) # ip access-group 107 in
```

```
router (config) # 107 remark allow traffic to Gil's PC
router (config) # 107 ip any host 197.78.46.8
router (config) # 107 remark allow only web traffic to web server
router (config) # 107 tcp any host 197.78.46.12 eq 80
router (config) # 107 remark block everything else
router (config) # 107 deny ip any any
router (config) # exit
router #
```

Named Access Lists

When you use a numbered access list with an enterprise router, it is possible, although probably unlikely, that you could run out of numbers. Another limitation of numbered access lists is that although the number informs you of the type of list, until you read the statements in the list, it is difficult, if not impossible, to differentiate the general function of one list from another. Perhaps recognizing this problem, Cisco introduced named access lists in IOS version 11.2.

Overview

A named access list lets you create an access list referred to by a name instead of a number. Named access lists are applicable to both standard and extended lists. The name used is case sensitive and must begin with an alphabet character. Within the name you can use just about any alphanumeric character, including [,], {, }, _, -, +, /, \, ., &, $, #, @, !, and ?. Although the authors have successfully used names up to 100 characters in length, from a practical standpoint, 20 to 25 characters should be more than sufficient for creating a meaningful access-list designation.

Standard Named IP Access Lists

The format for a standard named IP access list is shown here:

```
ip access-list standard name
```

where name is the name assigned to the standard named IP access list. That statement is followed by one or more permit and deny statements, as illustrated by the following example where we decided to allow packets from three specific hosts, perhaps in the accounting department, since that is the name assigned to the access list.

```
ip access-list standard accounting
permit 198.78.46.8 0.0.0.0
permit 198.78.46.12 0.0.0.0
permit 198.78.46.30 0.0.0.0
```

Application

Since we have not yet applied the named access list to an interface, at this point we do not know if packets are allowed to or from hosts with the three IP addresses listed in the previous example. To apply a named access list, we need to specify an interface as well as use the `ip access-group` command to define the direction of packet filtering with respect to the router's interface. The format of the `ip access-group` command, when used in conjunction with standard and extended named IP access lists, is shown here:

```
ip access-group <name> [in|out]
```

where `<name>` is the name of the named access list. Assuming we want to apply the previously created accounting access list to the serial0 interface to filter outbound packets, the statements would be as follows:

```
interface serial0
ip access-group accounting out
!
ip access-list standard accounting
permit 198.78.46.8 0.0.0.0
permit 198.78.46.12 0.0.0.0
permit 198.78.46.30 0.0.0.0
```

Now that we understand standard named IP access lists, let's look at extended named IP access lists.

Extended Named IP Access Lists

Similar to a standard named IP address list, the extended version uses `extended` followed by the name of the list to identify the access list. The format of the extended `ip access-list` command is shown here:

```
ip access-list extended <name>
```

where `<name>` is the name of the extended IP access list.

Application

An extended named IP access list is applied in the same manner as a standard IP named access list by using the `interface` command to define the interface and applying an `ip access-group` command with the name of the access list and the direction of packet filtering to be applied to the list.

The following example illustrates the commands required to apply an extended named IP access list called server-security to a router's serial0 port in the inbound direction. This example assumes the server is located on the class C network 198.78.46.0 and has the host address of .20. It is also assumed that because the Web server supports public access, the organization placed the server on a segment by itself, as illustrated in Figure 5-2.

Based upon the preceding, the extended IP access list would be applied as follows:

```
interface ethernet1
ip access-group server-security out
!
ip access-list extended server-security
ip permit tcp any host 198.78.46.20 eq 80
```

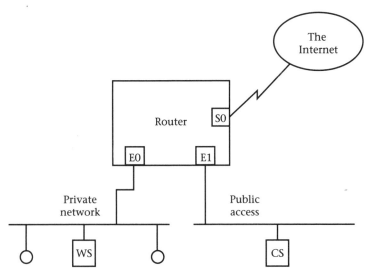

Figure 5-2 Using a router to control access to public and private networks operated by an organization. WS = Web server with address 198.78.46.20. CS = corporate server.

This example used an extended named IP access list to restrict packets flowing out of the Ethernet1 port to those transporting Web traffic to the host whose address is 198.78.46.20. Note we did not apply the access list to the serial interface because if we did, it would, in effect, bar all Internet traffic flowing into the router other than Web traffic to the specified server IP address. Also note the direction the access list was applied to is out, since filtering is required for packets flowing out of the router onto the 198.78.46.0 network. Last but not least, also note that both standard named IP access lists and extended named IP access lists follow the same construction rules as numbered access lists, with the numbers replaced by the name of the list in both the `access list` and `ip access-group` commands.

Editing

Until now, we concentrated on the format and construction of named access lists and briefly mentioned a few reasons for the use of them. However, when you edit a named access list, another advantage can be noted— specific entries in the access list can be deleted. In comparison, you cannot delete specific entries in a numbered access list. Although you can add entries to the bottom of a numbered access list, if you need to revise one or more entries, you must first create a new list, delete the existing list, and then apply the new list. This action is alleviated when you are working with a named access list since you can simply enter the `no` version of an access-list statement to remove the statement from the list.

However, it is important to note that named access lists are similar to numbered access lists in that neither supports the selective addition of statements. To add statements to a named access list you must delete an existing list and reapply a new or modified list with appropriate entries.

To illustrate how to selectively remove statements from a named access list, consider the following console operation in which the show command is used to display the named extended IP access list called server-security. Note that after the extended IP access list is given, the configure terminal command is used to define the named access list to be modified and then the no version of the command to be removed is entered.

```
router # show access-list server-security
Extended IP access-list server-security
permit tcp any host 198.78.46.20 eq 80
permit icmp any host 198.78.46.20 echo-reply
router # configure terminal
router (config) ip access-list extended server-security
router (config-int) # no permit icmp any host 198.78.46.20 echo-reply
router (config-int) # exit
router (config) # exit
router # show access-list server-security
permit tcp any host 198.78.46.20 eq 80
```

In this listing, note that the use of the no version of the second permit statement to remove it from the access list named server-security. The removed statement, permit icmp any host 198.78.46.20 echo-reply, was placed in the list to enable responses to pings from the server to flow back to the server. ICMP stands for the Internet Control Message Protocol, and an ICMP message type can be specified using either numerals or mnemonics. Table 5-3 summarizes ICMP message type codes and the corresponding name of the message.

Table 5-3 ICMP Type Numbers

Type	Name
0	Echo reply
1	Unassigned
2	Unassigned
3	Destination unreachable
4	Source quench
5	Redirect

Type	Name
6	Alternate host address
7	Unassigned
8	Echo
9	Router advertisement
10	Router selection
11	Time exceeded
12	Parameter problem
13	Timestamp
14	Timestamp reply
15	Information request
16	Information reply
17	Address mask request
18	Address mask reply
19	Reserved (for security)
20–29	Reserved (for robustness experiment)
30	Traceroute
31	Datagram conversion error
32	Mobile host redirect
33	IPv6 where-are-you
34	IPv6 I-am-here
35	Mobile registration request
36	Mobile registration reply
37	Domain name request
38	Domain name reply
39	SKIP
40	Photuris
41–255	Reserved

Since it is common practice for an unsophisticated hacker to go to a computer laboratory on a Friday evening and initiate pings with the program's continuous option to attack a target, it is also common for many organizations to block pings at the router. To do so you use a deny statement specifically prohibiting ICMP echo-request messages similar to the following statement:

```
deny icmp any any echo-request
```

or

```
deny icmp any any eq 8
```

The first deny statement uses the name of the ICMP message, while the second example shows the use of the message type number. The reason why you would more than likely include a specific deny icmp statement in your access list is because ICMP is transported via IP. Thus, if you wanted to allow IP traffic but exclude echo-request packets, you would first deny ICMP echo-requests prior to permitting IP.

Facilitating the Editing Process

Cisco routers support the tftp protocol as a client, so you can create configuration files on a PC operating as a tftp server and download applicable files into the router. As indicated earlier, you should save any configuration file you create using a word processor or text editor as ASCII text.

To illustrate the use of tftp to download a configuration into a router, we need a configuration file. Thus, let's assume you created the following short access-list configuration file which we appropriately named acl.txt.

```
acl.txt
interface serial0
IP access-group 101 in
access-list 107 permit tcp any host 198.78.46.20 eq 80
access-list 107 permit tcp any any established
access-list 107 permit icmp any any echo-reply
```

In the preceding access list the first statement allows Web traffic to the specified host. The second statement permits TCP packets that have their RST or ACK bits set, which means the packet is a response to a session initiated on the trusted side of the router. Finally, the third statement permits ICMP echo-reply packets from any host outside the network to flow to any host on the network.

To load the previously created file, let's assume it was stored on the host 198.78.46.12. The following instructions would be typed at the router console:

```
router # configure net
Host on network configuration file[host]?host
Address of remote host[255.255.255.255]?198.78.46.12
Name of configuration file[router-config]?acl.txt
Confirm using acl.txt from 198.78.46.12?[confirm]
Loading acl.txt from 198.78.46.12 [via e0]:
[ok - xxx bytes]
router #
```

Rules to Consider

This initial section on IP access lists concludes with a discussion of rules for success. These rules are a mixture of fact and suggestion. The factual portion of a rule is based on the manner by which access-list processing occurs, while the suggestion portion is the opinion of the authors based on the processing of access lists.

Top-Down Processing

Access-list entries are evaluated top down, sequentially commencing with the first entry in the list. This means you must carefully consider the order in which you place statements in an access list.

Adding Entries

New entries are added to the bottom of an access list. This means it may not be possible to change the functionality of an existing access list, requiring creation of a new list, deletion of the existing list, and application of the new list to an interface.

Standard List Filtering

Standard IP access lists are limited to filtering on source address. This means you may need an extended IP access list to satisfy organizational requirements.

Access-List Placement

Place extended access lists as close as possible to the source being filtered because then you can create filters that do not adversely affect the data flow on other interfaces. Place standard access lists as close as possible to the destination because a standard access list only uses source addresses. If the list is placed too close to the source, it can block the flow of packets to other ports.

Statement Placement

Since IP includes ICMP, TCP, and UDP, place more specific entries in an access list before less specific entries to prevent one statement ahead of another from negating the effect of a statement appearing later in the list.

List Application

Apply an access list using an `access-group` command. Remember, until the access list is applied to an interface, no filtering will occur.

Filtering Direction

The filtering direction defines whether inbound or outbound packets are examined. Always double check the filtering direction, since it defines which packets are examined.

Router-Generated Packets

Packets generated by a router, such as routing table updates, are not operated on by an outbound access list. Thus, you can only control router table updates and other router-generated packets using inbound access lists. Now that we understand the operation and utilization of Cisco IP access lists, lets look at the more powerful features incorporated into access lists. Collectively, these features are referred to as enhanced access lists.

Enhanced Access Lists

This section examines the operation and utilization of relatively new access-list features. Since Cisco refers to each feature as new access lists, we will do so as well. However, they are actually not separate access lists but features incorporated into traditional access lists that extend their capability. Each of these features is a relatively recent update to the Cisco Internetwork Operating System (IOS). The four additions examined in this section are: dynamic access lists, reflexive access lists, time-based access lists, and TCP intercept. In actuality, these additions provide additional capabilities, not new types of access lists.

Dynamic Access Lists

Dynamic access lists, the first new feature added to Cisco's IOS, are exactly what you would think; they are access lists that create dynamic entries. Traditional standard and extended access lists cannot create dynamic access-list entries. Once an entry is placed in a traditional access list, it remains there until you delete it manually. With dynamic access lists, you can create specific, temporary openings in an access list in response to a user authentication procedure.

Users open a telnet session to the router to authenticate themselves, normally by providing a userid and password. The router can also be configured to request only a password, but this is not recommended. Once the user is authenticated, the router closes the telnet session and places a dynamic entry in an access list to permit packets with a source IP address of the authenticating user's workstation. This allows you to configure an access list at a security perimeter that would only allow inbound packets from a workstation after the user on that workstation has completed the user authentication phase.

The benefits of this feature are obvious. With traditional access lists, if users on the untrusted side of a router needed access to internal resources, it would be necessary to open up permanent holes in your access list to allow packets from those users' workstations to enter the trusted network. By opening up permanent holes in your access lists, you create the opportunity for an attacker to send packets through your security perimeter to your inside network at any time. You can mitigate this problem to a certain degree by allowing inbound access only to certain, trusted source IP addresses. However, suppose the users you want to allow access don't have static IP addresses? This would be the case, for example, if the users were dialed up to an *Internet service provider* (ISP). Typically, home users get a different IP address every time they dial their ISP, so it is exceedingly difficult to create access-list entries that permit packets from these users without simultaneously creating large holes in your security perimeter that an attacker could exploit. In this situation, the use of dynamic access lists provides a significantly higher degree of security than using traditional IP access lists.

Note that even if you could limit the entries in a traditional extended access list to trusted source IP addresses, these entries could be exploited by an attacker using IP spoofing.

IP spoofing refers to the procedure whereby an attacker will change the source IP address of packets sent from their machine to that of an IP address they believe is trusted by the network they are attempting to breach. This danger is always present. It is nearly impossible to determine if the packets which arrive at your security perimeter are from the "real" host they claim to be from. Dynamic access lists only mitigate this problem by creating openings that are very temporary, lowering the probability that an attacker would be able to determine the trusted source IP addresses in time to exploit the openings.

Overview

As stated earlier, dynamic access lists are a new type of access list. However, the syntax of dynamic access lists is very similar to that of traditional access lists. The syntax of a dynamic access-list entry is shown here:

```
access-list <access-list number> dynamic <name> [timeout n]
[permit!deny] <protocol> any <destination IP> <destination mask>
```

The first entry, `<access-list number>`, is the same format as for a traditional extended access list, that is, a number between 100 and 199. The second parameter, <name>, is an alphanumeric string that designates the name of the dynamic access list. The [timeout] parameter is optional. If specified, it designates an absolute time-out for dynamic entries. The <protocol> parameter can be any of the traditional TCP/IP protocols such as IP, TCP, UDP, and ICMP. The source IP address is always replaced by the IP address of the authenticating host, so you should use the keyword any for the source IP address of your dynamic entries. The destination IP and mask are the same format as for traditional extended access lists.

It is safest to specify a single subnet for the destination IP address if possible or even to a specific host. You cannot specify more than one dynamic access-list entry per access list, so it is typical to specify IP or TCP as the protocol. In actuality, you can specify more than one entry, but additional dynamic entries do not create additional dynamic openings, so specifying multiple dynamic entries is meaningless. Interested readers are encouraged to experiment to see what happens when you place multiple dynamic entries in an access list. The router will accept the commands, but if you examine the results of show access-list, you will see interesting results as indicated by the following example:

```
access-list 100 permit tcp any host 160.50.1.1 eq telnet
access-list 100 dynamic test permit tcp any any
access-list 100 dynamic test permit udp any any
!
!
Router# show access-list
Extended IP access list 100
    permit tcp any host 160.50.1.1 eq telnet (332 matches)
    Dynamic test permit tcp any any
        permit tcp host 10.1.1.50 any idle-time 5 min.
    Dynamic test permit udp any any
        permit tcp host 10.1.1.50 any idle-time 5 min.
```

Pay close attention to the entries in bold.

As you can see, the dynamic access-list entry is part of a traditional extended access list. You would add the dynamic access-list entry in the desired place in your access list, specify the remaining traditional access-list entries, and then apply the access list to an interface. Typically, your dynamic access-list entry will appear toward the beginning of your access list, typically after any antispoofing entries. You will need, as a minimum, to allow incoming telnet to the router so the user authentication procedure can occur. If you do not allow incoming telnet connections, users will not be able to create dynamic entries in your access list. It is not necessary to create the telnet entry prior to the dynamic entry. As long as you explicitly allow inbound telnet connections to the router, the dynamic entries will be created appropriately.

In addition to creating a dynamic access-list entry, one additional step is needed in order to create dynamic entries. The autocommand parameter must be added beneath the vty lines as indicated here:

```
Line vty 0 2
  login local
  autocommand access-enable host timeout 5
```

Notice the use of the host parameter when using autocommand. Without the host parameter, the dynamic entries would not substitute the source IP address of the authenticating host in our dynamic entries and any host will be allowed through our dynamic entries, eliminating most of the reason for using dynamic access lists in the first place. It is very important that you not forget the host parameter when configuring the autocommand entry.

The time-out value is optional and specifies an idle time-out. It is recommended that either the absolute or idle timer value be configured, otherwise the dynamic entries will not be removed until the router is rebooted. If the absolute and idle timers are both used, the idle timer should be less than the absolute timer.

One additional point: if additional steps are not taken, all incoming telnet sessions will be treated by the router as attempts to open dynamic access-list entries. Since the telnet session is closed immediately after authentication, administrators would not be able to manage their routers via telnet. The way around this is to specify the rotary 1 command beneath some of the vty ports. The " command enables normal telnet access to the router on port 3001. An administrator would need to specify the use of port 3001 when attempting to access the router via a telnet session. The administrator would specify the port number immediately after the destination IP address:

```
telnet 160.100.1.1 3001
```

The commands to enable this feature are

```
Line vty 3 4
  Login local
  Rotary 1
```

Notice that only vty lines 3 and 4 are specified and that the autocommand does not appear. Make sure that your vty lines look like this before you save your configuration. If your vty lines are not configured properly, you could completely disable the ability to telnet to the router for management purposes. If the router is remote and you didn't have remote access via the auxiliary port, you could find yourself on a long road trip to visit your router. As a side note, it's always a good idea to test your access lists before saving new additions to your configuration. This way, if your access lists do not perform as expected and you accidentally lock yourself out of your own router, a simple reboot is all that is necessary.

Here is a complete sample configuration for reference; only relevant parts of the configuration are shown:

```
Username test password cisco
!
interface serial0
  description connection to the Internet
  ip address 160.50.1.1 255.255.255.0
  ip access-group 100 in
!
access-list 100 permit tcp any host 160.50.1.1 eq telnet
access-list 100 dynamic test 10 permit ip any any
!
line vty 0 2
  login local
  autocommand access-enable host timeout 5
line vty 3 4
  login local
  rotary 1
```

Notice that we have created the username test in the router configuration and refer to it in the second access-list command. You could specify only the password on the vty lines and not use a username, but then it is very easy for an intruder to run a password-guessing program against your router, trying successive passwords from a dictionary or password list. Unless you have chosen an exceptionally good password, the chances that an attacker would ultimately obtain the correct password are high. It also makes it impossible to track individual user actions, so you would not even know if an attacker had breached your security perimeter because you could not track an individual user's actions. Using only a password for authentication is not recommended.

Usage Guidelines

Dynamic access lists are a significant enhancement to IP extended access lists. Additional security concerns result from this increased functionality. Although dynamic access lists can restrict incoming access based on an external user's ability to provide a userid and password, this information is passed from the user's workstation to the router in clear text. This means that if anyone were to intercept the packets in transition from the user's workstation to the router by using a packet-sniffing program, he or she could read the username and password combination and duplicate it later to obtain access to your internal resources. This is, obviously, a potentially huge security risk. You would have no way of knowing that a user's authentication information had been captured by an attacker. The attacker could use the captured user information for a long period of time, perhaps indefinitely, before being noticed.

It may seem unlikely that this could happen, however, it is very common for an ISP server to be compromised by an attacker and for that attacker to place a packet-sniffing program on the compromised machine. The attacker then collects a large number of packets and searches for keywords like `userid` and `password`. For example, Kevin Mitnick, perhaps the world's most infamous hacker, used this technique. The bottom line is that although there is an authentication process for external users to gain access, you should be very careful when deploying dynamic access lists. Here are a few tips to follow when configuring dynamic access lists:

- Do not assign a name to a dynamic access list that you used with another access list (for example, a named access list).

- Define at least the idle time-out or the absolute time-out. If both are defined, the idle time-out should be less than the absolute time-out.

- Limit, if possible, the dynamic access-list entries to particular protocols and particular destination IP addresses.

- Change user passwords frequently. A maximum lifetime of 30 days is recommended; a shorter period is better if your environment permits it.

- Deploy dynamic access lists in conjunction with time-based access lists. This will limit the times that users are allowed to create dynamic entries and could alert you if someone has captured userid and password information. (For example, if you notice repeated attempted logins for a certain user during unauthorized access hours. Only authorized users would be aware of the hours that access is permitted.)

- Deploy logging to either the router's buffer or, preferably, to a separate syslog server. Review these logs at least weekly for suspicious activity. What counts as suspicious activity will vary, so you'll have to establish a baseline for what the normal network activity is for your particular site.

Now that we understand dynamic access lists and their capabilities, let's look at another relatively new feature of access list—reflexive access lists.

Reflexive Access Lists

One of the limitations that is associated with the use of the keyword `established` in an extended IP access list is that it is only applicable to TCP. If you wish to control other upper-layer protocols, such as UDP and ICMP, you have to either permit all incoming traffic or define a large number of permissible source/destination host/port addresses. Besides being a very tedious and time-consuming task, the resulting access list could conceivably require more memory than available on your router. Perhaps recognizing this problem, Cisco introduced reflexive access lists in IOS version 11.3.

Overview

A *reflexive access list* creates a dynamic, temporary opening in an access list. That opening results in the creation of a mirror image or reflected entry in an existing access list, hence the name of this list. The opening is triggered when a new IP traffic session is initiated from inside the network to an external network. The temporary opening is always a `permit` entry and specifies the same protocol as the original outbound packet. The opening also swaps source and destination IP addresses and upper-layer port numbers and exists until either the session initiated on the trusted network is closed or an idle time-out value is reached.

Tasks for Creating a Reflexive Access List

Four general tasks are associated with the creation of a reflexive access list. First, you create an extended named access list. In an IP environment you would use the following command format:

```
ip access-list extended <name>
```

where `<name>` is the name of the access list.

Next, you create one or more `permit` entries to establish reflected openings. Since a reflexive access list is applied to outbound traffic, it results in temporary openings appearing in an inbound access list. When defining `permit` statements for your outbound access list, you use the following statement format:

```
permit protocol any any reflect name [timeout seconds]
```

You can use the keyword `timeout` to assign a time-out period to each specific reflexive entry created in the inbound direction. If you elect not to use this option, a default time-out of 300 s is used for the opening. You can also elect to place a global time-out on all reflexive statements. To do so you use the following global command:

```
ip reflexive-list timeout value
```

where `value` is the global time-out value in seconds.

A third task is the creation of an access list for inbound filtering into which dynamic reflexive entries would be added. The following command concludes the operation:

```
evaluate name
```

where `name` is the name of the access list and causes packets to be evaluated by reflexive entries.

The following example illustrates the creation of a reflexive access list where the reflected openings are limited to 180 s of idle time. In the following statements note that the three `deny` statements in the extended access list named inbound are conventional statements that are not reflected. Also note that those statements are commonly referred to as antispoofing entries. That is, many times hackers use RFC 1918 private network IP addresses in an attempt to preclude network operators from identifying the source address of an attack.

```
!
ip reflexive-list timeout 180
!
ip access-list extended outbound
 permit tcp any any reflect my_session
 permit udp any any reflect my_session
 permit icmp any any reflect my_session
!
ip access-list extended inbound
 deny ip 10.0.0.0 0.255.255.255 any
 deny ip 172.16.0.0 0.31.255.255 any
 deny ip 192.168.0.0 0.0.255.255 any
 evaluate my_session
```

Before moving on, note that while reflexive access lists extend considerably the capability of packet filtering, they are limited to single-channel connections. Thus applications, such as FTP, that use multiple port numbers or channels cannot be supported by reflexive access lists. However, a special release of IOS initially referred to as the *firewall feature set* (FFS) introduced support for dynamic openings in access lists for multichannel applications. Now referred to as *context-based access control* (CBAC) in IOS release 12.0, CBAC also adds Java blocking, denial-of-service prevention, and detection, real-time alerts, and audit trails. (CBAC is covered in detail in *Cisco® Access Lists Field Guide*, the first volume in this series.)

Time-Based Access Lists

Until IOS version 12.0, no easy method existed for an administrator to establish different security policies based on the time of day or date. Although an administrator could create multiple access lists and apply them at different times, doing so could be a complex process. In addition, do you really want to stay in the office until 6 p.m. on a Friday to implement a new security policy? In IOS version 12.0 time-based access lists permit implementation of different policies based on time.

Creation Steps

In the wonderful world of IP time-based access lists is a relatively easy two-step process. First, you define a time range. Next, you refer to the time range in an access-list entry. You can specify a time range by using a time-range statement whose format is shown here:

```
time-range time-range-name
```

where time-range-name is the name you assign to the time range.

Once this is accomplished, you can specify a time range in one of two ways. You can use an absolute statement or a periodic statement, and the format of each is shown here:

```
absolute [start time date] [end time date]
periodic days-of-the-week hh:mm to [days-of-the-week] hh:mm
```

The time parameter is entered in the format hh:mm where hours (hh) is expressed in a 24-h format. You can list the days of the week separated by spaces or use the keywords daily or weekend. Once the time range is created, you can refer to it through the optional keyword time-range in a traditional access-list entry. The following example illustrates the creation of a time-based access list which restricts Web access to Monday through Friday from 8 a.m. to 5 p.m.

```
time-range allow-http
 Periodic weekdays 8:00 to 17:00
 !
access-list 101 permit tcp any any eq 80 time-range allow-http
```

TCP Intercept

In concluding our examination of enhancements to access lists let's now look at TCP intercept. This feature was added in IOS version 11.3 to alleviate a special type of denial-of-service attack referred to as SYN flooding.

TCP's Three-Way Handshake

Under TCP's three-way handshake, the first packet in a session has the SYN bit sent. The recipient of this initial packet requesting a service, such as HTTP, responds with a packet in which the SYN and ACK bits are set and waits for an ACK from the originator of the session. If the originator of the request fails to respond, the host times out the connection. However, while the host is waiting for the conclusion of the three-way handshake, the half-open connection consumes resources.

Suppose an unscrupulous person modifies software to transmit tens of thousands of packets with their SYN bit set, using forged IP source addresses. The result would be that the attacked host would never receive a response to its request to complete each three-way handshake. Thus, its resources are consumed as it times out each session only to be faced with a new flood of additional bogus packets with their SYN bit set. As host resources are consumed, its usefulness decreases to a point where little or no useful work occurs. Since this method of attack is popular, TCP intercept was added to limit half-open connections flowing through a router.

Feature Overview

The TCP intercept feature works by intercepting and validating TCP connection requests. TCI intercept can operate in one of two modes: intercept or watch. When in intercept mode, the router intercepts inbound TCP synchronization requests and establishes a connection with the client on behalf of the server and with the server on behalf of the client, in effect functioning as a proxy agent. If both connections are successful the router will merge them. To prevent router resources from being fully consumed by a SYN attack the router has aggressive thresholds and automatically deletes connections until the number of half-open connections falls below a particular threshold.

The second mode of operation of TCP intercept is watch mode. Under watch mode, the router passively monitors half-open connections and actively closes connections on the server after a configurable length of time.

Enabling TCP intercept is a two-step process. First, you configure either a standard or extended IP access list, permitting the destination address you wish to protect. Once this is accomplished, you enable TCP intercept using the following statement:

```
ip tcp intercept list list#
```

Since the default mode of operation of TCP intercept is intercept mode, a third step may be required to set the mode. To do so you would use the following command:

```
ip tcp intercept mode {intercept | watch}
```

As previously mentioned, TCP intercept includes aggressive thresholds to prevent router resources from being adversely consumed by a SYN attack. Four thresholds are maintained by routers that you can adjust. Those thresholds are set using the following TCP intercept commands, with the default value indicated for each setting:

```
ip tcp intercept max-incomplete low number 90
ip tcp intercept max-incomplete high number 1100
ip tcp intercept one-minute low number 900
ip tcp intercept one-minute high number 1100
```

To illustrate the use of TCP intercept assume you wish to protect the host 198.78.46.8. To do so while selecting default thresholds requires the following access-list statements:

```
ip tcp intercept list 107
access-list 107 permit tcp any host 198.78.46.8
```

As indicated in this chapter, the use of access lists is a valuable feature to control the flow of packets through your network. By carefully configuring your router and taking advantage of relatively recent additions to access-list features, you can satisfy a variety of security-related organizational requirements.

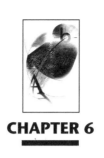

CHAPTER 6

IP Routing Protocols

his chapter examines several different routing protocols that are available for use with TCP/IP. We begin by discussing the functions a routing protocol performs and why they are useful in modern internetworks. We discuss how routing information is collected by a Cisco router and how to view and interpret the contents of the routing table. Additionally, we discuss load sharing, static routing, and the use of floating static routes.

Once we understand the basic routing process, we discuss the different types of routing protocols used in IP networks: distance vector and link state. Then we examine several specific routing protocols, including RIP version 1 and 2, interior gateway routing protocol (IGRP), enhanced interior gateway routing protocol (EIGRP), and open shortest path first (OSPF). After discussing each of these routing protocols, this chapter concludes with a discussion of route redistribution and filtering.

Overview

What is a routing protocol, and why is one needed? Answering this question is tantamount to understanding all the complexities associated with the many IP routing protocols found in modern internetworks. It is a fair question, and one we attempt to answer in this section. We begin our answer by using an analogy. Picture in your mind your neighborhood, and think of all of the houses and the streets that join them together. Now imagine that there are no maps or street signs and the only way anyone knows how to get from one street to another is by asking a neighbor which streets they are connected to. In turn, each neighbor asks another neighbor what street they are connected to and so on and so on. If the residents of each house communicate with one another and inform each of their neighbors which streets they are connected to, eventually every resident will learn the location of all of the streets in their neighborhood, their names, and how to reach them. This assumes, of course, that each neighbor knows the names of the connecting streets. For the purposes of this analogy we assume this to be the case.

For example, you might receive information from your neighbor that to get to Oak Street, you must go down five houses, make a left, go four more houses, and make a right. Your neighbor knows this information because a neighbor told them, whose neighbor told them, and so on and so forth. This all seems very straightforward and simple, and given a small neighborhood, it probably would be. However, potential problems exist even in this simple scenario. What if a neighbor isn't home? How do we establish contact with that neighbor? How often do we talk to our neighbors, and do we talk to them even if we have no new information to report? If I have four neighbors, do I have to talk individually to each of them or can I just post the information on my mailbox so each of them can read it at once? How do I know that the information my neighbor is giving me is correct? How do my neighbors know that the information they received is accurate?

The list of possible things that could go wrong is nearly endless. In order to overcome most of these difficulties, we would need to have a neighborhood meeting at which everyone would agree on procedures and policies, so that a resident could have a certain degree of assurance that the information received is accurate and timely. These specifications could be called a *protocol*. In fact, since the specifications tell a resident the route to a street, it could even be called a *routing protocol*. This simple analogy illustrates the reason why routing protocols exist and the motivation for studying and learning about the complexities of modern IP routing protocols.

This is all well and good, you might say, but it seems a little unnecessary. The streets in my neighborhood don't change often enough for all of this complexity, you might say. All that I really need is to be told once how to reach a street and I'll remember that information and keep using it. This is a valid point. In fact, as we'll see later, this is exactly what *static routing* is all about. When you create a static route, you simply tell the router "go to this next hop router for this address." It's a little like saying go to the fifth house and make a right to get to Elm Street and never getting any new information. Static routing has the great benefit that once it's configured, you never have to worry about configuring your routing again, assuming nothing changes in your network. It also has the great downfall that when things change in the neighborhood or network, the new information must be learned and acted on without benefit of protocols or procedures.

For simple networks, like a small five-router lab, static routing is fine and perhaps even desirable. However, imagine that you live in a neighborhood that is constantly undergoing new construction where new streets are added, old streets are changed, and street names are changed. Going through the process of discovering the correct information and updating your street routing information can become a significant burden. Now imagine that you live in a large city like New York and that street information is constantly undergoing changes and you begin to see that the overhead associated with establishing a routing protocol in advance and maintaining it outweighs the burden of constantly manually updating your information.

In a sense this problem has been experienced by anyone who has ever tried to call someone and gotten a wrong number. The static information the caller had is no longer valid. Typically, the protocol is to call information and request the new number. However, assume for a moment that the information number didn't exist, now what would you do? It hardly seems acceptable to wait for the next directory assistance book to be issued since they are issued so infrequently. Perhaps if the telephone company issued weekly updates containing only changes? In fact, this process is exactly what is done at large companies. A yearly telephone book is issued, and weekly updates are issued with changes. If people changed homes as frequently as they changed jobs, this routing protocol might have to be adopted nationwide.

From this simple introduction, the motivation for the creation and implementation of routing protocols should be clear. It should also be clear that in internetworks consisting of thousands of routers and tens of thousands of networks, procedures for maintaining this information can be complex. However, while the intricacies of some routing protocols are indeed complex, the basic principles of the protocols are not. Our goal in the rest of this chapter is to provide a familiarity with the different types of routing protocols used in modern internetworks and a solid understanding of the principles associated with each.

IP Path Determination

We begin our discussion of routing protocols by examining exactly how a router determines a path to a network. To facilitate our discussion, we will use Figure 6-1, a simple five-router network. Using this simple diagram, we can discuss many of the complex topics associated with IP routing protocols. Looking at Figure 6-1, we can see that each router, except R5, is connected to three links. Two of the three links connect to other routers and one link does not. If we assume that no routing protocol or static

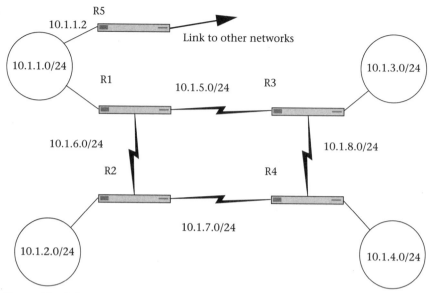

Figure 6-1 A five-router network.

routes have been configured, it should be obvious that each router can only be aware of the networks to which it is directly connected. We can see that by issuing the show ip route command on each router. A sample output of this command from router R1 is shown in Figure 6-2.

We can see that the router has only learned about the subnets to which it is directly connected. The C in the far left-hand column indicates that each subnet was learned by the router being directly connected to it. An

Figure 6-2 Output from a show ip route command issued on router R1.

```
r1#show ip route
Codes: C - connected, S - static, I - IGRP, R - RIP, M - mobile, B - BGP
       D - EIGRP, EX - EIGRP external, O - OSPF, IA - OSPF inter area
       N1 - OSPF NSSA external type 1, N2 - OSPF NSSA external type 2
       E1 - OSPF external type 1, E2 - OSPF external type 2, E - EGP
       i - IS-IS, L1 - IS-IS level-1, L2 - IS-IS level-2, ia - IS-IS inter area
       * - candidate default, U - per-user static route, o - ODR
       P - periodic downloaded static route
Gateway of last resort is not set
     10.0.0.0/24 is subnetted, 3 subnets
C       10.1.1.0 is directly connected, Ethernet0/0
C       10.1.6.0 is directly connected, Serial0/0
C       10.1.5.0 is directly connected, Serial0/1
r1#
```

important point to note here is that all networks are considered to have been "learned" by the router, even those directly connected. This has important consequences for distance vector routing protocols that we will see later. We discuss the specifics of each field on the routing table later in this chapter, but for now the information in Figure 6-2 should be fairly obvious. The router has learned three subnets, and they are directly connected through three different interfaces.

Another important point about routes that appears in the routing table is that even directly connected routes do not appear if the interface connected to that network is down. In Figure 6-2, all three interfaces were up/up, so all appeared in the routing table. Figure 6-3 illustrates the output from show ip route after unplugging the Ethernet0/0 interface.

Notice that the route for subnet 10.1.1.0 no longer appears in the routing table. The interface on which it was connected is down and the router has flushed it from the routing table. In fact, the router will not install a route in the routing table if the interface the router would reach that network on is down. For example, we can attempt to create a static route on R1 by using the following command:

```
ip route 192.168.1.0 255.255.255.0 10.1.1.2
```

We examine each of the parameters associated with the ip route command in this section, but this example is straightforward. It tells the router that to reach network 192.168.1.0/24, send packets to 10.1.1.2. Recall from our earlier analogy, this is like telling your neighbor to reach

Figure 6-3   Output from a show ip route command issued on router R1 after unplugging Ethernet0/0.

```
r1#
00:31:43: %LINEPROTO-5-UPDOWN: Line protocol on Interface Ethernet0/0,
changed s
tate to down
r1#show ip route
Codes: C - connected, S - static, I - IGRP, R - RIP, M - mobile, B - BGP
       D - EIGRP, EX - EIGRP external, O - OSPF, IA - OSPF inter area
       N1 - OSPF NSSA external type 1, N2 - OSPF NSSA external type 2
       E1 - OSPF external type 1, E2 - OSPF external type 2, E - EGP
       i - IS-IS, L1 - IS-IS level-1, L2 - IS-IS level-2, ia - IS-IS inter
area
       * - candidate default, U - per-user static route, o - ODR
       P - periodic downloaded static route
Gateway of last resort is not set
10.0.0.0/24 is subnetted, 2 subnets
C    10.1.6.0 is directly connected, Serial0/0
C    10.1.5.0 is directly connected, Serial0/1
r1#
```

Figure 6-4 Output from a `show ip route` command issued on router R1 after configuring a static route pointing 192.168.1.0/24 to 10.1.1.2.

```
r1#conf t
Enter configuration commands, one per line. End with CNTL/Z.
r1(config)#ip route 192.168.1.0 255.255.255.0 10.1.1.2
r1(config)#
r1#sho
00:42:51: %SYS-5-CONFIG_I: Configured from console by consolew ip
r1#show ip route
Codes: C - connected, S - static, I - IGRP, R - RIP, M - mobile, B - BGP
       D - EIGRP, EX - EIGRP external, O - OSPF, IA - OSPF inter area
       N1 - OSPF NSSA external type 1, N2 - OSPF NSSA external type 2
       E1 - OSPF external type 1, E2 - OSPF external type 2, E - EGP
       i - IS-IS, L1 - IS-IS level-1, L2 - IS-IS level-2, ia - IS-IS inter area
       * - candidate default, U - per-user static route, o - ODR
       P - periodic downloaded static route
Gateway of last resort is not set
10.0.0.0/24 is subnetted, 1 subnets
C     10.1.6.0 is directly connected, Serial0/0
C     10.1.5.0 is directly connected, Serial0/1
r1#
```

Oak Street, go down four houses and make a left and never giving them any additional updates. We might expect that network 192.168.1.0/24 would appear in our routing table. However, as you can see in Figure 6-4, it does not since our Ethernet0/0 interface is down and that is the interface through which the next hop, 10.1.1.2, would be reached.

A further point of interest in Figure 6-4 is the line in bold type. Often when configuring a router via its console connection, messages will pop up on the screen informing you of a configuration change. While these messages can be useful, they can also be annoying if they pop up as you are trying to type additional commands. If this happens, stop typing and enter the key sequence <CTL>+R (that is, press the <CTL> key and the R key at the same time) and the line you were typing will be repasted to the command line. In our case, we had entered `sho` when the pop-up messages appeared and had entered `w ip` before we stopped typing and entered the <CTL>+R key sequence. This key sequence repasted `show ip` to the next line and we continued typing `route` to complete the command. This little trick can save some frustration, especially if you're not a fast typist.

Entering Static Routes

We have seen one simple example of how to configure a static route. This section discusses all of the options available for configuring static routes

Figure 6-5 Output from a `show ip route` command issued on router R1 after configuring a static route pointing 192.168.1.0/24 to 10.1.1.2 and bringing Ethernet0/0 active.

```
r1#sh ip ro
Gateway of last resort is not set
10.0.0.0/24 is subnetted, 2 subnets
C    10.1.1.0 is directly connected, Etherne0/0
C    10.1.5.0 is directly connected, Serial0/0
C    10.1.6.0 is directly connected, Serial0/1
S  192.168.1.0/24 [1/0] via 10.1.1.2
r1#
```

and how they can prove useful even in networks where a routing protocol is in use. We begin by bringing back our Ethernet0/0 interface on router R1 to active. We can now issue a `show ip route` command and the static route for network 192.168.1.0/24 which was entered earlier is now in our routing table (see Figure 6-5).

NOTE
From this point forward, we abbreviate all show commands as `sh`. In general, you can usually abbreviate a command with the first two or three letters. If the router cannot determine your command , it will report ambiguous command. You can then type the first two or three letters followed by ? and the router will show you the commands available to complete the characters entered. The ? is the contex-sensitive help, and is one of the most powerful features of the Cisco IOS.

Note that we have removed the initial lines of the output in the interest of conserving space and avoiding redundancy and can now see that our static route to network 192.168.1.0/24 is in the routing table. Also, we now see a few new fields describing the static route that we did not see with our directly connected routes. The description of each of these fields is described in Figure 6-6.

Determining the Best Match

Several key points can be seen in Figure 6-6. A router may receive identical routes from different sources, especially if it is running multiple routing protocols. The router uses the *administrative distance* (AD) to determine which of the identical routes it should use. The AD of some

Figure 6-6 Description of the fields in a Cisco routing table.

```
1     2        3 4      5
S  192.168.1.0/24 [1/0] via 10.1.1.2
```

Field 1. Indicates the method by which the route was learned. Common indicators are C for connected, S for static, R for RIP, and I for IGRP.

Field 2. Indicates the network or subnet for this routing entry. The number after the / indicates how many bits are in the mask. In this example, the mask is 255.255.255.0, or 24 bits. A route that matches more bits is always preferred. For example, a route matching 25 bits of the address would be preferred over a route matching 24 bits of the address, regardless of the administrative distance or the metric (see Field 3).

Field 3. Indicates the administrative distance (AD) of a route. The AD is a weight that the router uses to prioritize identical routes received from different sources. For example, a connected route has an AD of 0 and a RIP route has an AD of 120. A lower AD is preferred, so the connected route would be preferred over the RIP-learned route. Connected routes always have an AD of 0 and this cannot be altered. Static routes pointing to an interface are listed as connected in the routing table, but will have an AD of 1, not 0. Static routes pointing to a next hop IP address will also have an AD of 1 unless otherwise configured.

Field 4. Indicates the metric of the route. The metric value will vary depending on the means by which the route was learned. RIP-learned routes will use a different metric than IGRP-learned routes and it is difficult to compare the metrics of the two routing protocols. The metric is used as a method to prefer one route over another if the routes match the same number of address bits and the AD is the same. Static routes always have a metric of 0.

Field 5. Indicates the next hop IP address to send packets for this destination. For directly connected routes, this field will indicate the interface to forward the packets to.

routing protocols is preferred over the AD of others. This is especially important to understand when you are redistributing routes learned from one routing protocol into another routing protocol. Once the routes can be seen in the new routing protocol, the AD will be changed to the AD of the new routing protocol, not the originating routing protocol. If a route learned via routing information protocol (RIP) is redistributed into OSPF, routers that learn the route via OSPF list the AD of that route as 110 (the default AD of OSPF), not 120 (the default AD of RIP).

If identical routes are learned using methods with the same AD, for instance, two routes learned using RIP, the route with the lowest metric is preferred. As seen in Figure 6-6, different routing protocols use different metrics. For example, RIP uses hop count while OSPF uses a dimensionless value called cost. We examine the metrics used by each routing protocol later in this chapter. For now, it is only important to understand that metrics for routes can only really be compared when the routes are learned through the same routing protocol. It doesn't make much sense to compare RIP metrics with OSPF metrics; this is why the AD is important.

The Longest Match Rule

A final critical point is that regardless of the AD or metric of a route, a longer matching route is always preferred. For example, a route to subnet 165.10.1.0/25 would always be preferred over a route to subnet 165.10.1.0/24. For example, 25 bits is a longer match than 24 bits. This rule is called the *longest match rule*, and it is impossible to fully understand routing in a Cisco network without understanding this concept. A simple example should suffice to drive this point home. Recall from Figure 6-1 that router R1 is directly connected to subnet 10.1.1.0/24. What happens if we configure a static route for 10.1.1.0/25? 10.1.1.0/25 is a subnet of 10.1.1.0/24 because we are matching 25 bits of the IP address instead of 24 bits. The 25 bits of matching equates to a subnet mask of 255.255.255.128. The 24 bits of matching equates to a subnet mask of 255.255.255.0, so 255.255.255.128 is obviously a longer matching mask. Figure 6-7 illustrates this scenario.

Notice that even though 10.1.1.0/24 is a directly connected route, the new route is in the routing table because 10.1.1.0/25 is a more specific route than 10.1.1.0/24. If we issue a debug ip packet command and attempt to

Figure 6-7   Illustration of the longest match rule.

```
r1#conf t
Enter configuration commands, one per line. End with CNTL/Z.
r1(config)# ip route 10.1.1.0 255.255.255.128 serial 0/0
r1(config)#
r1#
r1#sh ip ro
Gateway of last resort is not set
10.0.0.0/8 is variably subnetted, 3 subnets, 2 masks
S    10.1.1.0/25 is directly connected, Serial0/0
C    10.1.1.0/24 is directly connected, Ethernet0/0
C    10.1.5.0/24 is directly connected, Serial0/0
C    10.1.6.0/24 is directly connected, Serial0/1
r1#
```

Figure 6-8 Illustration of the debug ip packet command showing the use of the longest matching route.

```
r1#ping 10.1.1.2
Type escape sequence to abort.
Sending 5, 100-byte ICMP Echos to 10.1.1.2, timeout is 2 seconds:
02:05:03: IP: s=10.1.5.1 (local), d=10.1.1.2 (Serial0/0), len 100, sending
02:05:05: IP: s=10.1.5.1 (local), d=10.1.1.2 (Serial0/0), len 100, sending
02:05:07: IP: s=10.1.5.1 (local), d=10.1.1.2 (Serial0/0), len 100, sending
02:05:09: IP: s=10.1.5.1 (local), d=10.1.1.2 (Serial0/0), len 100, sending
02:05:11: IP: s=10.1.5.1 (local), d=10.1.1.2 (Serial0/0), len 100, sending
```

ping an address in the 10.1.1.0/25 range, 10.1.1.1 through 10.1.1.127, the router attempts to use the serial 0/0 interface (see Figure 6-8). This is because the 25-bit match for the route out that interface is a longer match than the 24-bit match out the directly connected Ethernet0/0.

Notice that the router is sending packets out the serial0/0 interface and not the Ethernet0/0 interface. The longest match rule overrides all other considerations such as the AD and the metric. The AD of the connected route is 0, the best value possible, but the longer matching route prevails even though its AD is higher. It is critical that you understand the longest match rule when examining entries in the routing table.

Using the Default Route

In most cases, the longest matching rule always applies. The only exception to this rule is when classful routing is used. We examine the exception of classful routing in the next section, after examining the use of default routes. To see why default routes are useful, we need to first examine how a router performs lookups in the routing table. When a router needs to forward a packet, it first tries to find an exact match in the routing table. For example, if the destination is 10.1.1.2, the router looks for a 10.1.1.2 in the routing table. If it cannot find an entry for 10.1.1.2, it looks for the next closest match, such as 10.1.1.0/25, 10.1.0.0/16, 10.1.0.0/15, etc. If no match exists for the subnet or network for the destination, the route would use a default route.

A default route is an indicator to a router where it should send packets for which it has no explicit destination. If the router cannot find a match for a destination and a default route has been configured, it forwards the packets to the IP address identified as its default route. In our earlier figures, note that the output from sh ip route always displays gateway of last resort not set. A gateway of last resort is another term for a default route. The router displays this information if no default route has been configured. You can configure a default route by entering a default to the 0.0.0.0/0 network. The 0.0.0.0 network is a numeric way of referring to the default route.

```
ip route 0.0.0.0 0.0.0.0 10.1.1.2
```

Entering this command on router R1 sets the gateway of last resort and is the location the router forwards packets to if it has no more specific match. Figure 6-9 illustrates the output from debug ip packet when trying to ping 174.3.1.1 before and after the default route has been configured.

Notice that the debug command shows unroutable before the default route is configured, indicating it could not find a match in the routing table for the destination 174.3.1.1. After configuring the default route, the router simply forwards any packets for which it does not have a specific route to next hop 10.1.1.2.

Figure 6-9 Illustration of the debug ip packet command when used with a default route.

```
r1#debug ip pack
IP packet debugging is on
r1#ping 174.3.1.1

Type escape sequence to abort.
Sending 5, 100-byte ICMP Echos to 174.3.1.1, timeout is 2 seconds:

02:27:20: IP: s=10.1.1.1 (local), d=174.3.1.1, len 100, unroutable.
02:27:22: IP: s=10.1.1.1 (local), d=174.3.1.1, len 100, unroutable.
02:27:24: IP: s=10.1.1.1 (local), d=174.3.1.1, len 100, unroutable.
02:27:26: IP: s=10.1.1.1 (local), d=174.3.1.1, len 100, unroutable.
02:27:28: IP: s=10.1.1.1 (local), d=174.3.1.1, len 100, unroutable.
Success rate is 0 percent (0/5)
r1#conf t
Enter configuration commands, one per line. End with CNTL/Z.
r1(config)#ip route 0.0.0.0 0.0.0.0 10.1.1.2
r1(config)#
r1#
02:27:42: %SYS-5-CONFIG_I: Configured from console by console
r1#ping 174.3.1.1

Type escape sequence to abort.
Sending 5, 100-byte ICMP Echos to 174.3.1.1, timeout is 2 seconds:

02:27:51: IP: s=10.1.5.1 (local), d=174.3.1.1 (Serial0/0), len 100, sending
02:27:53: IP: s=10.1.5.1 (local), d=174.3.1.1 (Serial0/0), len 100, sending
02:27:55: IP: s=10.1.5.1 (local), d=174.3.1.1 (Serial0/0), len 100, sending
02:27:57: IP: s=10.1.5.1 (local), d=174.3.1.1 (Serial0/0), len 100, sending
02:27:59: IP: s=10.1.5.1 (local), d=174.3.1.1 (Serial0/0), len 100, sending
```

Classless Routing Table Lookups

The process just described is not exactly the entire story. As discussed previously, when IP addressing was originally designed, there were different classes of addresses. IP routing took the idea of different classes of addresses into account when performing routing table lookups. In classful routing, when a routing table lookup is performed, the router first looks for an exact match for the destination, what is referred to as a host route since the destination address is normally a specific host IP address. If a host route is not found, the router then looks for a match on the classful network address. If a match is not found for the classful network, for example, 10.0.0.0/8, the packet is forwarded to the default route.

If a match for the classful network is found, the router then looks for a match of the subnet based on its knowledge of the manner in which the classful network is subnetted. If no match is found for the subnet, the packet is dropped. Notice that the default route is not considered in the routers'

Figure 6-10 Illustration of the debug ip packet command when classful routing is used and there is no entry for the destination subnet.

```
R1#sh ip ro
Gateway of last resort is 0.0.0.0 to network 0.0.0.0

10.0.0.0/24 is subnetted, 1 subnet
S    10.10.1.0 is directly connected, Ethernet0
C  192.168.1.0/24 is directly connected, Ethernet0
S*  0.0.0.0/0 is directly connected, Ethernet0
R1#debug ip pack
IP packet debugging is on
R1#ping 172.16.1.1

Type escape sequence to abort.
Sending 5, 100-byte ICMP Echos to 172.16.1.1, timeout is 2 seconds:

2d19h: IP: s=192.168.1.1 (local), d=172.16.1.1 (Ethernet0), len 100, sending
2d19h: IP: s=192.168.1.1 (local), d=172.16.1.1 (Ethernet0), len 100, sending
2d19h: IP: s=192.168.1.1 (local), d=172.16.1.1 (Ethernet0), len 100, sending
2d19h: IP: s=192.168.1.1 (local), d=172.16.1.1 (Ethernet0), len 100, sending
2d19h: IP: s=192.168.1.1 (local), d=172.16.1.1 (Ethernet0), len 100, sending
R1#ping 10.10.4.1

Type escape sequence to abort.
Sending 5, 100-byte ICMP Echos to 10.10.4.1, timeout is 2 seconds:

2d19h: IP: s=137.4.1.1 (local), d=10.10.4.1, len 100, unroutable.
2d19h: IP: s=137.4.1.1 (local), d=10.10.4.1, len 100, unroutable.
2d19h: IP: s=137.4.1.1 (local), d=10.10.4.1, len 100, unroutable.
2d19h: IP: s=137.4.1.1 (local), d=10.10.4.1, len 100, unroutable.
2d19h: IP: s=137.4.1.1 (local), d=10.10.4.1, len 100, unroutable.
Success rate is 0 percent (0/5)
```

examination if classful routing table lookups are performed and a route for the classful network exists in the routing table. This concept is best illustrated with an example. Figure 6-10 illustrates what happens to a packet when a match is found in the routing table for the classful network address.

Notice that the first ping we send is normal. There is no match in the routing table for network 172.16.0.0/16, so the packet is forwarded according to the default route out interface Ethernet0. However, when the second ping is initiated, subnet entries for the classful network 10.0.0.0/8 exist in the routing table, so the router looks for subnet 10.1.4.0/24. Notice that the router has an entry for the 10.1.1.0/24 subnet on a directly connected interface. Since the subnet 10.1.1.0 has a 24-bit subnet, the router assumes that all subnets of the 10.0.0.0/8 network use a 24-bit subnet mask and looks for a subnet routing entry 10.1.4.0/24 for the destination 10.1.4.1. Since no entry exists for subnet 10.1.4.0/24 in the routing table, the router reports that it cannot forward the packet with the error message unroutable.

There are two ways around this problem. First, we could place an entry in the routing table that explicitly informs the router of the route to the 10.1.4.0/24 subnet. This would work, however, it becomes an administrative burden to have to enter all of the subnet routes. A better solution is to use the global command ip classless. This tells the router to perform routing table lookups regardless of the class of the destination address. The router will just look for the best matching address. Figure 6-11 illustrates what occurs after entering this command into the router and repeating a ping to IP address 10.1.4.1.

Notice that after the ip classless command is entered, the router no longer reports the unroutable error message. Instead, the router uses the default route out the Ethernet0 interface. The default route is the best

Figure 6-11   Illustration of the debug ip packet command when classless routing is used and there is no entry for the destination subnet.

```
R1#conf t
Enter configuration commands, one per line. End with CNTL/Z.
R1(config)#ip classless
R1(config)#
R1#
R1#ping 10.1.4.1
Type escape sequence to abort.
Sending 5, 100-byte ICMP Echos to 10.1.4.1, timeout is 2 seconds:
2d19h: IP: s=192.168.1.1 (local), d=10.1.4.1 (Ethernet0), len 100, sending
2d19h: IP: s=192.168.1.1 (local), d=10.1.4.1 (Ethernet0), len 100, sending
2d19h: IP: s=192.168.1.1 (local), d=10.1.4.1 (Ethernet0), len 100, sending
2d19h: IP: s=192.168.1.1 (local), d=10.1.4.1 (Ethernet0), len 100, sending
2d19h: IP: s=192.168.1.1 (local), d=10.1.4.1 (Ethernet0), len 100, sending
R1#
```

match because no entry exists for the host 10.1.4.1, no entry exists for the subnet 10.1.4.0/24, and no specific route exists for the classful network 10.0.0.0/8 (only the subnet 10.1.1.0/24 is known). If an entry did exist for the 10.0.0.0/8 network, this entry would be a more specific match than the default route, and it would be used instead of the default route. The central point to remember is that when using the `ip classless` command, the router only cares about making the most specific match it can, based on the information in the routing table.

Classless Routing Protocols

The idea of classful and classless also applies to routing protocols. A routing protocol is said to be *classless* if it carries subnet information in its routing table updates. It is said to be *classful* if it does not carry subnet information in its routing updates. If a routing update does not contain subnet information, the router must assume that the subnet masks configured on its own interfaces are the same masks that are used throughout the network. For example, the router in Figure 6-12 is configured with an address 10.1.1.0/24, and it receives an update for subnet 10.1.2.0 from a neighboring router. Router R1 must assume that the router from which it received the update is using a 24-bit subnet mask as well.

If the other routers in the network are not using a 24-bit subnet mask, routing problems can occur. In fact, RIP will not send an update for a subnet whose mask is inconsistent with other subnets configured on the router. If we were to use, for example, a 25-bit subnet mask on router R2 in Figure 6-12, the router would never send an update for network 10.1.2.0, which is obviously a problem. Using different subnet masks in an internetwork is called using *variable length subnet masks* (VLSM). The use of VLSM is only supported when using a classless routing protocol. We will see later in this chapter that RIPv1 and IGRP are classful routing pro-

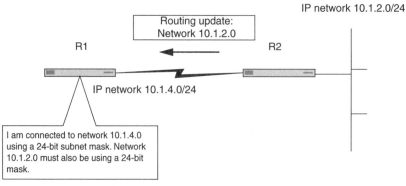

Figure 6-12   The use of a classful routing protocol.

tocols, while RIPv2, EIGRP, and OSPF are classless routing protocols. We examine the problems that can occur when using a classful routing protocol later in this chapter.

Another consequence of using a classful routing protocol is that you cannot divide portions of your classful address space. In other words, you cannot have two parts of your network using IP addresses from the 10.0.0.0/8 network range separated by IP addresses from another classful network range such as 172.16.0.0/16. The reason is that classful routing protocols summarize the entire classful network range at classful network boundaries. That is, a router connected to a subnet of the 10.0.0.0/8 and 172.16.0.0/16 networks would send a route for the entire 10.0.0.0/8 network out interfaces connected to the 172.16.0.0/16 network. Likewise, the router would send a route for the entire 172.16.0.0/16 network out any interface connected to the 10.0.0.0/8 network. If the 10.0.0.0/8 network were separated by subnets of the 172.16.0.0/16 network, routers in the 172.16.0.0/16 network would receive multiple routes for the 10.0.0.0/8 network and would believe that all subnets of that network were reachable via either path. Since this is probably not the case, many packets would fail to reach their destination. This situation is referred to as *discontiguous networks* and is illustrated in Figure 6-13.

Notice that router R3 is receiving routes for the 10.0.0.0/8 network from both R1 and R2. R1 and R2 are summarizing at the classful network boundary to the 172.16.0.0/16 network. Since R3 believes it can send packets to either R1 or R2, it could attempt to reach subnet 10.1.3.0/24 through R1. Since subnet 10.1.3.0/24 is only reachable via router R2, packets to this destination would fail. It is possible that router R3 would send some packets for subnet 10.1.3.0/24 to router R2 and some to R1 in an attempt to load balance, in which case some packets would be routed correctly and some would not. We examine load sharing in the next section. For now, the important point to remember is that classful routing

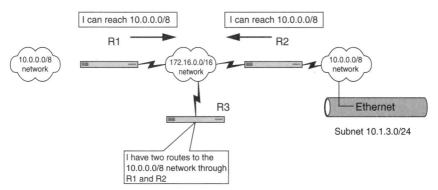

Figure 6-13 The use of discontiguous networks with a classful routing protocol.

protocols summarize at classful network boundaries and therefore do not support discontiguous networks.

Load-Sharing Packets

The previous section mentioned load-sharing packets. Load sharing occurs when a router has multiple paths to a destination and sends a portion of each packet across each path. Load sharing can increase throughput and provides hot redundancy. If one path fails, the other path is used immediately without the router having to determine if there is an alternate path to a destination. Cisco routers can load share across up to six paths, with the default being four paths. The default value can be changed with the routing protocol command maximum-paths #, where number is an integer between 1 and 6:

```
r4#conf t
Enter configuration commands, one per line. End with CNTL/Z.
r4(config)#router rip
r4(config-router)#maximum-paths ?
 <1-6> Number of paths
```

Fast Switching

An important topic that is closely related to load sharing is fast switching. A fast-switching cache is a memory cache populated by a router when it performs a routing table lookup for a destination address. The router caches the destination IP address and the interface to which packets should be forwarded for the destination. The fast-switching cache allows the router to forward packets from one interface to another without having to interrupt the CPU to perform a routing table lookup. Use of fast switching can greatly increase the speed with which a router can forward packets. When fast switching is enabled and there are multiple paths to a destination, the router will cache host entries. For example, if there are multiple routes to the 10.1.1.0/24 subnet out interfaces serial0 and serial1, the router would send packets for 10.1.1.1 out serial0, packets for 10.1.1.2 out serial1, and so on. This is called *load sharing on a per destination basis*. If fast switching is disabled, the router will load share on a per packet basis and simply send successive packets out each available path.

While turning off fast switching results in more evenly balanced load since it is per packet, it also slows down the speed with which the router can forward packets. Additionally, it will cause the load on the router's CPU to increase substantially due to the increased number of routing table lookups. In almost all cases, it is better to leave fast switching enabled and accept that your load sharing will not be exact. Fast switching is enabled by default for IP, but can be disabled on a per interface basis with the interface command no ip route-cache.

Floating Static Routes

Before we leave this section, floating static routes should be discussed. Recall our earlier discussion of AD and its use by the router to determine which route to choose from a list of candidate routes learned from different sources. For example, the AD of OSPF is lower than that of RIP, so OSPF routes are preferred over RIP-learned routes. Recall that we stated that the AD of static routes is 1. This is true for the default setting, but the AD of static routes can be set to a higher value when a static route is configured. The reason this is useful is that there are times when you want to use a dynamically learned route in preference to a static route, and only want to use the static route in the event the dynamically learned route disappears. This is the advantage of dynamic routing. Routes will disappear when they are unavailable and reappear when they are available.

The need for a backup static route is very common in dial backup scenarios, for example. You may have a primary serial interface through which you receive dynamically learned routes and which is the preferred path for all packets. However, if the serial interface fails, you would like to use a dial-up line for all packets. You don't want to leave your dial-up line active to receive routes, so the logical course of action is to point a static default route out the dial-up line. However, by default, the static router AD is 1, so it would be preferred over any dynamically learned route and all packets would be sent over the dial-up.

The solution to this problem is to set the AD on the static route out the dial-up line to a higher value than that of the dynamically learned routes. This way, if the serial line goes down, the dynamically learned routes disappear and the router uses the static route. However, when the dynamically learned routes are being received, they are preferred over the static route with the higher AD and the serial interface. Static routes that are configured with a higher AD than that of dynamically learned routes are called *floating static routes* because they float in and out of the routing table, depending on whether a dynamically learned route is present or not. Figure 6-14 illustrates the use of a floating static.

Notice that the AD of the static route is configured to 200 and the route only appears after the interface on which a dynamically learned route is being received goes down. The selection of the AD value is somewhat arbitrary, so long as the value chosen is higher than the AD value of the routing protocol in use. Values between 150 and 200 are typical. The AD values of the most common routing protocols are shown here:

```
EIGRP, 90
IGRP, 100
OSPF, 110
RIP(versions 1 and 2), 120
```

Figure 6-14 The use of a floating static route.

```
r1#sh ip ro
Gateway of last resort is not set

     172.16.0.0/24 is subnetted, 1 subnets
C    172.16.1.0 is directly connected, FastEthernet2/0
     10.0.0.0/24 is subnetted, 2 subnets
R    10.1.2.0 [120/1] via 10.1.1.4, 00:00:07, Ethernet0/0
C    10.1.1.0 is directly connected, Ethernet0/0
R 192.168.1.0/24 [120/2] via 10.1.1.4, 00:00:07, Ethernet0/0
r1#conf t
Enter configuration commands, one per line. End with CNTL/Z.
r1(config)#ip route 10.1.2.0 255.255.255.0 fastethernet 2/0 200
r1(config)#
r1#
r1#sh ip ro
Gateway of last resort is not set

     172.16.0.0/24 is subnetted, 1 subnets
C    172.16.1.0 is directly connected, FastEthernet2/0
     10.0.0.0/24 is subnetted, 2 subnets
R    10.1.2.0 [120/1] via 10.1.1.4, 00:00:22, Ethernet0/0
C    10.1.1.0 is directly connected, Ethernet0/0
R 192.168.1.0/24 [120/2] via 10.1.1.4, 00:00:23, Ethernet0/0
r1#conf t
Enter configuration commands, one per line. End with CNTL/Z.
r1(config)#int e 0/0
r1(config-if)#shut
r1(config-if)#
r1#
04:07:09: %LINK-5-CHANGED: Interface Ethernet0/0, changed state to
          administratively down
04:07:10: %LINEPROTO-5-UPDOWN: Line protocol on Interface Ethernet0/0,
          changed state to down
r1#sh ip ro
Gateway of last resort is not set

     172.16.0.0/24 is subnetted, 1 subnets
C    172.16.1.0 is directly connected, FastEthernet2/0
     10.0.0.0/24 is subnetted, 1 subnets
S    10.1.2.0 is directly connected, FastEthernet2/0
```

Types of Routing Protocols

To this point, we have talked about routing protocols as if they all performed in pretty much the same manner. In fact, this is not the case. The two distinct classes of routing protocols are distance vector (DV) and link state (LS). The manner in which these two classes of routing protocols perform is very different and is discussed in the following sections. RIP versions 1 and 2 and IGRP are examples of distance vector routing protocols. OSPF is an example of a link state routing protocol. EIGRP is unique in that in most respects it is a distance vector routing protocol, but it employs some special features not found in other traditional DV protocols such as RIP and IGRP. For this reason, EIGRP is often called a hybrid or an advanced distance vector routing protocol.

Distance Vector (DV) Routing Protocols

DV routing protocols perform in much the same manner as that discussed in our neighborhood analogy earlier in this chapter. A router informs its neighbor routers about all of its directly connected subnets. These neighbor routers, in turn, inform their neighbors of this information and so on. DV routing is referred to as "routing by rumor," since each router is only aware of what its direct neighbors tell it. No information is obtained from routers that are not direct neighbors. Neighbor routers pass along information received only after they have absorbed the information received. A router must process the update from its neighbor and add any additional information, such as increasing the metric, before sending this information on to its other neighbor routers. This process is illustrated in Figure 6-15.

Notice that at time $t1$, R1 sends a routing table advertisement to R2 that is processed by the router. After R2 has processed the routing update, it adjusts its routing table and includes this route in its routing table advertisement to router R3 at time $t1 + n$, where n is some value on the order of many seconds. The central point is that the new route is not sent from R2 to R3 immediately. Additionally, the information sent contains only the destination address and a metric. R3 has no way of knowing that the route sent by R2 originated from R1. All it knows is the metric and that it reaches the route through R2. When a router receives a route via a DV routing protocol, the only information the router gets is the distance to a destination and the next hop router to reach that destination (the next hop information is usually implied by the source of the routing update).

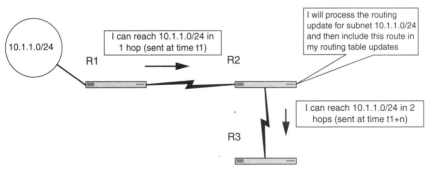

Figure 6-15 The routing update process used by DV routing protocols.

This is the origin of the term distance vector. A vector can be thought of as just a directional indicator, so a distance vector tells the router the direction (next hop) and the distance and nothing more. A router does not know what other routers in the path it must use to reach a particular destination. As stated previously, R3 does not know that the route from R2 originated from R1. Only the next hop router is known. We will see in the next section that when using link state routing protocols, each router knows the exact path through the network to each destination. This has important ramifications when there are failures in a network, as we will see later in this section.

Several other factors are key characteristics of DV routing protocols. DV protocols usually inform their neighboring routers of routing information by sending periodic broadcast updates containing their entire routing table. Periodic means that an update occurs whether any information has changed or not. The entire routing table is usually sent and the update is usually sent to the broadcast address. The reason for this behavior is that DV routing protocols do not usually establish a neighbor relationship between routers (we will see later that EIGRP does establish a neighbor relationship). Each router is not directly aware of the presence of other routers on its network and may only detect that a route is unavailable when it stops hearing periodic broadcasts from a neighbor.

Route Invalidation Timers

In order for a router to discover that a route is no longer available, it is necessary to have a route invalidation timer. A *route invalidation timer* is a length of time that can expire without an update before a route is removed from the routing table. This value is typically 3 to 6 times as long as the update period. A route invalidation timer is needed so that in the event that a router fails, neighboring routers can detect that the routes that were previously available through the failed router are no longer being advertised and remove them from the routing table. The neighboring routers do not know that a router has failed per se, they just know that they are no longer receiving broadcast updates about particular routes.

In practice, multicast updates can be used in preference to broadcast, and we will see that RIPv2 uses multicast instead of broadcast. However, the updates still contain the entire routing table and are sent at periodic intervals, regardless of whether any changes have occurred.

Split Horizon

There is one exception to the statement the entire routing table is sent. Most modern DV routing protocols employ a technique known as *split horizon*. Split horizon means that the router will not send updates about a network out the interface on which the network was learned. For example, in Figure 6-16, router R1 will not send a routing update out its

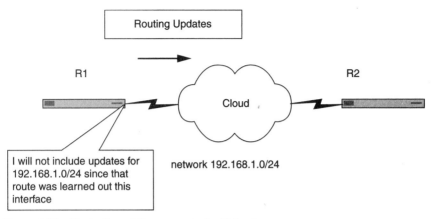

Figure 6-16   Illustration of the concept of split horizon.

Ethernet0 interface for subnet 192.168.1.0/24 because 192.168.1.0/24 is configured on that interface. Since 192.168.1.0/24 was learned on the link between router R1 and R2, the logic is that there is no reason to send an update regarding this subnet out that interface.

Any routers on that link should also have learned about the subnet already since they are directly connected as well. This has ramifications when using secondary IP addresses. If a secondary address is configured on a router interface, all other routers on that segment should also be configured with secondary IP addresses in the same subnet. Otherwise, the router with the secondary address will not inform other routers about this secondary subnet due to split horizon rules. Split horizon can be disabled with the interface command `no ip split-horizon`, but this is not recommended.

Routing Loops

Besides the fact that it reduces the number of routes sent in a routing update, split horizon serves another very valuable function. It allows for routers running DV protocols to detect the loss of a network in a more timely fashion. The time between the failure of a link or the loss of a route, such as a router failure, and the time until every router in the internetwork is aware of the change is called the *convergence time*. Before a network has converged, some routers in the internetwork will have incorrect routing information. This is obviously a bad situation, so ideally we would like a routing protocol that converges as quickly as possible. Anything that we can do to speed up convergence is considered a good thing. So how exactly does split horizon speed up convergence?

Consider Figure 6-17. Router R2 is advertising a route to R1 for subnet 10.1.1.0/24. The link on R2 fails, so R2 needs to inform R1 about this fail-

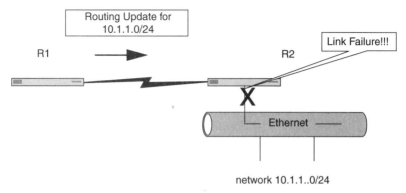

Figure 6-17   A routing loop caused by the absence of split horizon.

ure. However, just before R2 sends its update, R1 sends an update to R2 informing it that it has a route to 10.1.1.0/24 (this assumes that split horizon is not enabled).

R1 has learned the route from R2, but R2 has no way of knowing that the update received from R1 is not legitimate. Remember that when using DV routing protocols, routers typically do not know who their neighbors are. R2 does not know that R1 is informing it about the same route that just failed. R2 believes that it now has a legitimate route to 10.1.1.0/24 through R1. R2 now sends an update to R1 informing it that it has a route to 10.1.1.0/24, only now the metric is higher.

R1 dutifully records this information and sends an update back to R2 informing it that it has a route to 10.1.1.0/24. Every time a router sends an update, it increments the metric for the route based on its cost. When using RIP, for example, the cost is simply hop count, so each router would add one hop to the metric. You can see that since routers R1 and R2 are simply telling each other the same information over and over, a routing loop exists. If you tried to send a packet through R1 to subnet 10.1.1.0/24, it would forward it to R2. R2 would forward the packet to R1 and so on until the TTL value of the packet was reached.

This unhappy situation will eventually be corrected when the metric value for the route to 10.1.1.0/24 reaches its maximum. Because of situations like the one just described, DV routing protocols typically have a maximum value beyond which a route is considered unreachable. For RIP the maximum value is 15 hops, so 16 hops is considered an unreachable value for a route. Once the 16-hop count is reached, a router marks the route as unreachable. However, this process can take a long time. In our example, it would take 14 update periods to reach this value. RIP updates are every 30 s, so it would take about 7 min for routers R1 and R2 to determine that subnet 10.1.1.0/24 was unreachable. Seven minutes is an extremely long time in data networks. Ideally, we would like our network to converge in seconds, not minutes. This situation of having metrics increased to a maximum is called *counting to infinity*, and it always exists when using DV routing protocols. All that can be done is to mitigate its effects.

Poison Reverse

There is a final point to be made concerning split horizon. In addition to the form of split horizon discussed in this section, there is also a form of split horizon called split horizon with poison reverse. The idea of *poison reverse* is that a router does advertise routes out interfaces on which they were learned, however, it advertises the routes learned on those interfaces with an infinite metric. For example, RIP-learned routes would be advertised with a metric of 16, which is considered unreachable. The advantage to using poison reverse is that it handles situations where a route is corrupted. In our previous example, if R1 had received misinformation from another router indicating an alternate route to the 10.1.1.0/24 subnet, split horizon alone would not correct this problem. However, split horizon with poison reverse could correct the situation quickly.

Additional DV Protocol Features

In addition to the DV protocol features we have seen, two additional features are worthy of note. The first feature is called triggered updates. Remember we noted that DV protocols send their routing updates at set intervals. Sometimes, however, it can be advantageous to inform neighbors immediately if a route has failed or if a metric has changed. A DV routing protocol may, in this case, send an update immediately without waiting for the standard update period. An update that is sent immediately in response to a change in the network is referred to as a *triggered update*. Triggered updates can help speed up convergence time when using a DV routing protocol.

In addition to triggered updates, another useful feature is holddown timers. *A holddown timer* is a timer that is used by the router to place a hold on a route. New information concerning that route is not accepted from a neighboring router unless the metric is better than the metric the router currently has. This is useful in situations where a potential routing loop can occur. In Figure 6-18, suppose that the route to network 172.16.1.0/24 has failed on router R1.

R1 sends an update to this effect to its neighboring routers, R2 and R3. Just before R3 receives the new routing information, it sends an update to R4 with the old information about the route to 172.16.1.0/24. R2 receives the new information before it's timed update and will send the new information in its next update to R4. However, before it can do so, R4 sends an update to R2 informing R2 that it can reach 172.16.1.0/24. R2

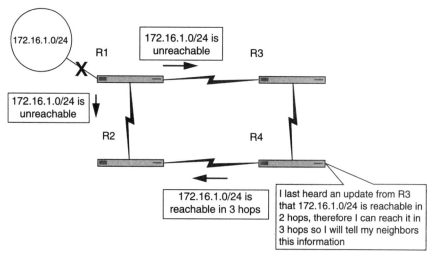

Figure 6-18 A routing loop caused by the absence of holddown timers.

would place this information in its routing table. R2 would then inform R1 and so on. When holddown timers are in place, R2 and R3 would have placed the route to 172.16.1.0/24 in a hold state due to the increase in the metric of the information received from R1. R2 would not accept any new routing information about 172.16.1.0/24 until the timer expired. The goal is that the routing information will have converged by the time the holddown timer has expired, so that a router does not accept incorrect routing information. In our example, R2 would not accept the route from R4 and when R2 sent out its next update, R4 would be informed that 172.16.1.0/24 was unreachable. Holddown timers decrease the likelihood that a router will accept incorrect routing information, but they slow convergence.

It should be clear by now that DV routing protocols have some inherent problems. Under certain conditions, routing loops and other misinformation can occur. The features that have been implemented to help avoid these problems, such as holddowns, alleviate some of these issues but they tend to slow convergence. We will see in the next section that link state (LS) routing protocols avoid many of the problems associated with DV routing protocols, but introduce some new problems of their own.

Link State (LS) Routing Protocols

LS routing protocols vary considerably in their design from DV routing protocols. In a DV routing protocol, each router is only aware of informa-

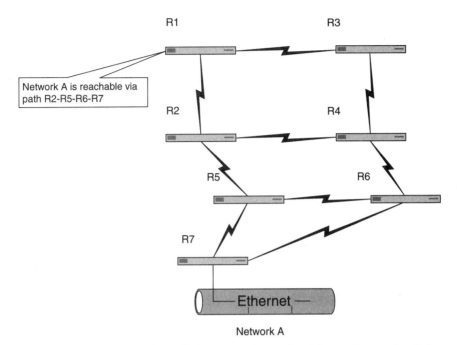

Network A

Figure 6-19   A router running a link state routing protocol knows the exact path to each destination in the internetwork.

tion obtained from directly connected neighbors. The information regarding a route only tells the router how far the route is and in which direction. In LS routing protocols, a router has a complete picture of the entire network. Each router has an exact path through the internetwork to reach each destination. Every router knows exactly which routers and which links on those routers must be traversed to reach each network and subnet. This process is illustrated in Figure 6-19.

LS Routing Protocol Procedures

LS routing protocols accomplish this by implementing the following procedures:

1. Each router establishes a neighbor relationship with other routers on its network segment. Small update packets, called hello packets, are exchanged between routers at short intervals so that a neighbor router is aware almost immediately of the loss of a neighbor.

2. Each router sends a *link state advertisement* (LSA) to each of its neighbors informing it of the links the router has and the neighboring routers it is aware of.

3. Each router immediately forwards these received LSA packets to all of its neighbors, except the one from which the LSA was received. This process is referred to as *LSA flooding*.

4. When the flooding process is complete, each router in the internetwork should have received identical LSA information that it will store in a database called the *link state database* (LS database).

5. Each router uses the Dijkstra algorithm to calculate a shortest cost path to each network or subnet in the internetwork. Each router performs this calculation independent of other routers.

Once these procedures are complete, each router in the internetwork should have a route to each destination. When there is a change on a router's link, the router immediately forwards this new information to its neighbors as an updated LSA. The new LSA information is flooded throughout the internetwork, so all routers are informed of the update very rapidly. If a router fails, its neighbor routers are informed of this failure very quickly due to the neighbor relationship and the neighbor routers will flood new LSA information concerning the loss of their neighbor. Notice that there are no holddown timers and no split horizon issues. Each router has an exact path to every subnet in the entire internetwork. For this reason, LS routing protocols typically converge must faster than DV routing protocols.

LS Routing Protocol Issues

Despite their advantages, LS protocols are not without their problems. LS protocols place additional CPU demands on each router since the Dijkstra algorithm must be recalculated every time a new LSA is received. In an unstable, large network, LSAs may be received at a rate that is so frequent that the router's CPU is too busy running the Dijkstra algorithm to perform any other tasks. Additionally, the memory requirements are higher on a router running an LS routing protocol due to the need to receive and maintain the LS database. While these factors cannot be ignored, in well-designed networks it should not be a deciding factor not to use LS routing protocols unless the routers in use have very slow CPUs and a very small amount of memory. For example, a 1000-node network, composed of 800 series Cisco routers, would probably not be a good choice to run OSPF as the routing protocol.

Sequence Numbers and LSA Aging

As noted, LSAs are flooded throughout an internetwork. At some point, it is likely that a router may receive duplicate LSAs that were flooded over different paths. How is a router that receives a duplicate LSA to determine that a newly received LSA is a duplicate? This is important because a router will forward any new LSAs it receives and it will also recalculate the

Dijkstra algorithm, so we want to avoid forwarding duplicate LSAs and unnecessarily burdening the routers' CPU. The answer to the problem is to give each LSA a sequence number that uniquely identifies each LSA. This way a router will be aware if it receives a duplicate LSA and can discard it.

The one problem with this is how a router selects what sequence numbers to use. If a router simply starts at the lowest sequence number when it is power cycled, its sequence numbers may be interpreted by other routers as old and would be ignored until an age out value is reached for the LSAs already in its neighbor routers' LS database. This is not very appealing. An alternative approach is for a router to initially use a sequence number that can be identified by its neighbors as unique to a router that has just been initialized.

If the neighbor routers have information about a sequence number the router was previously using, they inform the starting router what sequence number to begin with. If there is no previous sequence number, the startup router simply begins incrementing the sequence numbers up to a maximum value. Once the maximum sequence number value is reached, a router must flush the LSA from the database of other routers and reset its sequence number to a beginning value.

In addition to sequence numbers, an LSA aging process occurs on each router. An age out value is set for LSAs to prevent old LSA information from remaining in the LS database past its useful lifetime. To prevent a router's LSAs from timing out, each router resends all its LSA information on a periodic basis, even if no change has occurred. In OSPF, the resend period is 30 min and the age out value is 1 h. If an LSA reaches the age out period without being refreshed by the originating router, it is flushed from a router's LS database table.

In this section we have discussed the different categories of routing protocols, distance vector and link state and the special characteristics of each. The remainder of this chapter examines specific routing protocols and the features of each, specifically the packet format of each routing protocol, whether the routing protocol is classful or classless, and any features unique to each routing protocol.

RIP Version 1 and 2

In this section we discuss both version 1 and version 2 of the venerable RIP routing protocol. RIP versions 1 and 2 are often abbreviated simply as RIPv1 and RIPv2, and we will follow this convention in this section. RIP routing is enabled on a router through the use of the 'router' command:

```
r4#conf t
Enter configuration commands, one per line. End with CNTL/Z.
r4(config)#router rip
r4(config-router)#network 10.0.0.0
```

The network subcommand tells the router which interfaces will be configured for RIP processing. Notice that there is no subnet mask associated with the network statement. All interfaces on the router using addresses that are subnets of the 10.0.0.0/8 network would be enabled for RIP processing. If we desired not to run RIP on an interface with an IP address in this range, we would have to use the router command passive-interface <interface>.

We will see later in this section that the passive-interface command disables the sending of routing protocol information, but does not disable the router from listening to routing updates on an interface. If we wanted to prevent any routing updates from being learned on an interface, we would have to use the router command distribute-list to filter incoming routing updates:

```
r4#conf t
Enter configuration commands, one per line. End with CNTL/Z.
r4(config)#access-list 1 deny 0.0.0.0 255.255.255.255
r4(config)#router rip
r4(config-router)#distribute-list 1 in ethernet 0/0
```

Access-list 1 matches any routing update and we use the distribute-list command to apply it to routes arriving on the Ethernet0/0 interface. No routes will be accepted through this interface.

RIPv1

RIP is one of the oldest and best known IP routing protocols. It is at once very simple and easy to understand and ubiquitous. Nearly every major operating system supports at least the ability to listen to RIP routing updates, including most flavors of UNIX and NT. RIP was originally included with the 4.2 distribution of Berkeley standard distribution (BSD) in 1982, but a standard specification of RIP was not released until RFC 1058 in 1988. By this time, RIP was in widespread use in many UNIX environments, and was for all intents and purposes the only game in town as far as IP routing protocols were concerned.

RIP conforms very closely to the traditional DV routing protocol described earlier. It uses broadcast updates and sends its entire routing table in the updates. Routing updates are sent every 30 s with a time-out value of 180 s, or six routing periods. That is, if an update is not heard for a route in six updates, that route is marked unreachable. After another 60 s, the route is flushed from the routing table. RIP uses a simple hop count as its metric and has a maximum hop count of 15. Sixteen hops is considered an infinite distance, so all unreachable routes are given a metric of 16 to indicate that they are inaccessible. The timer values for RIP can be adjusted with the routing protocol command timers basic (see Figure 6-20).

The command is shown with its default values. The update parameter

Figure 6-20 The use of the `timers basic` command.

```
r4#conf t
Enter configuration commands, one per line. End with CNTL/Z.
r4(config)#router rip
r4(config-router)#timers basic ?
 <0-4294967295> Interval between updates
r4(config-router)#timers basic 30 ?
 <1-4294967295> Invalid
r4(config-router)#timers basic 30 180 ?
 <0-4294967295> Holddown
r4(config-router)#timers basic 30 180 180 ?
 <1-4294967295> Flush
r4(config-router)#timers basic 30 180 180 240
```

indicates how often routing updates are sent. The `invalid` parameter is the period of time that must expire without an update before a route is considered unreachable. The `holddown` value is the amount of time to place a route into a holddown state after receiving an update for the router with a larger metric. The `flush` parameter indicates how long after a route is marked inaccessible to wait before removing the route from the routing table. If these values are changed on one router, they should be changed on all routers in the internetwork. You should only consider changing these values if you have very specific reasons for doing so since any changes to these values could wreak havoc in a production network.

The RIP protocol uses user datagram protocol (UDP) as its transport and operates on port 520. The packet format for RIP updates is illustrated in Figure 6-21. Notice that there are many unused fields in the RIP update

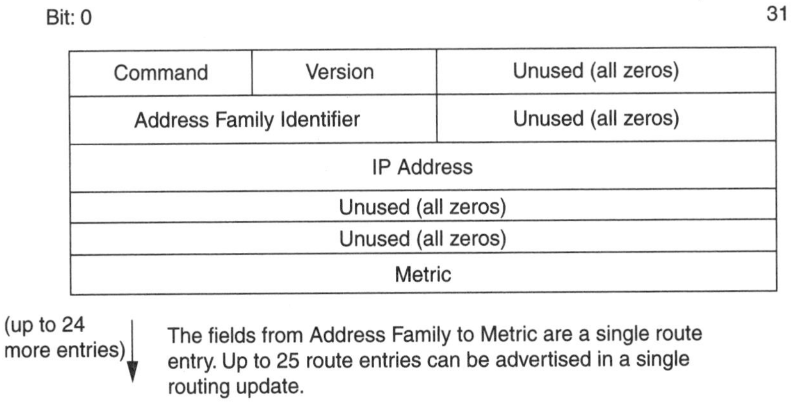

Bit: 0   31

Command	Version	Unused (all zeros)
Address Family Identifier		Unused (all zeros)
IP Address		
Unused (all zeros)		
Unused (all zeros)		
Metric		

(up to 24 more entries) → The fields from Address Family to Metric are a single route entry. Up to 25 route entries can be advertised in a single routing update.

Figure 6-21 The format of an RIP update packet.

packet. These fields were intended for future use. RIPv2 takes advantage of these fields and uses them to provide enhancements to RIPv1. A single RIP update can contain up to 25 routes.

RIP uses split horizon and triggered updates to speed convergence and avoid routing loops, as discussed earlier. RIPv1 uses classful routing and summarizes on classful network boundaries, so it does not support VLSM or discontiguous networks. RIP can be configured so that a router listens to RIP updates but does not advertise RIP routing updates. This mode of RIP is often referred to as *silent mode*. You configure RIP to run in silent mode on an interface by interface basis with the routing protocol command `passive-interface`.

```
r4#conf t
Enter configuration commands, one per line. End with CNTL/Z.
r4(config)#router rip
r4(config-router)#passive-interface ethernet0/1
r4(config-router)#
```

This tells the router to accept RIP updates on interface Ethernet 0/1, but not to send updates out this interface. The `passive-interface` command can be used in this manner with both versions 1 and 2 of RIP and IGRP. If used with EIGRP or OSPF, it completely disables both listening and sending of routing updates on the passive interface. This is because EIGRP and OSPF require a two-way hello process to function properly. By disabling the router from speaking EIGRP or OSPF on an interface, you prevent the sending of hello packets and the formation of neighbor relationships.

Another interesting note on the use of the `passive-interface` command is that it doesn't exactly disable the sending of updates on an interface. It disables the sending of routing protocol broadcast or multicast updates on that interface. Even when the `passive-interface` command is used, you can still enable the sending of unicast routing updates with the routing protocol command `neighbor a.b.c.d`:

```
r4#conf t
Enter configuration commands, one per line. End with CNTL/Z.
r4(config)#router rip
r4(config-router)#neighbor ?
 A.B.C.D Neighbor address
r4(config-router)#neighbor 10.1.1.1
r4(config-router)#
r4#
```

This would cause a unicast update to be sent to IP address 10.1.1.1.

A final topic that is worth discussing is the `offset-list` command. The `offset-list` command can be used to increase the metric of an advertised route or to increase the metric of a received route. For example, if we wished to set the metric for 172.16.1.0/24 to 3 before it was advertised to our neighbors out Ethernet0/0, we could use the `offset-list` command in the following manner:

```
r4#conf t
Enter configuration commands, one per line. End with CNTL/Z.
r4(config)#access-list 1 permit 172.16.1.0 0.0.0.255
r4(config)#router rip
r4(config-router)#offset-list 1 out 3 ethernet0/0
r4(config-router)#
```

Note the use of an access list to define the routes for which we are increasing the metric and the setting of the metric to 3. We also increase the metric of received routes by using the keyword `in` instead of `out`.

RIPv2

RIPv2 is much like RIPv1, but it introduces some important new features. First, RIPv2 is a classless routing protocol. The routing updates carry the subnet mask as a field in each update. Also, it sends its routing updates to the reserved multicast address 224.0.0.9. This has the advantage that devices not participating in the RIP routing protocol do not have to examine the packet. Broadcast packets must be examined by every device on a segment, whereas multicast packets can be discarded by the Ethernet drivers before any upper-layer protocols examine the packet.

A third important feature of RIPv2 is the ability to provide authenticated updates. This means that a password can be configured on each RIPv2 speaking router so that only routers that have the shared password are allowed to send and receive routes. This feature can be useful in situations where there may be devices outside of your control that you don't want to be allowed to participate in the RIP routing protocol. RFC 1723, the RIPv2 specification, describes only a simple password authentication. However, Cisco supports the use of an encrypted MD5 password. The use of an encrypted password means that the password will not be revealed if someone were to use a sniffer to capture the RIPv2 routing updates.

Two additional features of RIPv2 are the ability to specify an explicit next hop router in a routing update and the inclusion of a route tag field that allows groups of routes to be tagged for easier control by route maps. The RIPv2 packet format is shown in Figure 6-22. Notice that many of the fields that were reserved in the RIPv1 packet are being used in the RIPv2 packet.

Specifically, notice there is now a field for the inclusion of the subnet mask in a routing update. Since RIPv2 updates include subnet mask information, it supports VLSM and is considered a classless routing protocol. RIPv2 also supports the use of discontiguous networks. By default, RIPv2 will summarize on classful network boundaries like RIPv1. However, this

Bit: 0   31

Command	Version	Unused (all zeros)
Address Family Identifier		Route Tag
IP Address		
Subnet Mask		
Next Hop		
Metric		

(up to 24 more entries) → The fields from Address Family to Metric are a single route entry. Up to 25 route entries can be advertised in a single routing update.

Figure 6-22   The format of an RIP version 2 update packet.

behavior can be overridden by using of the routing protocol command no auto-summary:

```
r4#conf t
Enter configuration commands, one per line. End with CNTL/Z.
r4(config)#router rip
r4(config-router)#version 2
r4(config-router)#no auto-summary
```

When no auto-summary is configured, RIPv2 does not summarize at classful network boundaries. This command is also used with EIGRP to disable the automatic summarization at classful network boundaries. By specifying the command version 2, we configure RIP so that it will only send and receive RIPv2 updates. If the version command is not configured, the router will send only RIPv1 packets, but will listen to both RIPv1 and RIPv2 updates.

RIPv2 is backward compatible with RIPv1 and the router can be configured to send and receive for each version on a per interface basis with the interface commands ip rip send version and ip rip receive version. In the following commands, we configure Ethernet0/0 to send version 1 but receive versions 1 and 2 (note that this is the default behavior if the routing protocol command version is not used):

```
r4#conf t
Enter configuration commands, one per line. End with CNTL/Z.
r4(config)#interface ethernet 0/0
r4(config-if)#rip send version 1
r4(config-if)#rip receive version 1 2
```

Although RIPv2 provides some substantial enhancements to RIPv1, it is still limited by its use of a maximum 15-hop count limit. In modern internetworks, routers may be many more than 15 hops away from each other.

However, in small networks, the additional features of RIPv2 make it a viable alternative to more complicated protocols such as OSPF.

Interior Gateway Routing Protocol (IGRP) and Enhanced Interior Gateway Routing Protocol (EIGRP)

This section looks at two proprietary routing protocols from Cisco: IGRP and EIGRP. These routing protocols were developed by Cisco and, with rare exception, are only available on Cisco routers.

IGRP

IGRP was developed by Cisco in the mid-1980s as an alternative to RIPv1. The main limitations of RIPv1 that IGRP was designed to overcome were the use of hop count metrics and the restriction of internetworks to 15 hops. Instead of using a hop count metric, IGRP uses a composite metric that takes into account factors such as the smallest bandwidth in a path and the delay of each link in the path. IGRP does not use hop count as part of its metric, but it does track the hop count and supports internetworks up to 255 hops in diameter. IGRP additionally has a longer update interval, a more efficient routing update packet, and can load share across unequal cost paths. IGRP update periods are 90 s, with an invalid timer of 270 s. IGRP uses a flush timer of 630 s and a holddown time-out of 280 s.

Despite these advantages, IGRP does not include subnet mask information in its routing updates, so it is a classful routing protocol. It does not support the use of VLSM or discontiguous networks. Like RIPv1, it summarizes at classful network boundaries. Also like RIPv1, IGRP sends its updates to the broadcast address. However, IGRP does not use UDP as its transport. Instead, IGRP uses IP directly and operates on IP protocol 9.

IGRP Process Domains

In addition to its other features, IGRP supports the use of multiple process domains within an internetwork. When IGRP is defined, a process number is specified. All routers in a common AS must use the same process number for routing information to be propagated correctly. A single IGRP router can support processes for multiple process domains. This allows you to create border routers that redistribute routes from one IGRP process domain to another IGRP process domain in a controlled fashion. This is illustrated in Figure 6-23.

Router R1 is running multiple IGRP processes and has routes from each process domain. Routers R2 and R3 are participating in only a single IGRP process and have only routes from their respective IGRP process domains and any that R1 chooses to redistribute from one IGRP process to another.

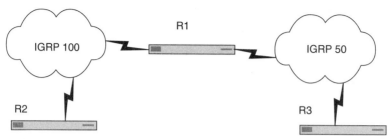

Figure 6-23 The use of multiple process domains in IGRP.

Administrators can choose the routes they want redistributed, so the propagation of routing information from one IGRP process domain to another can be tightly controlled. Router R1's IGRP configuration is shown here:

```
router igrp 100
 Network a.b.c.d
 !
router igrp 50
 network a.b.c.d
```

Like RIP, when configuring an IGRP process, the network statement determines what interfaces are enabled for IGRP processing. Only classful network addresses can be specified as in RIP. For example, you could only specify 10.0.0.0 as the network and not subnets of the 10.0.0.0/8 network. If an interface falls into this address range and you don't wish to run IGRP on that interface, the `passive-interface` command must be used. If you don't want to receive routing updates on that interface, you must use filtering to block incoming routing updates, as illustrated in the section on RIP.

IGRP Metrics

Unlike RIP, IGRP does not use a hop count metric. Instead, IGRP is capable of taking several factors into account when calculating metrics. The composite metric for IGRP is

$$\text{Metric} = [k1*\text{BWmin} + (k2*\text{BWmin})/(256\text{-load}) + k3*\text{DLYsum}] *[k5/(\text{reliability} + k4)]$$

where

> BWm = minimum bandwidth value of the outgoing interface to a destination.
>
> DLYsum = sum of all the delay values of the outgoing interface to a destination
>
> load = measure of the amount of traffic on an interface
>
> reliability = measure of whether an interface has experienced any outages
>
> $k1 - k5$ = constants with the default values $k1 = k3 = 1$ and $k2 = k4 = k5 = 0$.

Note the following:

- The bandwidth is not the actual bandwidth of the links but uses whatever value is configured with the bandwidth interface command. Note that only the outgoing interface bandwidth values going in the direction of the destination and only the minimum of these values are used.

- The delay of an interface is a measure of how quickly an interface can place packets on the wire. A faster interface has a lower delay. Unlike the bandwidth, the delay values of all outgoing interfaces to a destination are used, not just the minimum.

- Load is a measure of the amount of traffic on an interface. This is the same load parameter displayed when the sh interface command is used. It is a 5-minute weighted average and a number between 1 and 255. A value of 255 indicates a line that is fully loaded.

- Reliability is a measure of whether an interface has experienced any outages or not. It is a number between 1 and 255, with 255 indicating that the interface has never experienced any outages.

Notice when these values are plugged into the IGRP equation, only bandwidth and delay are used in metric calculations:

$$\text{Metric} = [1 * \text{BWmin} + (0)/(0) + 1 * \text{DLYsum}] * [k5/(0) + 0)]$$

$$\text{Metric} = \text{BWmin} + \text{DLYsum}$$

The values for the constants $k1$ through $k5$ can be changed with the command metric weights:

metric weights tos $k1$ $k2$ $k3$ $k4$ $k5$

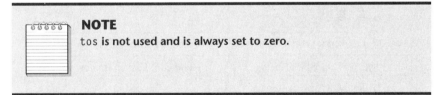

NOTE
tos **is not used and is always set to zero.**

While you might think that using the load and reliability of interfaces is a good idea, in practice their use can lead to route flapping. As the load on a line changes, routing information could change and alternate routing paths are selected. Once the load of the lines on that path increases and the load on the original path decreases, the router flaps back to the original path and so on. Cisco chose not to use the load and reliability values in the default IGRP metric calculations for this reason. You should think very carefully before manipulating these metric constants and should only do so if you have a very specific reason for changing them.

Manipulating Metrics

We should note that the BW_{min} value is not the actual bandwidth configured on an interface, but is actually 10^7 divided by the bandwidth. Similarly, the DLY_{sum} value is not the actual delay of an interface as displayed with the `sh interface` command but is the delay value divided by 10. If you are calculating IGRP metrics by hand, make sure to take this into account or you will have discrepancies between the values you calculate and the values the router displays. You can change the bandwidth and delay values for an interface easily:

```
r4#conf t
Enter configuration commands, one per line. End with CNTL/Z.
r4(config)#interface serial0/0
r4(config-if)#bandwidth 576
r4(config-if)#delay 55
```

However, if you are changing the values to influence a metric, it is best to manipulate the delay value and not the bandwidth. The bandwidth value is used by other processes on the router, such as OSPF, so manipulating the bandwidth can have unexpected consequences. Additionally, changing the bandwidth parameter can confuse someone who examines the router configuration and expects the bandwidth statement to reflect the actual bandwidth of the interface.

IGRP Packet Format

The format of an IGRP packet is shown in Figure 6-24.

The version field is always 1 and the OPcode is 1 for a request packet and 2 for an update packet. The process number has been discussed previously. A few words need to be said about the Number of Interior Routes, Number of System Routes, and Number of Exterior Route fields.

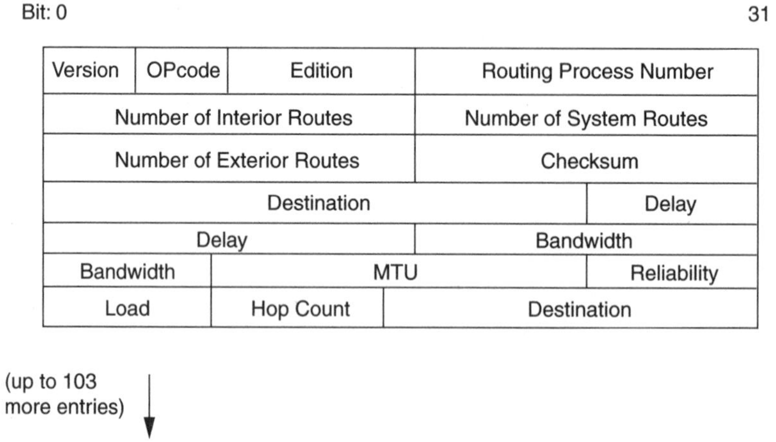

Bit: 0   31

Version	OPcode	Edition	Routing Process Number	
Number of Interior Routes			Number of System Routes	
Number of Exterior Routes			Checksum	
Destination				Delay
Delay			Bandwidth	
Bandwidth		MTU		Reliability
Load		Hop Count	Destination	

(up to 103
more entries)

Figure 6-24   The format of an IGRP packet.

IGRP classifies a route as interior, system, or exterior. An *interior route* is one that is local to the classful network on which the subnet is being advertised. For example, the subnet 10.1.1.0/24 being advertised on a link that is itself a subnet of 10.0.0.0/8 is considered an interior route. A *system route* is a route that has been summarized on a classful network boundary. For example, the route 10.0.0.0/8 advertised on a subnet of the 192.168.1.0/24 network would be classified as a system route.

An *exterior route* is a network advertisement that has been flagged as a default network. You can configure default routes in IGRP by using the `ip default-network a.b.c.d` command. When a router running IGRP or EIGRP is configured with a default network statement, it will advertise the network defined with this command to other IGRP routers as an external route. Routers receiving this advertisement install a default route in their routing table pointing in the direction from which the routing update was received. Recall our earlier discussion of the default route, also referred to as a gateway of last resort.

Since IGRP classifies routes into these three categories, it becomes possible to advertise an IP address with only 3 octets instead of all 4. If a route is interior, at least the first octet is known since the router is connected to the same classful network, so only the last 3 octets are needed. If the route is a system or exterior route, at least the last octet must be 0, so only the first 3 octets must be sent. This system allows IGRP to make more efficient use of the fields in an update packet. Notice that up to 104 IGRP routes can be sent in a single packet versus only 25 for RIP. Also notice that IGRP does not require that route entries fall on a 32-bit boundary and that every field is used, unlike RIPv1, which has several unused fields.

The remaining fields in the IGRP packet are self-explanatory. Notice that the hop count and MTU values are tracked, but they are not used in the IGRP metric calculation.

Variance

One additional feature of IGRP is unequal cost load sharing. IGRP and EIGRP are unique among IP routing protocols in that they allow you to load share across unequal cost paths. Recall from our earlier discussion that Cisco can load share across up to six equal cost paths and the default value is four. By using the router subcommand `variance`, you can specify an integer value that will indicate by how great a factor a higher cost metric can vary and still be used for load sharing.

```
r4#conf t
Enter configuration commands, one per line. End with CNTL/Z.
r4(config)#router igrp 1
r4(config-router)#variance 2
r4(config-router)#
```

For example, if the variance is set to 2, the metric for alternate paths can vary by a factor of 2 and still be used for load sharing. If the lowest cost path is 16,542, any path with a metric less than or equal to (2*16,542 = 33,084) will be used for load sharing. The router sends a proportionate number of packets across each path. Using a variance of 2 means that twice as many packets would be sent over the lowest-cost path as any other higher-cost paths. If fast switching is used, twice as many cache entries are set for the interface toward the lowest-cost path as are set for any higher-cost paths. The variance command is available for use only with IGRP and EIGRP.

EIGRP

Enhanced IGRP was introduced by Cisco in IOS version 9.21. Unlike RIPv2, which is very similar to RIPv1 with a few extensions, EIGRP is dramatically different from IGRP. EIGRP uses the same composite metrics and is still a distance vector protocol, but it varies considerably from IGRP and all other DV routing protocols in its behavior. Recall our earlier discussion of the behavior of DV routing protocols and their susceptibility to routing loops and slow convergence. In contrast to the periodic broadcasting of full routing tables, EIGRP routing updates are nonperiodic, partial, and bounded. Updates are sent only when changes occur, so they are nonperiodic unlike RIP and IGRP.

These updates only contain routing information that has changed, not the entire routing table. Additionally, these updates are sent only to affected routers and not as broadcasts. The updates are, therefore, bounded and are not sent to routers that do not need to receive the update. As we will see, EIGRP forms neighbor relationships with other EIGRP routers so it can quickly determine when a router has failed like a link state routing protocol. EIGRP additionally uses a Diffusing Update Algorithm (DUAL) to allow for very fast convergence. The DUAL algorithm is the key to EIGRP's performance and it is discussed later in this section.

EIGRP includes the subnet mask in its routing updates and is, therefore, a classless routing protocol. It supports the use of VLSM and discontiguous networks like RIPv2. Additionally, EIGRP allows you to summarize subnet address ranges on any interface, not just on classful network boundaries as is the case with RIPv2. As we will see later in this section, this can be an important benefit. Finally, EIGRP can be used for the routing of not only the IP protocol but IPX and Appletalk as well. We do not cover the use of EIGRP for protocols other than IP.

EIGRP Operations

EIGRP uses reliable multicast to disseminate routing information. When an EIGRP router needs to send an update to multiple neighbors, it sends an update to the reserved multicast address 224.0.0.10. Each neighbor sends a unicast reply indicating its reception of the update. EIGRP, like IGRP, uses IP as its transport protocol and operates on IP protocol 88. In addition to reliable multicast, EIGRP uses unicast updates as well. EIGRP sends a unicast routing update if a specific request is received from a neighboring router. Otherwise, it uses reliable multicast as described previously. Other types of packets used by EIGRP include:

Hellos. Used by EIGRP in neighbor discovery. Hellos are multicast and use reliable delivery.

Acknowledgments (ACKs). Unicast replies used by EIGRP to acknowledge receipt of a neighbors packets.

*Queries and Replies.*Used by the DUAL algorithm to perform diffusing computations. The behavior of DUAL is described in the next section.

EIGRP discovers and tracks its neighbors through use of hello packets. Hello packets are sent out at regular intervals to ensure that neighbor routers are still active. On LAN interfaces, the update interval is 5 s. On NBMA links, such as frame relay and ATM, the interval is 60 s. Neighbor routers are declared inactive if three hello packets are missed. You can see the neighbors that an EIGRP router has discovered by using the sh ip eigrp neighbors command shown in Figure 6-25.

This command is very useful for determining if an EIGRP router is properly communicating with its neighbor routers. The next section shows that the use of the DUAL algorithm depends on an EIGRP router establishing and maintaining neighbor relationships.

The DUAL Algorithm

The DUAL algorithm can seem complicated, but in fact it is based on very simple principles. The first principle is that each router keeps a record of the routing information sent by each neighbor router. This may not seem very unique since it would seem that all DV routing protocols do this. However, other DV routing protocols like RIP and IGRP take the routing information advertised by neighbor routers, add their own metric to it, and

Figure 6-25 The output of sh ip eigrp neighbors.

```
r1#sh ip eigrp neigh
IP-EIGRP neighbors for process 1
H  Address         Interface Hold Uptime  SRTT  RTO Q Seq Type
                   (sec)    (ms)    Cnt Num
1  10.1.2.2        Se1/2    13 00:04:54  0 4500 0 2
0  10.1.1.4        Et0/0    12 00:05:04 728 4368 0 2
r1#
```

Figure 6-26 The output of `sh ip eigrp topology`.

```
r1#sh ip eigrp topology
IP-EIGRP Topology Table for AS(1)/ID(192.19.15.1)
Codes: P - Passive, A - Active, U - Update, Q - Query, R - Reply,
    r - Reply status
P 10.1.3.0/24, 1 successors, FD is 20512000
        via Connected, Serial1/1
        via 10.1.1.4 (537600/512000), Ethernet0/0
P 10.1.2.0/24, 1 successors, FD is 25600
        via Connected, Serial1/2
P 10.1.1.0/24, 1 successors, FD is 281600
        via Connected, Ethernet0/0
        via 10.1.3.4 (537600/25600), Serial1/1
P 10.1.5.0/24, 2 successors, FD is 537600
        via 10.1.1.4 (537600/512000), Ethernet0/0
        via 10.1.2.2 (537600/512000), Serial1/2
        via 10.1.3.4 (1024000/512000), Serial1/1
P 192.168.1.0/24, 1 successors, FD is 51200
        via 10.1.1.4 (51200/25600), Ethernet0/0
        via 10.1.3.4 (537600/25600), Serial1/1
r1#
```

place the route in the routing table. They typically only place the best route to a destination in the routing table and discard any additional higher-cost routes. EIGRP is different. EIGRP records all of the routes advertised by neighbors in a special database called the *topology database*. EIGRP uses this topology database to look for other available routes to a destination if the best route fails. You can view the EIGRP topology table with the command `sh ip eigrp topology`, as shown in Figure 6-26. Notice the information in bold. The route to 10.1.5.0/24 is our main interest. Notice that EIGRP reports that there are two successors. This means that there are two next-hop neighbors with equal cost paths to subnet 10.1.5.0/24. If we look up the route to 10.1.5.0/24 in the routing table, we find that indeed two equal-cost paths are recorded, as shown in Figure 6-27.

Notice that the metric shown for the route to 10.1.5.0 in Figure 6-27 is the same reported as the `FD` value for 10.1.5.0/24 in Figure 6-26. This is no accident.

Feasible Distance (FD)

FD is critical to the operation of the DUAL algorithm because it is the best route to a destination. In simplest terms, it is just the smallest metric to reach a given destination. Any next hop through which the router calculates a route that is equal to the FD is considered a successor. All this means is that the router uses that next hop to send packets for a particular destination. Remember that when a DV routing protocol receives a

Figure 6-27   The output of sh ip ro for subnet 10.1.5.0.

```
r1#sh ip ro 10.1.5.0
Routing entry for 10.1.5.0/24
 Known via "eigrp 1", distance 90, metric 537600, type internal
 Redistributing via eigrp 1
 Last update from 10.1.1.4 on Ethernet0/0, 00:03:52 ago
 Routing Descriptor Blocks:
 * 10.1.2.2, from 10.1.2.2, 00:03:52 ago, via Serial1/2
    Route metric is 537600, traffic share count is 1
    Total delay is 21000 microseconds, minimum bandwidth is 128 Kbit
    Reliability 255/255, minimum MTU 1500 bytes
    Loading 1/255, Hops 1
   10.1.1.4, from 10.1.1.4, 00:03:52 ago, via Ethernet0/0
    Route metric is 537600, traffic share count is 1
    Total delay is 21000 microseconds, minimum bandwidth is 128 Kbit
    Reliability 255/255, minimum MTU 1500 bytes
    Loading 1/255, Hops 1
 r1#
```

routing advertisement from a neighbor, it takes the advertised metric, adds its cost to reach the neighbor, and then uses this new cost to determine the best path. The FD value is the lowest metric the router has found after performing this process on all advertised paths to a destination.

Successors

In Figure 6-26, the router lists two successors. Notice the numbers in parenthesis for next-hop IP addresses 10.1.2.2 and 10.1.1.4. The first number, 537600, is the distance to subnet 10.1.5.0 through each next-hop IP address. Notice that this value is equal to the FD value. Both next-hop IP addresses 10.1.2.2 and 10.1.1.4 will be used to load share packets to 10.1.5.0/24 since the metrics are equal. This is why the router reports two successors for 10.1.5.0/24 in Figure 6-26 and why the router reports using two paths in the routing table in Figure 6-27.

Reported Distance

Notice the second number in parenthesis in Figure 6-26. This number is the cost to subnet 10.1.5.0/24 as advertised by our neighbor routers. Neighbors 10.1.1.4 and 10.1.2.2 are both advertising a metric of 512000 to reach subnet 10.1.5.0/24. The metric to a destination advertised by a neighbor is referred to as the *reported distance* and we will see its importance shortly. It should be noted that we have simplified our example so that only the delay variable is used to calculate our metric. Each successor, 10.1.1.4 and 10.1.2.2, is advertising a metric to subnet 10.1.5.0/24 with a value of 512000 and this number is based only on the delay of the interfaces to reach the subnet. Again, this is the second number in parenthesis in Figure

6-26. The delay on each interface of router R1 has been set to an equal value, so the calculated metrics are equal. In the real world, it is unlikely that you would set the delay on an Ethernet interface to the same value as that of a serial interface; we have done so here only to aid discussion.

Feasible Successor

We now understand that the FD is the best cost to a destination and for every neighbor that has this cost the router will record it as a successor, as shown in Figure 6-26. This is all very straightforward and doesn't seem all that unique. However, in addition to a successor, EIGRP will also track feasible successors. A *feasible successor* is a router that is advertising a metric, referred to as the reported distance, that is less than the router's FD. In Figure 6-26, while we have two successors, notice that there are actually three next-hop IP addresses reported. Next-hop IP 10.1.3.4 is a feasible successor because it is reporting a cost of 512000 to reach subnet 10.1.5.0/24 and the FD is 537600. The number 512000 is less than 537600 so 10.1.3.4 is a feasible successor. What this means in plain English is that 10.1.3.4 is metrically closer to 10.1.5.0/24 than router R1 since its advertised cost to reach 10.1.5.0/24 is less than R1's current minimum cost to reach the same destination.

This is another central principle of the DUAL algorithm. A router cannot form a loop by choosing a next-hop router that is metrically closer to a destination than its current calculated metric. Notice in Figure 6-26 that although the calculated metric to 10.1.5.0/24 through 10.1.3.4 is 1024000, the metric advertised by 10.1.3.4 is only 512000. Although the path through 10.1.3.4 is not the best path and it is not a successor, the metric advertised by this router is less than the FD. In the event of the failure of the paths through neighbors 10.1.1.4 and 10.1.2.2, the router would immediately switch to the path through 10.1.3.4 because it knows there cannot be a routing loop by choosing that path. A loop can never be formed if a router chooses a lower-cost next hop than its currently calculated metric. DUAL takes advantage of this fact and, by tracking the metric advertised by its neighbors, is able to almost instantaneously switch to an alternate path as long as a feasible successor is available.

Diffusing Computation

The question arises as to what occurs when there is no feasible successor. That is, what if there is no neighbor advertising a metric that is less than the router's current best metric. In this scenario, EIGRP marks a route as active and begins what is called a diffusing computation. The router sends a query to all of its neighbors asking if they have a feasible successor to the route in question. If they do, the neighbor router responds with this information and diffusing computation is completed. If the neighbor routers do not have a feasible successor to the destination, they, in turn, query their neighbors looking for a feasible successor. Each router keeps track of all of the queries sent and places a timer to determine when an expected reply has not been given. If a reply to a query has not been received within the time-out value, the route is marked as stuck-in-active. The default time-out value is 3 min.

When a router sends a query to its neighbors looking for a feasible successor, each of its neighbors removes the querying router as a feasible successor for the queried route. For example, if R2's best route for 10.1.5.0/24 was through R1, R2 would remove this information from its topology table if it received a query from R1 looking for a route to 10.1.5.0/24. This eliminates the possibility that R2 could supply bogus information to R1 that might cause a routing loop.

It should be noted that these diffusing computations may take a long time in large internetworks. If each router that is queried has no feasible successor to a destination and must query its neighbors, quite a bit of traffic could result. In a stable environment, the amount of this kind of traffic should be minimal, but it is best to try to limit the number of routers participating in this process. As with IGRP, you can split your internetwork into separate process domains by running separate EIGRP processes on some routers and redistributing certain routes between process domains.

Summary Routes

One final point about EIGRP is its ability to summarize routes on an interface-by-interface basis. For summary routes to work correctly, the automatic summarization on classful network may need to be disabled with the routing protocol subcommand `no auto-summary`. Recall that we discussed the use of this command in the RIPv2 section as well.

A summary route is also referred to as a *supernet route* as opposed to a subnet. In basic terms a summary or supernet route is a single route that includes many more specific routes. For example, Figure 6-28 has a summary route for 172.16.0.0/21. This route includes all of the more specific routes 172.16.0.0/24 through 172.16.7.0/24.

Notice that after configuring a summary route on the Ethernet interface, a new route automatically appears in the routing table pointing to `null0`. This is our summary route. Figure 6-29 shows the routing table of a downstream router before and after configuring the summary route on R1. Notice that after the summary route is configured, the more specific routes are no longer in the routing table.

This concludes our coverage of EIGRP and DV routing protocols. The next section looks briefly at OSFP, the most popular link state routing protocol used in contemporary internetworks.

Figure 6-28 The use of a summary route.

```
r1#sh ip ro
Gateway of last resort is not set

     172.16.0.0/24 is subnetted, 4 subnets
C       172.16.10.0 is directly connected, Serial1/2
D       172.16.1.0 [90/41728] via 10.1.2.2, 00:01:07, Serial1/2
D       172.16.2.0 [90/41728] via 10.1.2.2, 00:01:07, Serial1/2
D       172.16.3.0 [90/41728] via 10.1.2.2, 00:01:07, Serial1/2
r1#conf t
Enter configuration commands, one per line. End with CNTL/Z.
r1(config)#int e 0/0
r1(config-if)#ip summary-address eigrp 1 172.16.0.0 255.255.248.0
r1(config-if)#
r1#
r1#sh ip ro
Gateway of last resort is not set

     172.16.0.0/16 is variably subnetted, 5 subnets, 2 masks
C       172.16.10.0/24 is directly connected, Serial1/2
D       172.16.0.0/21 is a summary, 00:00:07, Null0
D       172.16.1.0/24 [90/41728] via 10.1.2.2, 00:01:32, Serial1/2
D       172.16.2.0/24 [90/41728] via 10.1.2.2, 00:01:32, Serial1/2
D       172.16.3.0/24 [90/41728] via 10.1.2.2, 00:01:32, Serial1/2
```

Figure 6-29 The effects of using a summary route on a downstream router.

```
r4#sh ip ro
Gateway of last resort is not set
172.16.0.0/24 is subnetted, 4 subnets
D       172.16.10.0 [90/51200] via 10.1.1.1, 00:00:01, Ethernet0/0
D       172.16.1.0 [90/67328] via 10.1.1.1, 00:00:01, Ethernet0/0
D       172.16.2.0 [90/67328] via 10.1.1.1, 00:00:01, Ethernet0/0
D       172.16.3.0 [90/67328] via 10.1.1.1, 00:00:01, Ethernet0/0
r4#sh ip ro
Gateway of last resort is not set

     172.16.0.0/16 is variably subnetted, 2 subnets, 2 masks
D       172.16.10.0/24 [90/51200] via 10.1.1.1, 00:00:13, Ethernet0/0
D       172.16.0.0/21 [90/67328] via 10.1.1.1, 00:00:13, Ethernet0/0
```

OSPF

As mentioned previously, OSPF is a link state routing protocol, not a DV routing protocol. LS routing protocols operate fundamentally differently than DV routing protocols. They establish neighbor relationships and send link state updates to their neighbors regarding the state of their links. These links are, in turn, flooded by neighboring routers through the internetwork. While the basic principles of OSPF are not complicated, there are many different topics related to its implementation in large internetworks. OSPF uses IP as its transport protocol like EIGRP and uses IP protocol 88. OSPF uses the reserved multicast addresses 224.0.0.5, AllSPFRouters, and 224.0.0.6, AllDRouters, to exchange LS information with its neighbors. This section discusses only the basic topics.

We first look at how OSPF is configured on a router and then examine the forming of neighbor relationships. We complete our discussion with the use of areas in an OSPF network, including the different types of OSPF areas.

Enabling OSPF

Figure 6-30 illustrates the enabling of an OSPF process on a Cisco router. The number specified with OSPF is not a process domain as with IGRP and EIGRP. It is referred to simply as a process ID and has only local significance. Routers in an OSPF network do not have to use the same process ID, but using the same process ID makes configuration simpler.

Notice that unlike RIP, IGRP, and EIGRP, we can specify a mask with the network statement. This means we can specify on a per-interface basis which interfaces will participate in OSPF and which will not. There is no need to use the passive-interface command, although its use is supported if you choose to use it. If the passive-interface command is used, it completely disables the use of OSPF on that interface as it does with EIGRP. Notice further that we specify an area number. We discuss areas in just a moment. For now, what is important to know is that each interface participating in OSPF must belong to an area and it can only belong to a single area. We will see why the specification of an area is important later.

Figure 6-30   Configuring OSPF on a Cisco router.

```
r1#conf t
Enter configuration commands, one per line. End with CNTL/Z.
r1(config)#router ospf 1
r1(config-router)#network 10.1.1.0 0.0.0.255 area 0
r1(config-router)#
r1#
```

Neighbor Relationships

As previously mentioned, OSPF routers discover and track neighboring routers. It was stated that OSPF routers establish this neighbor relationship with all neighboring routers and exchange link state information. The process of establishing a relationship with a neighboring router for the purpose of exchanging LS information is called forming an *adjacency*. Routers do not form adjacencies with all neighboring routers. On broadcast media such as Ethernet, if an OSPF router had to form an adjacency with each of its neighbors, it would lead to a large number of adjacencies and would place a large burden on each router. Since the media supports broadcast, it seems unnecessary to have all of these adjacencies. It would be better to simply select one router with which all other routers could form an adjacency that would act as a proxy to inform every OSPF router about the LS information of every other OSPF router. This is the function of the *designated router* (DR).

On broadcast media such as Ethernet, a DR router is elected. The function of the DR is to establish an adjacency with every other OSPF router on the network segment. The DR collects LS information from each OSPF router and passes this information on to other OSPF routers. This way, only the DR has to maintain a large number of adjacencies. A *backup DR* (BDR) is also elected so that the network is not disrupted in the event of a failure of the DR. Every router on a broadcast media forms an adjacency with the DR and BDR, and the DR and BDR form adjacencies with each other. The election of the DR and BDR is on a per-interface basis and can be influenced with the interface command `ip ospf priority`. The higher the priority, the more likely a router is to become the DR. If this value is set to 0, a router is not eligible to become a DR or BDR on that interface (but it could be a DR or BDR on another interface). There is no concept of a DR or BDR on point-to-point links. Routers on point-to-point links will always become adjacent and exchange LS information. This is true of routers on point-to-point subinterfaces as well as those used with frame relay and ATM.

Areas

LS information is flooded throughout an internetwork. Obviously, if the internetwork is very large, this can lead to a significant amount of LS traffic in an internetwork and a significant amount of CPU processing may be required by each router to process these LS floods. To combat this situation, OSPF uses the concept of areas. An OSPF *area* is a smaller collection of OSPF routers within an internetwork. LS information is flooded only to routers within the area and not to all routers in the internetwork. By creating areas that contain a fewer number of routers, the LS burden is reduced on each router in the area. Every area must have at least one router that is connected to multiple areas. This router is called the *area border router* (ABR). It is the responsibility of the ABR to handle interarea traffic. If multiple areas are used in an internetwork, one of the areas must be area 0. Area 0 is a special OSPF area. All areas must be connected to area 0 and all interarea traffic must flow through area 0. This is illustrated in Figure 6-31.

In Figure 6-31, traffic from area 1 to area 2 must flow through routers R1 and R2. Traffic cannot traverse directly from one area to another without crossing area 0. It is the responsibility of the ABR to ensure that traffic is properly forwarded from one area to another.

Summary Routes

An additional useful feature of an ABR is to send a summary route into an area. As with EIGRP, a summary route is a way for routers to send information about ranges of subnets to other routers. You configure an ABR to send a summary route into an area with the OSPF command `area range`:

```
r1#conf t
Enter configuration commands, one per line. End with CNTL/Z.
r1(config)#router ospf 1
r1(config-router)#area 0 range 10.1.0.0 255.255.0.0
r1(config-router)#
r1#
```

This tells ABR R1 that there is a summary range for the address 10.1.0.0/16 contained in area 0. This range is sent into areas other than

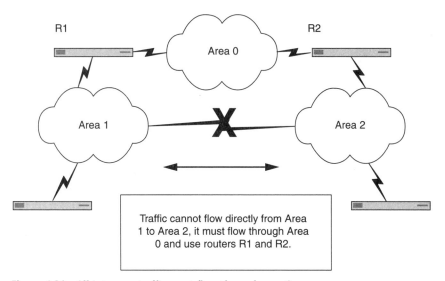

Figure 6-31   All interarea traffic must flow through area 0.

area 0. For example, if R1 were connected to area 1 and area 0. The preceding command would cause router R1 to send a summary LSA into area 1 and suppress more specific LSAs contained in the 10.1.0.0/16 range.

This means that if a network link using an IP address in the 10.1.0.0/16 range fails in area 0, the LSA information would not be flooded into area 1. Using the area range command is, therefore, very useful to limit the flooding of LSAs from one area to another. If you do not create area range summaries on ABR routers, all LSA information will be flooded throughout the internetwork from one area to another, eliminating most of the reason for creating areas to begin with. It is obvious then that the creation of area range commands is a critical step to proper OSPF design.

Types of Areas

Up to this point, we have discussed areas generically. However, not all areas are created equal. There are several different types of areas in an OSPF network.

Stub Areas

A *stub area* is an area into which external routes are not flooded. An external route is any non-OSPF–originated route. For example, a route redistributed from another routing protocol would be considered an external route. External routes are normally flooded throughout an OSPF internetwork. However, sometimes it is unnecessary to flood this information into an area. This would be the case, for example, if there were only a single ABR for an area. If there is only a single exit point from an area, there seems little reason to flood a lot of routes into that area. It makes more sense just to send a default route LSA into the area and suppress external routers. This is exactly what occurs in a stub area. You configure a stub area by adding the keyword stub to the end of the network statement. Every router in an area must be configured with the stub keyword.

Totally Stubby Areas

A *totally stubby area* takes the idea of a stub area one step further. In addition to not flooding external routes into the area, not even OSPF summary routes are flooded into an area. In fact, only a default LSA is sent into a totally stubby area by an ABR. This can be safely done on any area that has only a single ABR. If there are multiple ABR routers for an area, configuring the area as totally stubby may result in suboptimal routing. The reason for this is that one of the ABRs may have a better path to some of the summary addresses it would normally flood into an area. If this is not the case or if it is not a concern, you can make areas with multiple ABRs into totally stubby areas as well. You can configure an area as totally stubby by adding the keyword `stub no-summary` to the end of the network statement on the ABR only. All of the other routers in the area should have the `stub` keyword configured as with stub areas.

This concludes our brief overview of OSPF. There are many additional topics related to OSPF, and this section is intended only to provide an overview of the operation of OSPF. A detailed discussion of OSPF can, and has, filled entire books. For more information on OSPF, a good resource is *Cisco Router OSPF: Design and Implementation Guide* by William R. Parkhurst (McGraw-Hill 1998).

We have now completed our coverage of IP routing protocols. We hope that this chapter has provided at least a basic understanding of the need for routing protocols and their use in Cisco networks. This chapter was intended only as an overview of the workings of the most common routing protocols. Additional coverage for each of the routing protocols discussed in this chapter and much more can be found in *CCIE Professional Development: Routing TCP/IP Volume 1* by Jeff Doyle (Cisco Systems 1998).

CHAPTER 7

Additional IP Services

IP Functions

This section examines some of the key functions of the IP layer that provide additional services useful in internetworks.

Hot Standby Routing Protocol (HSRP)

The *hot standby routing protocol* (HSRP) provides a backup default gateway for your workstations and servers. Most of the time, workstations do not participate in routing protocols. You simply configure a default next-hop IP address to which the workstation sends packets for all IP destinations not on its directly connected subnet. This situation usually works well since it alleviates the burden of having each workstation keep track of all of the IP subnets that are in use in the internetwork. Problems arise however when the workstation's default gateway fails. Many workstations' operating systems only allow you to specify a single default gateway. Even those that allow you to specify more than one default gateway may not work in the manner you expect.

For example, Microsoft Windows allows you to specify multiple default gateways, but the MS TCP/IP stack uses TCP to detect the loss of a primary default gateway, not ICMP. What this means is that if there were a failure in the end-to-end path, MS would try to use the backup default gateway, even if the failure in the network was many hops downstream. Most administrators would like for their workstations to continue to use the primary default gateway as long as it is active or at least until there is a failure of a link on the default gateway itself, not a failure in a downstream link many router hops away. HSRP provides for this functionality.

You need at least two routers for HSRP to function, but you can use more than two if you wish. First select an IP address that will be the HSRP IP address, that is, the IP address you will point the default gateway of your workstations toward. One of the routers will be the active HSRP router and the remaining routers will be standby routers. As long as the active router is operating, it will answer IP requests for the HSRP IP address. In the event the active HSRP router fails, a backup HSRP router will begin answering requests for the HSRP IP address. This is illustrated in Figure 7-1.

The configuration for routers R1 and R2 is shown in Figure 7-2. Notice that the command `standby 1 IP` specifies the HSRP IP address. HSRP routers become aware of the presence of other HSRP routers on the same segment by sending out HSRP hello packets to multicast address 224.0.0.2. All HSRP routers listen for other HSRP neighbors on this multicast address. The information contained in the HSRP hello includes the standby group number, the standby IP address, the hello interval, the hold time, and the router's priority. The priority value determines which router becomes the active HSRP router. The default value is 100, and a higher value is preferred.

Notice that R1 has been configured with an HSRP priority of 110 so that it will become the active HSRP router. The default interval for HSRP hello packets is 3 s and the hold time is 10 s. If an HSRP router does not hear from a neighbor in three update periods, it assumes the neighbor has failed. Notice also in Figure 7-2 the use of the command `standby 1`

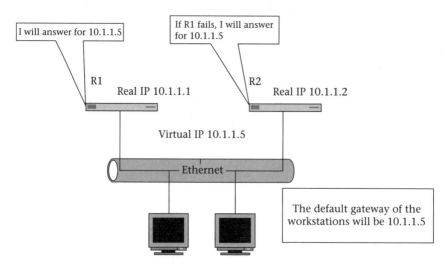

Figure 7-1 Using the hot standby routing protocol.

Figure 7-2 The configuration of two routes running HSRP.

```
Hostname R1
!
interface Ethernet0/0
 ip address 10.1.1.1 255.255.255.0
 no ip redirects
 standby 1 priority 110
 standby 1 preempt
 standby 1 ip 10.1.1.5
Hostname R2
!
interface Ethernet0/0
 ip address 10.1.1.2 255.255.255.0
 no ip redirects
 standby 1 preempt
 standby 1 ip 10.1.1.5
```

preempt. This command allows an HSRP router to assume the role of the active HSRP router from another HSRP router. Without this command, a router would have to wait for the active HSRP router to fail to assume the role of the active HSRP router. For example, if router R1 in Figure 7-1 were to fail, router R2 would assume the role of the active HSRP router with or without the preempt command. However, when router R1 becomes available again, it would not be allowed to resume its duties as the active HSRP router without the use of the preempt command, even though its priority is higher than R2.

You can see what the current state of the HSRP process on a route is by using the command sh standby. The output from this command is illustrated in Figure 7-3. Notice that router R1 reports that it is the active router and the active state is local. Also notice that the router reports the virtual Mac address. In addition to the virtual IP that is configured, the HSRP routers create a virtual Mac address. The virtual Mac address is used

Figure 7-3 The output from the sh standby command.

```
R1#sh stand
Ethernet0/0 - Group 1
 Local state is Active, priority 110, may preempt
 Hellotime 3 holdtime 10
 Next hello sent in 00:00:01.334
 Hot standby IP address is 10.1.1.5 configured
 Active router is local
 Standby router is 10.1.1.2 expires in 00:00:09
 Standby virtual mac address is 0000.0c07.ac01
```

Figure 7-4 The output from the sh standby command on a router with multiple HSRP groups.

```
R1#sh stand
Ethernet0/0 - Group 1
  Local state is Active, priority 110, may preempt
  Hellotime 3 holdtime 10
  Next hello sent in 00:00:02.331
  Hot standby IP address is 10.1.1.5 configured
  Active router is local
  Standby router is 10.1.1.1 expires in 00:00:08
  Standby virtual mac address is 0000.0c07.ac01
Ethernet0/0 - Group 2
  Local state is Standby, priority 100
  Hellotime 3 holdtime 10
  Next hello sent in 00:00:00.368
  Hot standby IP address is 10.1.1.10 configured
  Active router is 10.1.1.1 expires in 00:00:08
  Standby router is local
  Standby virtual mac address is 0000.0c07.ac02
```

by whichever router is the active HSRP router. When a backup HSRP router takes over for a failed HSRP router, it begins using the virtual Mac address. This process alleviates the need of the workstations to learn a new Mac address for the virtual IP address.

On some routers you can configure more than one HSRP group. You cannot configure multiple HSRP groups on all Cisco routers due to limitations in the hardware. Multiple HSRP groups can be configured on 2600, 3600, 4000, and 7x00 series routers. Figure 7-4 shows the output from the sh standby command issued on a 2600 series router.

Notice that router R1 is the active router for group 1 and the standby router for group 2. Using multiple HSRP groups can allow you to use one router as the primary HSRP router for one group and the backup HSRP router for another group so that you can load share across multiple routers. To do this, you need to have some of your workstations point their default gateway to the HSRP IP address of group 1 and some to the HSRP IP address of group 2. Whether or not the additional administrative burden associated with managing such a configuration is worth it depends on your environment.

IP Maximum Transmission Unit (MTU)

Every router interface has a maximum transmission unit (MTU) that specifies how large a packet can be before it must be fragmented. You can adjust the IP MTU set for an interface so that the IOS fragments IP packets

Figure 7-5 The use of the `ip mtu` command.

```
r4#conf t
Enter configuration commands, one per line. End with CNTL/Z.
r4(config)#int e 0/0
r4(config-if)#ip mtu 500
r4(config-if)#
r4#
2d19h: %SYS-5-CONFIG_I: Configured from console by console
r4#sh ip int e 0/0
Ethernet0/0 is up, line protocol is up
  Internet address is 10.1.1.4/24
  Broadcast address is 255.255.255.255
  Address determined by setup command
  MTU is 500 bytes
```

larger than the specified IP MTU size. You might want to do this, for example, if you suspect that equipment between two routers is having problems with large packets. By changing the IP MTU size, you can force the router to send only small packets. Use the interface command `ip mtu` to change the IP MTU size, as shown in Figure 7-5.

You can see that the router fragments packets that are larger than the 500-byte IP MTU by using the `debug ip packet` command, as shown in Figure 7-6. Notice that the IP packets are fragmented since we have configured the ping program to use 600-byte packets and the IP MTU of the interface was configured for only 500 bytes.

Ping

Most anyone who has ever worked with IP for any amount of time has used the ping program. In its simplest form, the ping program simply sends an ICMP `echo-request` packet to a destination address and expects an ICMP `echo-reply` in return. This simple use of ping is very useful for determining whether an IP device is alive. The ping program on a Cisco router allows you to do much more than this however. There are many options that you can use with the ping program, and we discuss a few of the most useful ones here.

Specifying the Source Address

There are many times when a user or another system administrator call you and say "I have a workstation that cannot get to X" where X may be a server in your network, a site on the Internet, etc. The person on the other end may say "I have checked everything on the workstation and it is correct and I can ping it from the router on its segment, so its IP con-

Figure 7-6 Illustration of the router fragmenting packets larger than the IP MTU.

```
r4#debug ip pack
IP packet debugging is on
r4#ping
Protocol [ip]:
Target IP address: 10.1.1.1
Repeat count [5]:
Datagram size [100]: 600
Timeout in seconds [2]:
Extended commands [n]:
Sweep range of sizes [n]:
Type escape sequence to abort.
Sending 5, 600-byte ICMP Echos to 10.1.1.1, timeout is 2 seconds:
!!!!!
Success rate is 100 percent (5/5), round-trip min/avg/max = 8/8/8 ms
r4#
2d19h: IP: s=10.1.1.4 (local), d=10.1.1.1 (Ethernet0/0), len 600,
          sending
2d19h: IP: s=10.1.1.4 (local), d=10.1.1.1 (Ethernet0/0), len 500,
          sending fragment
2d19h: IP: s=10.1.1.1 (Ethernet0/0), d=10.1.1.4 (Ethernet0/0), len 600,
          rcvd 3
2d19h: IP: s=10.1.1.4 (local), d=10.1.1.1 (Ethernet0/0), len 600,
          sending
2d19h: IP: s=10.1.1.4 (local), d=10.1.1.1 (Ethernet0/0), len 500,
          sending fragment
2d19h: IP: s=10.1.1.1 (Ethernet0/0), d=10.1.1.4 (Ethernet0/0), len 600,
          rcvd 3
2d19h: IP: s=10.1.1.4 (local), d=10.1.1.1 (Ethernet0/0), len 600,
          sending
2d19h: IP: s=10.1.1.4 (local), d=10.1.1.1 (Ethernet0/0), len 500,
          sending fragment
2d19h: IP: s=10.1.1.1 (Ethernet0/0), d=10.1.1.4 (Ethernet0/0), len 600,
          rcvd 3
2d19h: IP: s=10.1.1.4 (local), d=10.1.1.1 (Ethernet0/0), len 600,
          sending
2d19h: IP: s=10.1.1.4 (local), d=10.1.1.1 (Ethernet0/0), len 500,
          sending fragment
2d19h: IP: s=10.1.1.1 (Ethernet0/0), d=10.1.1.4 (Ethernet0/0), len 600,
          rcvd 3
2d19h: IP: s=10.1.1.4 (local), d=10.1.1.1 (Ethernet0/0), len 600,
          sending
2d19h: IP: s=10.1.1.4 (local), d=10.1.1.1 (Ethernet0/0), len 500,
          sending fragment
2d19h: IP: s=10.1.1.1 (Ethernet0/0), d=10.1.1.4 (Ethernet0/0), len 600,
          rcvd 3
```

figuration must be correct." In actuality, simply pinging a host from a router on its segment is not really testing everything.

Pinging from a router on the same segment only means that the router has an entry in its ARP table for the workstation and the workstation likewise has an entry in its ARP table for the router. All this means is

Figure 7-7 Specifying the source IP address for a ping packet.

```
r4#ping
Protocol [ip]:
Target IP address: 10.1.1.100
Repeat count [5]:
Datagram size [100]:
Timeout in seconds [2]:
Extended commands [n]: y
Source address or interface: 192.168.1.1
Type of service [0]:
Set DF bit in IP header? [no]:
Validate reply data? [no]:
Data pattern [0xABCD]:
Loose, Strict, Record, Timestamp, Verbose[none]:
Sweep range of sizes [n]:
Type escape sequence to abort.
Sending 5, 100-byte ICMP Echos to 10.1.1.100, timeout is 2 seconds:
.....
Success rate is 0 percent (0/5)
```

that ARP is working properly. In order to know if the workstation has its default gateway configured correctly, you need to send a packet to the workstation for which the workstation must use its default gateway. You can do this by sending a packet from an upstream router, or by using the ping option to specify the source address of the packet. Figure 7-7 illustrates what occurs when you attempt to ping a host on a directly connected subnet if you source the packet from an IP address on one of the router's other interfaces and the workstation has its default gateway set improperly.

Notice that there is no response from the workstation. If you perform these steps and the workstation does not respond, it almost always indicates the workstation's default gateway or subnet mask is set incorrectly.

Specifying the Data Pattern

Another very useful ping option is specifying the pattern of the bits in the data portion of the IP packet. Sometimes when a serial line is having problems, it is because some of the telco equipment is experiencing *bit sensitivity*. Bit sensitivity simply means that some equipment is failing in such a way that certain bit patterns cause errors on the line. You can test for bit sensitivity on a serial interface by specifying the bit pattern in the ping options, as shown in Figure 7-8.

The most common patterns to use are the all zeros, 0x0000, or all

Figure 7-8 Specifying the data pattern for a ping packet.

```
r4#ping
Protocol [ip]:
Target IP address: 10.1.1.1
Repeat count [5]:
Datagram size [100]:
Timeout in seconds [2]:
Extended commands [n]: y
Source address or interface:
Type of service [0]:
Set DF bit in IP header? [no]:
Validate reply data? [no]:
Data pattern [0xABCD]: 0x0000
Loose, Strict, Record, Timestamp, Verbose[none]:
Sweep range of sizes [n]:
Type escape sequence to abort.
Sending 5, 100-byte ICMP Echos to 10.1.1.1, timeout is 2 seconds:
Packet has data pattern 0x0000
!!!!!
Success rate is 100 percent (5/5), round-trip min/avg/max = 4/4/4 ms
```

ones, 0x1111. Another bit pattern the authors have found useful for testing is 0x2020. A 20 in hex equates to a space in ASCII. Some serial lines have shown sensitivity to large file transfers when the files contained a large number of spaces. These problems can usually be found, when they exist, by using a large number of ping packets with these different data patterns.

Setting the DF Bit

A final use of ping is the setting of the *don't fragment* (DF) bit in the IP packet. As we saw earlier, you can set the maximum IP MTU size on an interface. If you want to test all of the links in a path to see if they support a certain MTU size, you can specify the size of the ping packet (the default is 100 bytes) turn on the DF bit. If the packet reaches a router that has an interface with a smaller MTU than the size of the packet, the packet is dropped since the DF bit is set in the packet. The setting of the DF bit when using ping is illustrated in Figure 7-9.

Notice we have set the byte size to 600 and turned on the DF bit. All of our ping packets timed out after setting these parameters, yet a normal ping to 10.1.1.1 works. We can surmise from this that there is a link in the path to 10.1.1.1 that has its IP MTU set to something smaller than 600 bytes.

This completes our coverage of ping and IP services. The next section examines some of the additional configuration options available for the ICMP protocol.

Figure 7-9 Setting the don't fragment (DF)bit for a ping packet.

```
r4#ping
Protocol [ip]:
Target IP address: 10.1.1.1
Repeat count [5]:
Datagram size [100]: 600
Timeout in seconds [2]:
Extended commands [n]: y
Source address or interface:
Type of service [0]:
Set DF bit in IP header? [no]: yes
Validate reply data? [no]:
Data pattern [0xABCD]:
Loose, Strict, Record, Timestamp, Verbose[none]:
Sweep range of sizes [n]:
Type escape sequence to abort.
Sending 5, 600-byte ICMP Echos to 10.1.1.1, timeout is 2 seconds:
.....
Success rate is 0 percent (0/5)
r4#ping 10.1.1.1
Type escape sequence to abort.
Sending 5, 100-byte ICMP Echos to 10.1.1.1, timeout is 2 seconds:
!!!!!
Success rate is 100 percent (5/5), round-trip min/avg/max = 4/4/4 ms
```

ICMP Functions

While ICMP is a very simple protocol, it is also very powerful. This section looks at several ICMP configuration options.

IP Unreachables

When a router receives a packet for a destination address that it cannot forward, the router sends an ICMP destination unreachable message to the originator of the IP packet. This is illustrated in Figure 7-10.

Figure 7-10 A router sends an ICMP destination unreachable message to the origi-nator of the IP packet.

```
r1#debug ip icmp
ICMP packet debugging is on
r1#ping 172.17.1.1
Type escape sequence to abort.
Sending 5, 100-byte ICMP Echos to 172.17.1.1, timeout is 2 seconds:
U
02:05:36: ICMP: dst (10.1.1.1) host unreachable rcv from 10.1.1.4.U
02:05:38: ICMP: dst (10.1.1.1) host unreachable rcv from 10.1.1.4.U
Success rate is 0 percent (0/5)
```

Figure 7-11 A router sends an ICMP administratively prohibited message to the originator of the IP packet when an access list is violated.

```
r1#telnet 192.168.1.1
Trying 192.168.1.1 ...
% Destination unreachable; gateway or host down
r1#
02:15:18: ICMP: dst (10.1.1.1) administratively prohibited unreachable
  rcv from
10.1.1.4a
```

Router R1 is receiving a `destination unreachable` message from the
next hop router because it does not have a route to 172.16.1.1. Similarly,
a router will send an unreachable message in response to an access-list vio-
lation, as shown in Figure 7-11, where the next hop router is blocking telnet sessions, so it sends an ICMP administratively prohibited message in
response to our request to initiate a telnet session.

While these messages are helpful in most cases, they can be a little too
helpful and may reveal information that we don't wish to reveal. For
example, someone could use these features to determine what networks
our router knows about and what services it is blocking with an access list.
If enough traffic were sent to a router blocked by an access list, it could
place a large load on a router's CPU due to the large number of ICMP
unreachable messages being sent to the originator by the router. For these
reasons, on routers connected to hostile networks, such as the Internet, it
is recommended that you prevent the router from revealing this information by using the interface command `no ip unreachables`. After configuring this command on the next hop router, notice that we no longer
receive an `administratively prohibited` message in Figure 7-12.

Figure 7-12 After configuring `no ip unreachables` on the next hop router, we no
longer receive any ICMP unreachable messages.

```
r4#conf t
Enter configuration commands, one per line. End with CNTL/Z.
r4(config)#int e 0/0
r4(config-if)#no ip unreachables
r4(config-if)#
r4#
r1#telnet 192.168.1.1
Trying 192.168.1.1 ...
% Connection timed out; remote host not responding
```

Notice that no ICMP messages appear on the console of router R1. Also notice instead of the `destination unreachable` message recorded in Figure 7-11, this time the router simply records `connection timed out` because it never receives any response to its telnet request.

IP Redirects

IP redirects are sent from the router to a workstation or server when the router detects that a device is sending packets to it that should be sent to another router on the same segment. For example, in Figure 7-13 the workstations have been configured with R1 as their default gateway.

Any packets they need to send to devices on a subnet other than their own are sent to router R1. However, some destination subnets can only be reached through router R2. R1 is aware of this and will correctly route packets for those destinations through R2. But this is inefficient. The workstations would do better to send their packets directly to R2. Since this is the case, R1 sends an ICMP redirect to the workstations informing them that the destination they are sending packets to can best be reached through R2.

IP-Directed Broadcast

A directed broadcast is a packet that has a destination address of all ones in the subnet portion of the packet, for example, 192.168.1.255/24 or 10.1.255.255/16. There is usually very little reason for these packets to be

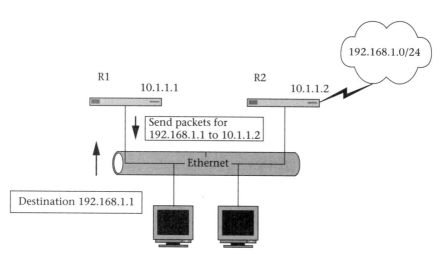

Figure 7-13 Router R1 sends an ICMP redirect message to hosts trying to reach 192.168.1.1.

forwarded through a router. These addresses are sometimes used to allow a station to send a ping to this address to see which hosts are available. On a router connected to an internal segment this may be allowed. However, any router connected to networks outside of your control, such as the Internet, should be prevented from forwarding these sorts of packets by using the interface command no ip directed·broadcast.

```
R1#conf t
Enter configuration commands, one per line. End with CNTL/Z.
R1(config)#interface ethernet0/0
R1(config-if)#no ip directed-broadcast
```

Subnet broadcast packets are used in some of the most notorious denial of service attacks (DoS), such as the smurf attack where an attacker floods your network with icmp echo-request packets with a spoofed source address. This attack can bring down a network in a matter of seconds, so disabling the forwarding of these kinds of packets is crucial. IP-directed broadcasts are disabled by default in IOS version 12.0.

Upper-Layer Services

This section briefly looks at some of the services provided for the upper-layer protocols such as TCP and UDP because they can greatly increase the functionality of a router in your internetwork.

TCP Header Compression

It can sometimes be useful to compress packets before they are sent through the router. By compressing the TCP headers of small packets, such as telnet, you can substantially reduce the overall size of the packet and increase the speed with which the packets traverse the network. Smaller packets can be moved faster than larger packets. Cisco supports the compression of TCP headers on serial lines using HDLC or PPP encapsulation. Both ends of the serial connection must have compression enabled. You enable TCP header compression with the interface command ip tcp header-compression

```
R1#conf t
Enter configuration commands, one per line. End with CNTL/Z.
R1(config)#interface serial0/0
R1(config-if)#ip tcp header-compression
```

Telnet Source Address

At times it can be useful to test TCP functions from the router to another device, for example, if you have *network address translation* (NAT) set up on a router and you want to test to see if it is working properly for TCP applications. Telnet is the most obvious selection for use as a TCP application since the router supports it and so do many other end devices. The problem is that in most cases any packets sourced from the router will have a source IP address of the interface from which the packet is sent. In most cases this is fine; however, there may be situations where you would like to specify the source IP address to be that of another interface on the router. You use the global command to specify what interface the router will use for telnet packets.

```
R1#conf t
Enter configuration commands, one per line. End with CNTL/Z.
R1(config)#ip telnet source-interface loopback0
```

IP Helper Address

Many applications use UDP-based broadcasts to locate servers. One of the most prevalent is *dynamic host configuration protocol* (DHCP), which allows workstations to obtain IP address information dynamically. Since UDP broadcasts are blocked at router interfaces, it would be necessary to have a DHCP server on each network segment. Needless to say, in a large network this could add up to a lot of DHCP servers. It would be helpful if there were a way to forward these UDP broadcasts in a limited fashion to a centrally located DHCP server. This is the function of the ip helper-address command. You can define single or multiple IP addresses that will receive UDP request packets. The router takes the UDP broadcasts and forwards them as a UDP unicast packet to the IP addresses you specify. You configure IP help addresses with the interface command ip helper-address:

```
R1#conf t
Enter configuration commands, one per line. End with CNTL/Z.
R1(config)#interface ethernet0/0
R1(config-if)#ip helper-address 172.16.1.1
```

You configure the IP helper address on the interface that will receive the UDP broadcasts. This is usually a LAN interface such as Ethernet or Token Ring.

IP Forward Protocol

By default several types of UDP broadcasts are enabled for forwarding when the IP helper address is configured: TFTP, TACACS+, DNS, Time services, NetBIOS (137 and 138), and Bootp (DHCP). You may not wish all of the default services to be enabled. For example, NetBIOS broadcasts are enabled for forwarding by default. You can selectively enable which services are enabled for forwarding by using the global command no ip forward-protocol udp and specifying which protocols you do not wish to be forwarded.

```
R1#conf t
Enter configuration commands, one per line. End with CNTL/Z.
r1(config)#no ip forward-protocol udp netbios-ns
```

Many UDP applications can be forwarded with the IP helper command. Any service that is not enabled by default would have to be explicitly enabled through the use of the ip forward-protocol udp command.

CHAPTER 8

Monitoring IP Network Traffic

This concluding chapter reviews another important IP-related topic that is valuable for learning about the operation of your network. This topic provides information about the operation of your router as well as the operation of different types of media to which your router is connected. After you have read this chapter, you will be able to identify potential problems before they become major problems, allowing you to take remedial action before network users are adversely affected and start to complain. This topic is the monitoring of network traffic and it not only identifies problems, but also gives you the ability to notice capacity issues that represent a two-edged sword. That is, while users normally complain when there is too little bandwidth, they never complain when there is too much bandwidth.

While monitoring of network traffic reduces the time network managers and administrators have to respond to customer queries, it can also indicate your organization has too much transmission capacity, with the result your organization may be able to reduce costs by converting to a more appropriate transmission facility. This means that you should carefully review statistical information obtained by traffic monitoring—both as a tool to denote potential network problems and a mechanism to verify the necessity of existing communications facilities.

Since network traffic obviously flows through a router, this chapter focuses on router monitoring of IP traffic. We use a number of router commands that provide information—both directly and indirectly—about network activity. In addition, since the utilization level of a router is an essential component of network activity, we also examine the use of the router to review the active processes being performed and how such processes could affect the flow of IP traffic.

Displaying Interface Statistics

This section reviews the display of interface statistics by examining certain metrics and how those metrics can be used to provide information about network activity.

Using the `show interfaces` Command

Interface statistics can be displayed by using the `show interfaces` command. This command is used at the `EXEC` prompt to display statistical information about a particular interface or all interfaces on your router. To do so, you enter the command using the following format:

```
show interfaces [interface type] [accounting]
```

In this format note that the keyword `interface` instead of `interfaces` produces the same results in recent versions of the IOS. If you do not specify a particular interface, such as `serial0/0/0`, information about all interfaces are displayed. The optional keyword `accounting` can be used to display the number of packets of different protocols transmitted through a particular interface or all interfaces. However, note that while the keyword `accounting` works with the `show interfaces` command, unless you turn on accounting for a specific protocol, such as IP, you will not be able to obtain an applicable display when you use other display commands, such as `show ip accounting`.

The interface accounting information only counts the number of packets and characters of an entire class of packets such as all IP or all IPX. The accounting which can be enabled on an individual interface for certain protocols, such as IP, will track the number of packets and bytes to individual addresses within a protocol, so it provides much more granular information than that shown with simple interface accounting.

Because the old adage "the proof of the pudding is in the eating" is applicable to most router operations, let's look at the use of the `show interface(s)` command to examine the statistics we can display.

Figure 8-1 shows an abbreviated portion of the results of the use of a `show interfaces` command, followed by two examples of the use of the `show interfaces` command, including the use of the keyword `accounting`.

Examining Serial Port Metrics

In Figure 8-1 the top portion is an example of the use of the `show interfaces` command without any parameters, which results in a display of information about all router interfaces. For brevity of discussion the display

Figure 8-1 Using the show interfaces command.

```
Cisco7500>show interfaces
Serial0/0/0 is up, line protocol is up
  Hardware is cyBus Serial
  Description: ATT KGBC673F00010002
  Internet address is 4.0.112.2/30
  MTU 1500 bytes, BW 1544 Kbit, DLY 20000 usec,
    reliability 255/255, txload 138/255, rxload 20/255
  Encapsulation HDLC, crc 16, loopback not set
  Keepalive set (10 sec)
  Last input 00:00:00, output 00:00:00, output hang never
  Last clearing of "show interface" counters 1w3d
  Input queue: 0/75/0 (size/max/drops); Total output drops: 7331
  Queueing strategy: weighted fair
  Output queue: 0/1000/64/7331 (size/max total/threshold/drops)
    Conversations  0/52/256 (active/max active/max total)
    Reserved Conversations 0/0 (allocated/max allocated)
  5 minute input rate 125000 bits/sec, 109 packets/sec
  5 minute output rate 836000 bits/sec, 124 packets/sec
    52161129 packets input, 1306513966 bytes, 0 no buffer
    Received 0 broadcasts, 0 runts, 0 giants, 0 throttles
    320 input errors, 319 CRC, 0 frame, 0 overrun, 0 ignored, 1 abort
    56644790 packets output, 4100337688 bytes, 0 underruns
    0 output errors, 0 collisions, 0 interface resets
    0 output buffer failures, 15155581 output buffers swapped out
    0 carrier transitions
    RTS up, CTS up, DTR up, DCD up, DSR up
Serial0/0/1 is up, line protocol is up
  .  .  .  .  .
  .  .  .  .  .

Cisco7500>show interfaces serial0/0/0 accounting
Serial0/0/0 ATT KGBC673F00010002
          Protocol    Pkts In    Chars In   Pkts Out  Chars Out
                IP   52065266 1300335224   56534267 4094010678
               CDP      14430    4761900      28884    8116404

Cisco7500>show interfaces accounting
Serial0/0/0 ATT KGBC673F00010002
          Protocol    Pkts In    Chars In   Pkts Out  Chars Out
                IP   52075490 1301720107   56543918 4102765133
               CDP      14432    4762560      28888    8117528
Serial0/0/1 ATT KGBC673F00020002
          Protocol    Pkts In    Chars In   Pkts Out  Chars Out
                IP   52075909 1302786494   58493070 2597191413
               CDP      14432    4762560      28888    8117528
Interface Serial0/0/2 is disabled

Serial0/1/0 ATT KGBC673F00030002
          Protocol    Pkts In    Chars In   Pkts Out  Chars Out
                IP   52130117 1308935767   62376410 2374918354
               CDP      14430    4776330      28888    8117528
Serial0/1/1 ATT KGBC673F00040002
          Protocol    Pkts In    Chars In   Pkts Out  Chars Out
                IP   52076943 1303731632   61455913 1769036975
               CDP      14432    4776992      28888    8117528
```

(Continued)

Figure 8-1 *(Continued)*

```
FastEthernet1/0
                Protocol    Pkts In    Chars In    Pkts Out   Chars Out
                      IP  270671551  3326047313   229869574   493584473
                 DEC MOP          0           0        1442      111034
                     ARP      63358     3807818       31678     1900680
                     CDP      14437     4634277       28888     8825284
Interface FastEthernet1/1 is disabled

TokenRing4/0/0
                Protocol    Pkts In    Chars In    Pkts Out   Chars Out
                      IP   18017669  2720198549    18244086  1505348553
                     ARP       1953       97730        2189      109450
                     CDP          0           0       14444     4362088
Interface TokenRing4/0/1 is disabled


Ethernet4/1/1
                Protocol    Pkts In    Chars In    Pkts Out   Chars Out
                      IP   74372072   244993828    67351336  2139924247
                 DEC MOP          0           0        1442      111034
                     ARP       8815      528900        5223      313380
                     CDP          0           0       14444     4419864
```

was terminated once all information about the first serial port was shown and the IOS began to display information about the next serial port. The two lines of dots indicate that additional interface information would continue to be displayed as a result of entering the show interfaces command.

In comparison, the bottom portion of Figure 8-1 illustrates two examples of the show interfaces command with the keyword accounting included in the command. In the first example a specific interface is included with the command, while in the second example the command was entered without specifying an interface, resulting in the display of packets for each protocol used by each interface.

In the top portion of Figure 81 the 5-min input and output rates are expressed in bits per second and packets per second. These two metrics are extremely valuable because they provide an indirect measurement of the utilization of the media to which an interface is connected. In this particular example the interface is connected to a T1 transmission facility that operates at 1.544 Mbps. Since this is a full-duplex transmission facility, we can compute inbound and outbound circuit utilization levels as follows:

$$\text{Inbound utilization} = \frac{125,000}{1,544,000} \times 100 = 8.09\%$$

$$\text{Outbound utilization} = \frac{836,000}{1,544,000} \times 100 = 51.15\%$$

Since T1 facilities are full duplex, the higher of these two numbers determines the utilization of the line. In this case, 51.15 percent is higher than 8.09 percent, so the utilization of the line is about 51percent. The idea of full duplex is a little confusing to some, and the confusion is compounded by vendors who make claims such as "it's 100-Mbps full duplex, so it's 200 Mbps." Having a full-duplex interface does not mean the interface can have twice the throughput. Data communications is, by necessity, two way, so if you have traffic in one direction, you must have corresponding traffic in the other direction if for no other reason than to transmit acknowledgment of the receipt of data.

There are very few applications and/or protocols that don't require an acknowledgment that data has been received at its destination. Keeping this in mind, it's very rare that you could have 100-Mbps of traffic in one direction and a completely different set of traffic in the other direction, and it's misleading to state otherwise. Do not be confused by the use of full duplex when calculating throughput, and resist the temptation to claim that since an interface is full duplex it yields twice the aggregate throughput, because it simply does not. Thus, we normally consider the highest level of utilization in one direction to represent the level of utilization on a circuit.

Returning to our discussion of our T1, in actuality the preceding computations are not fully correct and a word of explanation is required on the reason for this. Although the operating rate of a T1 line is 1.544 Mbps, this line has a framing rate of 8 kbps. Since you cannot transfer data on the framing portion of the T1 line, the data transfer capability of the line is reduced to 1.536 Mbps. Thus, a more accurate computation of line utilization becomes:

$$\text{Inbound utilization} = \frac{125,000}{1,536,000} \times 100 = 8.135\%$$

$$\text{Outbound utilization} = \frac{836,000}{1,536,000} \times 100 = 54.42\%$$

After a comparison of the two sets of computations, differences between the two become apparent, especially as the input and output rates build up. Thus, it is highly recommended by the authors to use a denominator of 1.536 Mbps when computing the level of utilization for a T1 line. Let's return to our discussion of the serial line. In this particular example the serial line provides an Internet connection for a LAN on which a publicly accessible Web server resides. Web server page requests are in the form of relatively short URL requests, while responses are in the form of Web pages, which explains the imbalance between inbound and outbound utilization levels. Since you must order symmetrical operating rates on a T1 line, unfortunately you cannot take advantage of this imbalance.

Since the show interface command displays the input and output rate on a 5-min basis, you would have to create a script to pipe the output 12 times per hour to a file and accumulate the results to display an hour of activity. Fortunately, several shareware and freeware programs are available that allow you to accumulate and display router statistics. For readers interested in such programs, you can search for the term MRTG with one of the many available search engines, and it will provide you with information on the *multirouter traffic generator* (MRTG) program. This program is a Perl script and you need to have Perl to run the script. The third book in this series of Cisco Field Guides, *Cisco Router Performance*, provides information on the operation and utilization of MRTG. The last chapter of that book focuses on the *simple network management protocol* (SNMP), including the public and Cisco's *private management information base* (MIB) object identifiers and the operation of MRTG using different MIB object identifiers.

Further examination of the statistics for the serial interface shown at the top of Figure 8-1 illustrates the following: After displaying the 5-min input and output rates, the router displays information about the quantity of packets received on the interface and then a summary of different types of errors encountered on the interface. Note that input errors define the total errors received on the interface, which in this example totals 320. Of the 320 errors, 319 are *cyclic redundancy check* (CRC) errors and one was an abort error. Since the line above the input error count indicates 52,161,129 packets were received, this is an extremely low error rate and not a cause for alarm. This brings up an important point: simply knowing the number of errors on an interface doesn't really provide you with much useful information.

If there were 100,000 errors on the interface, that would seem like a lot. However, suppose the router interface counters had not been cleared for 18 months and those 100,000 errors had accumulated over such a long period of time? Now the 100,000 number doesn't seem so bad. What if the counters had been cleared 10 days ago, but the 100,000 errors had all accumulated over a single week and the problem had been fixed and the errors weren't accumulating? Again, now those errors don't seem so important. The main point is that if you are going to watch for errors on a line, you should clear the counters on the interface and then monitor the interface. See if they are incrementing, how fast they are incrementing and track the percentage of errors to packets. If the percentage of errors on the line is 0.1 percent (errors per number of packets), it's probably not worth worrying about, no matter how many errors are on the line.

Now look a bit further down the top portion of Figure 8-1. The next three lines in the `serial0/0/0` interface display show the number of packets' output and outbound errors. Also, note the last line in the interface display shows the status of key serial interface control leads, in this example, *Request to Send* (RTS), *Clear to Send* (CTS), *Data Terminal Ready* (DTR), *Data Carrier Detect* (DCD), and *Data Set Ready* (DSR). Observation of these control leads often provides a quick insight into a problem. For example, assume network users called to complain about their inability to access the Internet. After receiving the call, you used the `show interfaces` command

and determined that DCD was down. This would indicate that either the line connection was inoperative or the Data Service Unit/Channel Service Unit had failed, with line connection failure being a much higher probability. In such a case, the interface would report itself as "down, down." If the first value is down, it indicates the interface has a physical-layer problem. On a serial interface, this typically means you have lost carrier (DCD) and the line is unplugged, the CSU/DSU has failed, or the line to the local telephone company office (called the "local loop") has failed.

If the interface reports it is up, down, it indicates a failure in the data-link layer such as a failure to receive HDLC or PPP keepalive messages from the opposite end of the circuit. This could mean the other end of the circuit has a wrong encapsulation or some other problem. The exceptions to this rule are Ethernet interfaces which report up, down even if they do not have a physical-layer connection. In fact, you can cause an Ethernet interface to turn to an up, up condition even if it is not physically connected to a hub or switch by issuing the interface command no keepalive. This feature can be useful in lab scenarios.

The next example in Figure 8-1 shows the use of the keyword accounting. Note in this example we are displaying the number of packets inbound and outbound as well as raw characters by protocol for a specific interface. The following example illustrates the use of the accounting keyword without specifying a particular interface.This action results in the display of accounting information for each router interface. To limit the size of the resulting display, only a portion of all router interfaces are contained in the lower portion of Figure 8-1.

Note that an interface will only display accounting information for protocols configured on that interface. For example, if your Ethernet interface is not configured to pass IPX traffic, you will not see a column for IPX traffic in the accounting information, even if IPX packets have arrived at the Ethernet interface. The accounting information therefore reflects only those packets that have actually been processed by the router.

Examining Ethernet Metrics

We continue our examination of various interface metrics and look at Ethernet. We use the show interface command, using a specific Ethernet interface for illustrative purposes.

Figure 8-2 illustrates the results of the show interface ethernet command and displays information about the Ethernet module installed in slot 4 in our router. In examining the entries in Figure 8-2 note the tx (transmit) and rx (receive) loads are 5/255 and 54/255, respectively. These loads are similar to the serial port loads in that they are an exponential average calculated over a 5-min period. According to Cisco literature, a period of four time constants must pass "prior to the average falling within 2 percent of the instantaneous rate of a uniform stream of traffic over that period."

Figure 8-2 Using the show interface ethernet command.

```
Cisco7500>show interface ethernet4/1/1
Ethernet4/1/1 is up, line protocol is up
  Hardware is cxBus Ethernet, address is 0010.7936.a889 (bia 0010.7936.a889)
  Internet address is 205.131.176.1/24
  MTU 1500 bytes, BW 10000 Kbit, DLY 1000 usec,
    reliability 255/255, txload 5/255, rxload 54/255
  Encapsulation ARPA, loopback not set
  Keepalive set (10 sec)
  ARP type: ARPA, ARP Timeout 04:00:00
  Last input 00:00:03, output 00:00:03, output hang never
  Last clearing of "show interface" counters 1w6d
  Queueing strategy: fifo
  Output queue 0/40, 63 drops; input queue 0/75, 0 drops
  5 minute input rate 2152000 bits/sec, 322 packets/sec
  5 minute output rate 230000 bits/sec, 310 packets/sec
    89154470 packets input, 3386899386 bytes, 0 no buffer
    Received 585582 broadcasts, 0 runts, 0 giants, 0 throttles
    84 input errors, 84 CRC, 0 frame, 0 overrun, 0 ignored
    0 input packets with dribble condition detected
    80872733 packets output, 3447488860 bytes, 0 underruns
    1036 output errors, 1036 collisions, 2 interface resets
    0 babbles, 0 late collision, 2544575 deferred
    0 lost carrier, 0 no carrier
    0 output buffer failures, 0 output buffers swapped out
```

What this means in plain English is that the number is a *weighted average* over the previous 5 min and may not necessarily reflect the current instantaneous load on an interface. This is not really a problem though because, in most cases, the instantaneous load on the interface isn't all that useful. Data traffic is by nature bursty, so the amount of traffic on an interface may vary by an order of magnitude from one second to the next, although it will be fairly uniform over longer periods of time such as minutes or hours. One other point of interest is that in previous versions of the IOS, only a single value was shown for the interface load; the addition of both input and output rates is a new feature so the output on your router may not exactly match what is shown.

If we look further down in Figure 8-2, after the display of ARP information, the following line indicates the number of hours, minutes, and seconds since the last packet was successfully received and transmitted via the interface. If this value remains high, it could indicate a dead interface. Similarly, the output hang indicator, which is shown as output hang never would indicate the hours, minutes, and seconds since the interface was last reset due to a transmission that took too long. In this example no such event occurred, resulting in the display message output hang never.

Now look at the line beginning Output queue and note the values 0/40. The first number indicates the number of packets in the queue and the second number indicates the size or length of the queue. Similarly, this information is repeated for the input queue. Note that after information about the number of packets in the queue and queue length, the display shows the number of dropped packets. You can use the number of dropped packets to determine whether or not to increase the queue length from its default. In our example there were 63 drops when the output queue was set to a length of 40. In this example an expanded queue length to 60 should be considered. Similar to our discussion of the serial port, the 5-min input and output rates are exponentially weighted averages and you should monitor them for four periods to obtain an average within 2 percent of the instantaneous rate of a uniform stream of traffic over a 20-min period.

After displaying the input and output rate, the display of the Ethernet interface produces a summary of different types of errors. Table 8-1 describes the terminology associated with various Ethernet interface error conditions.

While most of the entries in Table 8-1 are self-explanatory, the use of the statistics, as well as a few specific entries, deserve some further review.

First, unlike a protocol analyzer that can provide detailed information on different error conditions, the show interface command provides general summary information. Thus, if you note what appears to be a large number of errors, the display only lets you know you have a problem but not the location where the problem originated. For example, a high CRC value could result from a failing NIC, however, the quantity simply tells you some research is in order and not where the culprit resides.

Let's look at specific entries in Table 8-1. Note that frame errors typically result from collisions. However, if collisions are lower than frame errors, you probably have a malfunctioning Ethernet NIC on the network. Also note that the input and output error counts may not equal the sum of the respective error conditions. This is because some datagrams can have more than one type of error, while other datagrams can have errors that do not fall into one of the Cisco predefined categories. Thus, do not be alarmed if the individual error count does not add up to the total. Again, keep in mind that a few errors on an interface are normal, so don't be alarmed if each of your interfaces is not 100 percent error-free. However, an interface should not consistently report increasing errors (with the exception of collisions on an Ethernet interface, which is not really an error). An increasing error count on an interface may be symptomatic of larger problems within the network such as faulty hardware or cabling.

Table 8-1 Ethernet Interface Display Error Conditions

Condition	Description
Input errors	Total errors, including CRC, frame, overrun, runts, giants, no buffer, and ignored counts.
Runts	Packets discarded because they are less than Ethernet's minimum length of 64 bytes (not including the preamble).
Giants	Packets discarded because they are greater than Ethernet's maximum length of 1518 bytes (not including the preamble).
No buffer	Received packets discarded due to a lack of space in the router input queue.
CRC	The checksum computed at the receiver does not match the checksum added to the data by the originator.
Frame	Packets that have a CRC error and a noninteger number of octets.
Overrun	Condition where the receiver hardware was unable to pass received data to a hardware buffer because the input rate exceeded the receiver's ability to handle the traffic.
Ignored	Condition where packets were ignored by the interface when it ran low on internal buffers.
Dribble bit error	Condition where a frame is accepted even though it is slightly too long.
Underrun	Condition where the transmitter runs faster than the router can handle.
Output errors	Sum of all errors that prevent the transmission of datagrams via the interface.
Collisions	Condition where a message is retransmitted due to a collision.
Interface reset	Number of times the interface was reset.

Examining Fast Ethernet Metrics

The key difference between the use of the show interface command to display an Ethernet and a Fast Ethernet interface is in the value of the bandwidth and identity of the hardware. Otherwise, the resulting display resembles the Ethernet display shown in Figure 8-2, and the metric shown can be used as previously described. One additional difference worth noting is that most Fast Ethernet interfaces can operate in full-duplex mode, while most standard Ethernet interfaces cannot. What this means in practical terms is that you should not see any collisions on an interface that is operating in full-duplex mode. Cisco supports full-duplex Ethernet interfaces on some model routers, but most of their standard Ethernet interfaces do not support this functionality. All Cisco Fast Ethernet interfaces support full-duplex mode.

Examining Token Ring Metrics

Since Token Ring continues to be popular in certain types of organizations, our discussion of the show interface command with a review of the display of a token-ring interface. Figure 8-3 illustrates the use of the show interface tokenring command to view the state of one such interface.

In Figure 8-3 note that most fields in the display are very similar, if not the same, as the fields in the serial and Ethernet interface displays recently viewed. Except for a ring speed and mode definition, which denote a token-ring interface, the basic display fields and display structure are the same and use the displayed information in a manner similar to that previously described. If you look carefully at the fields in Figure 8-3, the one labeled *collisions* might appear awkward, because Token Ring cannot have collisions. Cisco uses this field to indicate occurrence of an unusual event, when a frame is either being queued or dequeued by router software. Other than this odd use of terminology, the other fields are used as indicated in Table 8-1. One additional field worth mentioning is the ring speed information. This value is either 4 or 16 Mbps, depending upon how your token-ring environment is configured. This parameter must match all stations on the Token Ring. If it is set incorrectly, the token-ring interface will constantly try to keep inserting itself into the ring and failing. If you see this behavior, make sure your ring speed is set correctly.

Displaying IP Protocol Statistics

Since this book focuses on the Internet Protocol (IP), we now narrow that focus of the use of the show command to the Internet Protocol.

Figure 8-3 Viewing a token-ring interface.

```
Cisco7500>show interface tokenring4/0/0
TokenRing4/0/0 is up, line protocol is up
  Hardware is cxBus Token Ring, address is 0008.9e6c.1501 (bia 0008.9e6c.1501)
  Internet address is 205.131.174.2/24
  MTU 4464 bytes, BW 16000 Kbit, DLY 630 usec,
     reliability 255/255, txload 5/255, rxload 1/255
  Encapsulation SNAP, loopback not set
  Keepalive set (10 sec)
  ARP type: SNAP, ARP Timeout 04:00:00
  Ring speed: 16 Mbps
  Duplex: half
  Mode: Classic token ring station
  Single ring node, Source Route Transparent Bridge capable
  Group Address: 0x00000000, Functional Address: 0x08000000
  Ethernet Transit OUI: 0x000000
  Last Ring Status 3d02h <Soft Error> (0x2000)
  Last input 00:00:00, output 00:00:00, output hang never
  Last clearing of "show interface" counters 1w6d
  Queueing strategy: fifo
  Output queue 0/40, 0 drops; input queue 0/75, 0 drops
  5 minute input rate 89000 bits/sec, 48 packets/sec
  5 minute output rate 359000 bits/sec, 61 packets/sec
     21433609 packets input, 4240641523 bytes, 0 no buffer
     Received 22233 broadcasts, 0 runts, 0 giants, 0 throttles
     0 input errors, 0 CRC, 0 frame, 0 overrun, 0 ignored, 0 abort
     21585987 packets output, 3308510107 bytes, 0 underruns
     0 output errors, 0 collisions, 0 interface resets
     0 output buffer failures, 0 output buffers swapped out
     0 transitions
```

Using the `show ip accounting` Command

Figure 8-4 illustrates the options associated with the `show ip accounting` command and a few uses of the command that are literally swallowed by the router and do not produce any output nor error messages, the reason for which will be shortly explained. In the top portion of Figure 8-4 note the use of the `show ip accounting` command, followed by a question mark to display the various command options. As noted, you can use the keywords `access-violations`, `checkpoint`, and `output-packets`.

The display of the command options is followed by the use of the command with the keyword `access-violations`, followed by the use of the command with the keyword `output-packets`. Note that, for both uses of the command, the IOS accepts the command but appears to do nothing! Since we might be a bit puzzled about what happened, next we use the `ip accounting checkpoint` command, followed by a question mark, and

Figure 8-4   Examining the use of the show ip accounting command.

```
Cisco7500>show ip accounting ?
  access-violations  show access violations in accounting database
  checkpoint         The checkpointed IP accounting database
  output-packets     show output packets in accounting database
  |                  Output modifiers
  <cr>

Cisco7500>show ip accounting access-violations
Cisco7500>show ip accounting output-packets
Cisco7500>show ip accounting checkpoint ?
  access-violations  show access violations in accounting database
  output-packets     show output packets in accounting database
  |                  Output modifiers
  <cr>

Cisco7500>show ip accounting checkpoint
Cisco7500>show ip accounting checkpoint output-packets ?
  | Output modifiers
  <cr>

Cisco7500>show ip accounting checkpoint output-packets
```

then entered that command with its keyword output-packets. Once again, the command was accepted by the IOS but no output appeared.

The reason why the use of the show ip accounting commands used in Figure 8-4 were accepted by the IOS but produced no output is because IP accounting has not been turned on. Thus, lets turn on IP accounting and revisit the use of the show ip accounting command.

Turning on IP Accounting

Figure 8-5 illustrates how to turn on IP accounting, followed by the use of the show ip accounting command which now produces a table of output. In Figure 8-5, note that you turn on IP accounting by going into the privilege exec mode of operation and then into the configuration mode. Once this is accomplished, you enter the command ip accounting. After turning on IP accounting and exiting the configuration mode, we then use the show ip accounting command to obtain a list of IP accounting information.

Viewing IP Accounting Data

In Figure 8-5 note that the use of the show ip accounting command results in a table of source and destination IP addresses as well as the total

Figure 8-5 Turning on IP accounting to use the show ip accounting command.

```
Cisco7500(config-if)#ip accounting
Cisco7500(config-if)#end
Cisco7500#show ip accounting
       Source          Destination        Packets            Bytes
  192.131.176.11   204.222.164.66          67                90761
  192.131.174.1    198.41.0.10             15                  795
  192.131.174.1    204.71.191.220         107                15064
  192.131.175.20   192.130.237.93          41                 6099
  192.131.175.20   206.38.157.138          47                 6536
  192.131.175.21   192.130.237.93           9                 1535
  192.131.175.20   192.243.160.106         13                18044
  192.131.175.23   207.133.68.245          17                17070
  192.131.175.20   55.64.154.22            11                10758
  192.131.176.11   131.87.111.65           35                45092
  192.131.175.20   199.128.124.220         35                17867
  192.131.175.23   155.76.36.16             8                 4658
  192.131.175.20   204.208.27.228          34                46075
  192.131.176.11   4.17.247.1             141                68992
  192.131.175.23   152.166.207.16           1                   41
  192.131.174.1    128.227.128.24           2                  550
  192.131.174.1    149.111.34.35           20                 2588
  192.131.175.23   192.160.47.153          58                86302
  192.131.175.23   131.64.11.26            25                37500
  192.131.174.1    198.3.98.99              7                  765
  192.131.175.20   147.71.29.20            17                21249
  192.131.176.11   192.128.215.66           9                 9439
       Source          Destination        Packets            Bytes
  192.131.176.11   165.83.219.245          18                21550
  192.131.175.20   137.243.44.144           4                  503
  192.131.174.1    207.46.185.138          20                 2886
  192.131.175.10   159.189.129.123         34                28384
  192.131.176.11   192.131.145.18          28                20781
  192.131.174.1    128.8.10.90              3                  159
  192.131.175.20   192.221.235.55          30                35615
  192.131.174.1    207.46.179.136           3                  466
  192.131.175.24   63.16.78.167            11                 2790
  192.131.176.11   141.116.67.12           93                11929
  192.131.175.10   136.177.96.245           1                   40
  192.131.174.1    24.1.240.67              1                  279
  192.131.175.20   131.46.41.61            33                 3729
  192.131.175.24   131.7.52.7              10                 7903
  192.131.174.1    199.114.8.10             1                  283
  192.131.174.1    192.153.39.200           1                   60
  192.131.176.11   209.117.138.129         21                25828
  192.131.175.19   158.68.33.84             1                 1052
  192.131.175.16   158.68.33.84            23                24196
  192.131.175.23   152.75.107.17            6                  240
  192.131.175.23   199.217.177.59          54                25060
  192.131.175.23   192.46.108.16           28                35368
       Source          Destination        Packets            Bytes
  192.131.175.5    168.179.169.60         189                62582
  192.131.174.1    128.231.200.34           4                  263
  192.131.175.20   199.196.144.11           8                 7656
  192.131.175.23   148.129.143.2            6                  240
```

Figure 8-5 (*Continued*)

Source	Destination	Packets	Bytes
192.131.175.23	199.196.144.11	13	13552
192.131.175.20	209.49.118.18	167	93842
192.131.174.1	216.33.148.250	17	1882
192.131.175.20	134.11.66.77	28	19407
192.131.175.20	63.21.80.14	40	21306
192.131.174.1	131.77.137.33	18	2419
192.131.175.20	206.229.210.131	116	81123
192.131.175.20	132.241.245.231	17	20741
192.131.174.1	136.192.248.207	1	271
192.131.176.11	204.34.211.82	180	56855
192.131.175.20	209.3.152.35	132	16236
192.131.176.11	33.56.100.43	21	2575
192.131.176.11	150.177.124.10	10	759
192.131.174.1	207.233.160.195	1	64
192.131.175.20	150.177.124.10	43	64500
192.131.175.20	150.226.93.122	24	19326
192.131.175.20	209.8.53.191	157	26899
192.131.174.5	140.221.9.20	1	76

Accounting data age is 2

number of packets and bytes flowing between each address pair. If the use of a show interfaces or a specific show interfaces command for a particular interface indicates a high level of utilization, you should not upgrade the LAN or transmission facility prior to using the show ip accounting command. The reason is because this command lets you determine if one or more IP addresses are accounting (no pun intended) for an abnormally large portion of network traffic. If you find this to be true, your next step is to determine the reason for the large proportion of network traffic flowing to or from those addresses. At the bottom of Figure 8-5, note accounting was only in effect for 2 min. To make an intelligent decision concerning network activity, as a minimum, you should examine network usage during the busy hour over a prolonged period of time such as several weeks or even a month of typical network utilization.

Viewing the IP Cache

Another tool you can use to monitor IP network traffic is the show ip cache command. Figure 8-6 demonstrates the use of the show ip cache command. The top portion of Figure 8-6 illustrates the command options displayed by the question mark appended to the command, followed by the command without options to obtain a display of the routing table cache that is used to fast switch Internet traffic.

Although we see a summary displayed, we also see what appears to be a table header without table entries in the display. The reason for this is

Figure 8-6   Examining the use of the show ip cache command.

```
Cisco7500>show ip cache ?
  A.B.C.D       prefix of entries to show
  Ethernet      IEEE 802.3
  FastEthernet  FastEthernet IEEE 802.3
  Null          Null interface
  Serial        Serial
  TokenRing     IEEE 802.5
  flow          flow cache entries
  policy        policy cache entries
  verbose       display extra information
  |             Output modifiers
  <cr>

Cisco7500>show ip cache
IP routing cache 0 entries, 0 bytes
   781 adds, 781 invalidates, 0 refcounts
Minimum invalidation interval 2 seconds, maximum interval 5 seconds,
   quiet interval 3 seconds, threshold 0 requests
Invalidation rate 0 in last second, 0 in last 3 seconds
Last full cache invalidation occurred 00:10:09 ago

Prefix/Length          Age        Interface        Next Hop
```

that two criteria must be met to obtain a full and relevant display in response to the use of the show ip cache command.

First, you must enable fast switching on your router, which results in a display of summary statistics, as shown in Figure 8-6. However, this by itself may not be sufficient to display the cache table. To be able to do so, you may have to enable IP accounting. On some routers the authors worked with, IP accounting did not have to be enabled to view IP cache; however, on one router, IP accounting did have to be enabled. Thus, if you cannot view IP cache on a particular router, consider enabling IP accounting.

Once we enable IP accounting, we can use the show ip cache command and obtain a summary of the fast switching of Internet traffic and the display of a table of routing cache entries. Figure 8-7 illustrates the use of the show ip cache command after IP accounting was enabled. In the table shown in Figure 8-7 note that the table entries were changed from earlier versions of the IOS, when the entries in the table included the destination IP address, interface, and Mac header. As indicated in Figure 8-7, under IOS version 12.0, which is used by the authors, the table contains the prefix length, age of the entry, interface, and next hop IP address.

An additional caching feature that is new on some router platforms in IOS version 12.0 is a caching method Cisco calls *Netflow*. In Netflow switching, the router caches not only the destination IP address, as with

Figure 8-7 Using the show ip cache command after accounting is enabled.

```
Cisco7500#show ip cache
IP routing cache 46 entries, 7416 bytes
   842 adds, 796 invalidates, 0 refcounts
Minimum invalidation interval 2 seconds, maximum interval 5 seconds,
   quiet interval 3 seconds, threshold 0 requests
Invalidation rate 0 in last second, 0 in last 3 seconds
Last full cache invalidation occurred 04:10:32 ago

Prefix/Length           Age         Interface      Next Hop
4.2.49.4/30             00:02:05    Se0/1/2        4.2.49.4
24.0.0.0/8             00:04:48    Se0/0/0        24.1.240.67
33.0.0.0/8             00:00:28    Se0/0/0        33.8.106.41
63.0.0.0/8             00:02:09    Se0/1/0        63.24.98.124
128.11.0.0/16          00:04:08    Se0/1/1        128.11.40.53
128.158.0.0/16         00:02:02    Se0/0/0        128.158.176.192
131.81.0.0/16          00:00:01    Se0/0/0        131.81.36.8
134.11.0.0/16          00:04:07    Se0/1/3        134.11.100.2
137.227.0.0/16         00:04:05    Se0/1/0        137.227.116.2
138.145.0.0/16         00:04:24    Se0/1/2        138.145.200.26
140.216.0.0/16         00:00:58    Se0/0/1        140.216.31.182
150.192.0.0/16         00:04:37    Se0/0/0        150.192.95.36
152.163.0.0/16         00:04:02    Se0/1/2        152.163.195.212
155.76.0.0/16          00:03:20    Se0/0/1        155.76.39.135
155.77.0.0/16          00:04:48    Se0/0/1        155.77.31.22
Prefix/Length           Age         Interface      Next Hop

158.72.0.0/16          00:03:47    Se0/0/1        158.72.76.135
164.66.0.0/16          00:03:46    Se0/0/0        164.66.10.118
165.224.0.0/16         00:04:07    Se0/0/0        165.224.109.18
166.4.0.0/16           00:04:30    Se0/0/1        166.4.171.50
168.99.0.0/16          00:03:27    Se0/0/0        168.99.133.109
170.104.0.0/16         00:04:32    Se0/1/0        170.104.35.62
192.54.138.0/24        00:03:28    Se0/1/2        192.54.138.84
192.131.145.0/24       00:04:07    Se0/0/1        192.131.145.18
198.17.189.0/24        00:02:38    Se0/0/0        198.17.189.235
198.207.223.0/24       00:01:40    Se0/0/0        198.207.223.251
199.131.125.0/24       00:04:16    Se0/1/0        199.131.125.129
199.169.208.0/24       00:04:30    Se0/1/3        199.169.208.133
199.173.224.0/24       00:04:56    Se0/1/3        199.173.224.20
199.196.144.0/24       00:00:09    Se0/0/1        199.196.144.12
204.34.201.0/24        00:03:10    Se0/0/0        204.34.201.69
204.71.105.0/24        00:00:59    Se0/1/0        204.71.105.63
204.151.230.0/24       00:02:39    Se0/0/1        204.151.230.2
204.222.168.0/24       00:01:05    Se0/0/0        204.222.168.82
205.131.175.20/32      00:01:27    FastEthernet1/0 205.131.175.20
205.131.188.0/24       00:01:05    Se0/1/3        205.131.188.1
205.188.209.0/24       00:04:09    Se0/1/3        205.188.209.72
206.166.238.0/24       00:04:14    Se0/0/1        206.166.238.34
```

standard fast switching, but also the source IP address and the upper-layer source and destination ports. This enables collection of much finer granularity caching information. Netflow switching was only available on higher-end platforms in prior IOS releases. In IOS version 12.0 it has been

Figure 8-8 Using the show ip cache flow command.

```
r1#sh ip cache flow
IP packet size distribution (42 total packets):
  1-32   64   96  128  160  192  224  256  288  320  352  384  416  448  480
  .000 .880 .095 .000 .000 .000 .000 .000 .000 .000 .000 .000 .000 .023 .000

   512  544  576 1024 1536 2048 2560 3072 3584 4096 4608
  .000 .000 .000 .000 .000 .000 .000 .000 .000 .000 .000

IP Flow Switching Cache, 278544 bytes
  1 active, 4095 inactive, 6 added
  94 ager polls, 0 flow alloc failures
  last clearing of statistics never
Protocol        Total    Flows   Packets Bytes  Packets Active(Sec)
Idle(Sec)
─────           Flows     /Sec    /Flow  /Pkt     /Sec    /Flow     /Flow
TCP-Telnet          1      0.0        7    47      0.0      2.1       1.5
UDP-other           4      0.0        1    52      0.0      0.0      15.2
Total:              5      0.0        2    49      0.0      0.4      12.5

SrcIf        SrcIPaddress    DstIf         DstIPaddress    Pr SrcP DstP  Pkts
Se1/2        10.1.2.1        Et0/0         10.1.1.4        06 0017 2AFA    31
```

included in lower-end platforms such as the 2600. The output from a show ip cache flow command from a Cisco 2600 router is shown in Figure 8-8. Notice the cache entry contains the source address and upper-layer port information.

Now that we understand the show ip cache command, let's look at how to obtain a display of a router's routing table.

Displaying the Routing Table

You can use the show ip route command to display a wide range of statistics about entries in your router's routing table. The basic format of this command is

```
Show ip route [address [mask]]|[protocol|keyword]
```

When entered without any options, this command displays information about each of a router's interfaces, including whether or not they are connected and, if so, the type of connection. Since the command supports a number of options, we use the command followed by a question mark at the top of Figure 8-9 to display the options supported. Note that there are a total of 19 options, which include entering the command by itself, followed by a carriage return.

In Figure 8-9 note that this command can be used to provide a sum-

Figure 8-9 Using the show ip route command.

```
Macon>show ip route ?
  Hostname or A.B.C.D  Network to display information about or hostname
  bgp                  Border Gateway Protocol (BGP)
  connected            Connected
  egp                  Exterior Gateway Protocol (EGP)
  eigrp                Enhanced Interior Gateway Routing Protocol (EIGRP)
  igrp                 Interior Gateway Routing Protocol (IGRP)
  isis                 ISO IS-IS
  list                 IP Access list
  mobile               Mobile routes
  odr                  On Demand stub Routes
  ospf                 Open Shortest Path First (OSPF)
  profile              IP routing table profile
  rip                  Routing Information Protocol (RIP)
  static               Static routes
  summary              Summary of all routes
  supernets-only       Show supernet entries only
  traffic-engineering  Traffic engineered routes
  |                    Output modifiers
  <cr>

Macon>show ip route summary
Route Source     Networks     Subnets     Overhead     Memory (bytes)
connected        3            6           504          1296
static           1            1           392          288
rip              0            0           0            0
internal         2                                     2328
Total            6            7           896          3912

Macon>show ip route
Codes: C - connected, S - static, I - IGRP, R - RIP, M - mobile, B - BGP
       D - EIGRP, EX - EIGRP external, O - OSPF, IA - OSPF inter area
       N1 - OSPF NSSA external type 1, N2 - OSPF NSSA external type 2
       E1 - OSPF external type 1, E2 - OSPF external type 2, E - EGP
       i - IS-IS, L1 - IS-IS level-1, L2 - IS-IS level-2, * - candidate default
       U - per-user static route, o - ODR, P - periodic downloaded static route
       T - traffic engineered route

Gateway of last resort is 0.0.0.0 to network 0.0.0.0

     4.0.0.0/30 is subnetted, 6 subnets
C       4.0.156.0 is directly connected, Serial0/0/0
C       4.0.156.4 is directly connected, Serial0/0/1
C       4.0.156.84 is directly connected, Serial0/1/0
C       4.0.156.104 is directly connected, Serial0/1/2
C       4.0.156.108 is directly connected, Serial0/1/3
C       4.0.156.100 is directly connected, Serial0/1/1
C     205.131.175.0/24 is directly connected, FastEthernet1/0
C     205.131.174.0/24 is directly connected, TokenRing4/0/0
      172.20.0.0/21 is subnetted, 1 subnets
S       172.20.8.0 [1/0] via 205.131.174.1
C     205.131.176.0/24 is directly connected, Ethernet4/1/1
S*    0.0.0.0/0 is directly connected, Serial0/1/0
                 is directly connected, Serial0/1/1
                 is directly connected, Serial0/1/2
                 is directly connected, Serial0/1/3
                 is directly connected, Serial0/0/1
                 is directly connected, Serial0/0/0
```

mary of static routes or you can use the command with a specific protocol to display information about routes supporting a specific routing protocol. You can also use a keyword instead of a protocol to obtain different information that spans multiple protocols, such as the keyword summary, which was used in the middle portion of Figure 8-9 to display a summary of the routing table. In the lower portion of Figure 8-9 we used the command without any parameters to display a summary of the routing table, including the status of interface connections.

Viewing IP Traffic

To conclude our discussion of the show ip command, we use the traffic subcommand to display statistics about IP traffic. The format of this EXEC command is shown here:

```
Show ip traffic
```

Unlike many other show commands, this particular command does not have any options and its use results in a display of statistics concerning IP traffic. Figure 8-10 illustrates the use of this command.

The display that results from issuing the show ip traffic command shown in Figure 8-10 primarily consists of IP, ICMP, UDP, TCP, and ARP statistics. The reason there is a conspicuous absence of routing statistics is because the router used by the authors to illustrate the use of several show ip–related commands was directly connected to an Internet service provider and configured for static routing. If the authors had used a router within the Internet or within a large corporate IP network, you would then see a significant amount of statistics for one or more routing protocols in the display. However, regardless of the location and routing protocols supported, certain statistics are common to all routers and whose observation can provide insight into certain types of potential network problems.

For example, received IP statistics indicates seven possible error conditions and counts for each condition. Those error counts include format errors, checksum errors, bad hop count, unknown protocol, not a gateway, security failures, and bad options. While some of these error conditions are self-explanatory, a few warrant further discussion.

A large unknown protocol count could indicate your router was not configured to support one or more protocols being used to transmit traffic. While a bad hop count sounds bad, in actuality it indicates that a datagram with a hop count of 1 reached the router, which decrements the count to zero and tosses the data into the bit bucket. When this situation occurs, ICMP generates a time to live exceeded message. Although almost 20,000 bad hop counts were shown in Figure 8-10, that number is

Figure 8-10 Using the show ip traffic command.

```
Cisco7500#show ip traffic
IP statistics:
  Rcvd:  2154922158 total, 4328377 local destination
         0 format errors, 0 checksum errors, 19390 bad hop count
         0 unknown protocol, 0 not a gateway
         0 security failures, 6 bad options, 3841 with options
  Opts:  227 end, 30 nop, 3 basic security, 6 loose source route
         0 timestamp, 0 extended security, 0 record route
         0 stream ID, 0 strict source route, 3605 alert, 0 cipso
         0 other
  Frags: 5921 reassembled, 12 timeouts, 0 couldn't reassemble
         16593 fragmented, 4403 couldn't fragment
  Bcast: 3274699 received, 213680 sent
  Mcast: 0 received, 0 sent
  Sent:  1194452 generated, 2118216862 forwarded
  Drop:  8036 encapsulation failed, 0 unresolved, 0 no adjacency
         40733 no route, 0 unicast RPF, 0 forced drop

ICMP statistics:
  Rcvd: 0 format errors, 5 checksum errors, 0 redirects, 34 unreachable
        292849 echo, 2280 echo reply, 0 mask requests, 0 mask replies, 0 quench
        0 parameter, 0 timestamp, 0 info request, 0 other
        0 irdp solicitations, 0 irdp advertisements
  Sent: 9 redirects, 379383 unreachable, 2318 echo, 292847 echo reply
        0 mask requests, 0 mask replies, 0 quench, 0 timestamp
        0 info reply, 19062 time exceeded, 0 parameter problem
        0 irdp solicitations, 0 irdp advertisements

UDP statistics:
  Rcvd: 3964520 total, 0 checksum errors, 2818851 no port
  Sent: 441642 total, 0 forwarded broadcasts

TCP statistics:
  Rcvd: 68639 total, 0 checksum errors, 28 no port
  Sent: 51426 total

Probe statistics:
  Rcvd: 0 address requests, 0 address replies
        0 proxy name requests, 0 where-is requests, 0 other
  Sent: 0 address requests, 0 address replies (0 proxy)
        0 proxy name replies, 0 where-is replies

EGP statistics:
  Rcvd: 0 total, 0 format errors, 0 checksum errors, 0 no listener
  Sent: 0 total

IGRP statistics:
  Rcvd: 0 total, 0 checksum errors
  Sent: 0 total

OSPF statistics:
  Rcvd: 0 total, 0 checksum errors
        0 hello, 0 database desc, 0 link state req
        0 link state updates, 0 link state acks
    Sent: 0 total
```

(Continued)

Figure 8-10 (*Continued*)

```
IP-IGRP2 statistics:
  Rcvd: 0 total
  Sent: 0 total

PIMv2 statistics: Sent/Received
  Total: 0/0, 0 checksum errors, 0 format errors
  Registers: 0/0, Register Stops: 0/0,  Hellos: 0/0
  Join/Prunes: 0/0, Asserts: 0/0, grafts: 0/0
  Bootstraps: 0/0, Candidate_RP_Advertisements: 0/0

IGMP statistics: Sent/Received
  Total: 0/0, Format errors: 0/0, Checksum errors: 0/0
  Host Queries: 0/0, Host Reports: 0/0, Host Leaves: 00
  DVMRP: 0/0, PIM: 0/0

ARP statistics:
  Rcvd: 183207 requests, 4759 replies, 42421 reverse, 0 other
  Sent: 12499 requests, 119150 replies (50369 proxy), 0 reverse
```

out of a total of over 2 billion datagrams, representing a negligible bad hop count.

As an educated guess, some stations accessing the network behind the router are located beyond the default setting of the hop count setting of their router, which should be increased. These messages might also be due to the use of the traceroute program, which functions by sending packets with a TTL of 1 toward a destination address. Since the TTL is decremented by 1 at each hop, the first router discards the packet and sends a time to live exceeded message. Traceroute then sends the next packet with a TTL of 2 to reach the second router and so on and so on until it reaches the final destination with each router recording a bad hop count and sending ICMP error messages. If you perform traceroutes through your routers, expect to see the bad hop count counter incremented.

Another error statistic that warrants attention is no route, which indicates that a router discarded a datagram it did not know how to route. You might see a lot of these sorts of errors if the router does not have a default route. If there is no default route, the router must have an explicit route to the IP network or subnet or it will not be able to forward the packet. In most networks, every router has a default route, so these messages should be infrequent.

Under the ARP statistics heading, a proxy reply represents the condition where the router transmits an ARP on behalf of another host. Proxy ARP can be useful in situations where you have a LAN with multiple routers and would like to institute load sharing and redundancy for your end stations. Most end stations can only use a single default gateway at a time, so you must choose a single router to use. If this router fails, you have to manually switch your end stations over to use another router. If, however, you point the default gateway of your end stations to their own IP address, they will ARP for every destination. If the routers are configured to perform proxy ARP, each router will respond to the ARP request and your end stations will survive the failure of a single router and also get some statistical load sharing across multiple routers.

Another error of interest is encapsulation failed, which is listed beneath the IP statistics section. An encapsulation failure is normally generated if a router has no ARP entry in its cache for the intended destination. This error may also be caused on NBMA WAN interfaces such as frame relay if there is no frame-relay mapping statement. Frame relay has no broadcast facility, so its correct operation relies on having specific IP addresses manually mapped to the correct DLCI. This is unlike LAN media such as Ethernet and Token Ring where a station simply issues a broadcast to populate its ARP cache with the destination station's Mac address.

By examining the IP statistics, you can easily get some idea of unicast, broadcast, and multicast traffic. Although the statistics shown in Figure 8-10 do not indicate any multicast traffic, suppose several network users joined different video broadcast sessions. In this situation the multicast received count would become significant. If your network had a high degree of utilization, you might then query the rationale for users becoming members of multicast groups. Thus, the use of statistics provided by the router should be used in conjunction with statistics obtained on the operation of attached networks to determine if potential problems could occur and to rectify such problems.

In examining the general statistics from the show ip traffic command, note the errors are exceedingly low in comparison to the traffic transported. Thus, in this particular example no unusual conditions warrant our attention.

We can summarize this chapter by pointing out that monitoring statistics plays an important role in examining the health of a network. Rather than waiting for problems to occur, it's a good idea to periodically use the show interfaces and other commands as preventive medicine.

Index

Abbreviation (of commands),
  39–40, 169
Access lists, 50, 133–163
  application of, 134, 143
  creation of, 143
  enhanced, 152–161
    dynamic access lists, 152–157
    reflexive access lists, 157–159
    and TCP intercept, 160–161
    time-based access lists,
      159–160
  extended IP, 135, 139–143
    fields in, 139–141
    keywords with, 142–143
    named access lists, 146–147
    options supported by,
      141–142
  interface, specification of,
    143–145
  named, 145–151
    editing, 147–151
    extended named IP access
      lists, 146–147
    standard named IP access lists,
      145–146
  purpose of, 133–134
  rules for success with,
    151–152
  standard IP, 135–139
    format, 135
    keywords with, 135, 137–139
    named access lists, 145–146
    protocols in, 135, 136
    source address of, 137
Acknowledgment Number field
  (TCP), 97, 99
AD (see Administrative distance)

Address Allocation for Private
  Internets (RFC 1918), 66
address interface command,
  126
Address resolution protocol
  (ARP), 15, 51, 83–90
Addressing, IP, 59–90
  basic addressing scheme, 61
  classes, address, 61–64
  and classless networking, 77–78
  configuration examples, 73, 76
  dotted-decimal notation, 64–65
  in IPv6, 78–82
  and networks, 66–75
  reserved addresses, 65–66
  resolution, address, 82–90
  router address assignment,
    76–77
  and subnetting, 68–75
Administrative distance (AD),
  169–170
any keyword, 138
Apple Talk, 1
ARP (see Address resolution
  protocol)
arp command, 87–88, 112
ASCII, 23, 32, 143
Asynchronous transmission
  mode (ATM), 83, 106

Bandwidth (BW), 109
bandwidth interface command,
  112, 118, 125
banner exec command, 41–43
Banners, 41–43
Banyan, 1

BGP (border gateway protocol), 2
Boot field, 21
Bootstrap loader, 20, 21
Border gateway protocol (BGP),
  2
Broadcasts, 88–90, 223–224
BW (bandwidth), 109

Cabling, 26
Calendar/clock settings, 43–44
Central processing unit (CPU),
  14
Checksum field:
  TCP, 100
  UDP, 103
Cisco Professional Reference
  Guide Series, 2
Class A addresses, 61–63
Class B addresses, 61–63
Class C addresses, 61–63
Class D addresses, 62–64
Class E addresses, 64
Classes, address, 61–64
Classless routing, 77–78,
  174–178
Code Bits field (TCP), 99–100
Code field (ICMP), 92–95
Command interpreter (*see* EXEC
  router command interpreter)
Configuration commands, 33–40
  (*See also* Router configuration)
  abbreviation of, 39–40
  global commands, 33–37
  interface commands, 37, 38
  line commands, 37, 38
  router commands, 38–39
Configuration file, 23–25
Configuration register, 20–21
configure command, 7
Console port, 26–28
Convergence time, 183
Counting to infinity, 185
CPU (central processing unit), 14

CRC (*see* Cyclic redundancy
  check)
Crossover cable, 26
Cyclic redundancy check (CRC),
  25, 124, 232

Data flow (within router), 24–25
Data terminal equipment (DTE)
  port, 26
Day/time settings, 43–44
DECnet, 1
delay interface command, 112,
  118, 125
description interface com-
  mand, 113, 118
Destination address field (IP
  header field), 59
DHCP (dynamic host configura-
  tion protocol), 225
Diffusing Update Algorithm
  (DUAL), 200–202
Dijkstra algorithm, 188
Directed broadcasts, 89–90,
  223–224
Distance vector (DV) routing
  protocols, 181–186
Domain name server (DNS), 73,
  76
Dotted-decimal notation, 64–65
DTE (data terminal equipment)
  port, 26
DUAL (*see* Diffusing Update
  Algorithm)
DV routing protocols (*see*
  Distance vector routing
  protocols)
Dynamic access lists, 152–157
Dynamic host configuration pro-
  tocol (DHCP), 225

early-token release interface
  command, 118

EIGRP (*see* Enhanced IGRP)
enable command, 7, 28–31
encapsulation interface command, 126
Enhanced access lists, 152–161
  dynamic access lists, 152–157
  reflexive access lists, 157–159
  and TCP intercept, 160–161
  time-based access lists, 159–160
Enhanced IGRP (EIGRP), 177,
  180–182, 192, 194, 200–206
Ethernet:
  interface configuration,
    107–115
  metrics, 233–236
EXEC router command interpreter, 2–9, 31–33
  access levels, 3–4
  configuration mode, 6–8
  error indications, 6
  online assistance for, 5–6
  privileged-mode operations,
    32–33
  syntax of, 4–5
  user-mode operations, 32
Extended IP access lists, 135,
  139–143
  fields in, 139–141
  keywords with, 142–143
  named access lists, 146–147
  options supported by, 141–142

Fast Ethernet:
  interface configuration,
    107–115
  metrics, 237
Fast switching, 17–19, 178
Fiber-distributed data interface
  (FDDI), 24–25, 87
Fifo queuing strategy, 109–110
File transfer protocol (FTP), 96
Flags field (IP header field), 54
Flash memory, 14–15

Floating static routes, 179–180
Flooding broadcasts, 89
Fragment offset field (IP header
  field), 53
FTP (file transfer protocol),
  96

Global configuration commands,
  33–37
Graphic user interface (GUI), 3

Hardware, router (*see* Router
  hardware)
HDLC (higher-level data-link
  control), 124
Header fields, IP, 52–59
Higher-level data-link control
  (HDLC), 124
High-speed serial interface
  (HSSI), 106, 129–131
Hlen field:
  IP, 52
  TCP, 99
Holddown timer, 185
hold-queue interface command,
  113, 119
host keyword, 137–138
Hostname, assignment of,
  40–41
hostname command, 40–41
Hot standby routing protocol
  (HSRP), 213–216
HSSI (*see* High-speed serial
  interface)
HyperText Transfer Protocol
  (HTTP), 160

IAB (*see* Internet Activities
  Board)
IANA (Internet Assigned
  Numbers Authority), 97

ICMP (*see* Internet Control Message Protocol)
Identification field (IP header field), 53
IEEE (*see* Institute of Electrical and Electronics Engineers)
IGRP (*see* Interior Gateway Routing Protocol)
Inbound interfaces, 134
incomplete command error message, 6
Initialization, router, 19–23
Input/output (I/O) ports, 15–17
Institute of Electrical and Electronics Engineers (IEEE), 82, 109–110
interface commands, 16, 37, 38, 105–106
Interface configuration, 105–131
high-speed serial interfaces, 129–131
LANs, 106–121
Ethernet/Fast Ethernet, 107–115
Token Ring, 115–120
WANs, 121–129
serial interface commands, 122–129
standard serial port configuration, 121–122
Interior Gateway Routing Protocol (IGRP), 176–177, 180, 192, 195–200
enhanced (*see* Enhanced IGRP)
metrics, 196–198
packet format, 198–199
process domains, 195–196
variance, 199–200
Internet Activities Board (IAB), 59–60
Internet Assigned Numbers Authority (IANA), 97

Internet Control Message Protocol (ICMP), 1, 51, 90–95
Code field, 92–95
configuration options, 221–224
directed broadcasts, IP, 223–224
redirects, IP, 223
unreachables, IP, 221–223
Type field, 90–92
Internet online service (IOS) commands, 1
Internet protocol (IP), 1, 51–90
addressing in, 59–90
basic addressing scheme, 61
classes, address, 61–64
and classless networking, 77–78
configuration examples, 73, 76
dotted-decimal notation, 64–65
IPv6, 59, 78–82
and networks, 66–75
reserved addresses, 65–66
resolution, address, 82–90
router address assignment, 76–77
and subnetting, 68–75
header fields in, 52–59
destination address field, 59
flags field, 54
fragment offset field, 53
Hlen field, 52
identification field, 53
protocol field, 54–58
service type field, 53
source address field, 59
time to live field, 53
total length field, 53
VERS field, 52
Internet service providers (ISPs), 124, 153
invalid input error message, 6
I/O ports (*see* Input/output ports)